D0915768

BLACK DIONYSUS

Also by Kevin J. Wetmore, Jr.

The Athenian Sun in an African Sky:
Modern African Adaptations of Classical Greek Tragedy
(McFarland, 2002)

BLACK DIONYSUS

Greek Tragedy and African American Theatre

Kevin J. Wetmore, Jr.

McFarland & Company, Inc., Publishers
Jefferson, North Carolina, and London

Library of Congress Cataloguing-in-Publication Data

Wetmore, Kevin J., Jr., 1969–
　　Black Dionysus: Greek tragedy and African American theatre /
Kevin J. Wetmore, Jr.
　　　　p.　　cm.
　　Includes bibliographical references and index.

　　ISBN 0-7864-1545-2 (softcover : 50# alkaline paper)

　　1. American drama—African American authors—History and
criticism.　2. American drama (Tragedy)—History and criticism.
3. Greek drama (Tragedy)—History and criticism.　4. Literature,
Comparative—American and Greek.　5. Literature,
Comparative—Greek and American.　6. American drama—
Greek influences.　7. African Americans in literature.
8. Mythology, Greek, in literature.　I. Title
PS338.N4W48　2003
812.009'896073—dc21　　　　　　　　　　　　　　　　2002156684

British Library cataloguing data are available

Cover photograph: The Darker Face of the Earth at the Oregon
Shakespeare Festival (photograph by T. Charles Erickson)

Manufactured in the United States of America

McFarland & Company, Inc., Publishers
　Box 611, Jefferson, North Carolina 28640
　　www.mcfarlandpub.com

To the memory of
Catherine Maher Fracasse
and Barbara Wetmore Hamilton

Acknowledgments

Once again, I find myself in deep debt to a number of people without whom this book could never have been written.

Thanks to those who have guided my research and thought-process through the years: Kiki Gounaridou, J. Thomas Rimer, Dennis Brutus, Atillio "Buck" Favorini, Paul Kuritz, Martin Andrucki, William Pope. L, and Martin Banham.

A special shout going out to Each One Tell One and the Pittsburgh Posse—Neilesh Bose, Javon Johnson, Derek Sanders, and Mark Clayton Southers. Many late night, post-rehearsal, and green-room discussions about African American theatre, pan–Africanism, post-colonialism, race relations, the nature of education, acting, directing, playwriting, and the future have informed the writing of this book, and I owe them much. An extra special thanks to Neilesh for his thoughts and insights on both books I have written on this subject. Stay Black, rafiki yangu!

My colleagues have also been extremely kind and supportive. Thanks to the good people in the Theatre Department at the California State University at Northridge. My gratitude extends to Jon Farris, Rob Gander, Peter Pauze, Cynthia Turnbull, and Marilyn Sundin, as well as the administration and staff of Denison University. A special thanks is extended to Pam Magelaner of the Denison University Library for her assistance in securing many difficult to find sources and Star Andrews, also of Denison University Library, for her assistance in the archives. Some of this research was also carried out under the auspices of the University of Pittsburgh, and its many fine libraries and librarians are owed thanks as well.

Part of the research for this volume was carried out through the gracious assistance of a grant from the Sherman Fairchild Foundation and Denison University. The author is duly grateful to the powers that be at both.

Gratitude must be expressed to those who graciously allowed the use of their texts and/or photographs in this book:

Father Ernest Ferlita was kind enough to answer many questions and provide two scripts and a photograph.

T. Charles Erickson provided a number of photographs.

Rhodessa Jones and Cultural Odyssey were kind enough to provide a script and information. Jeanie Garber went above and beyond the call of duty to arrange for it all.

Silas Jones graciously provided a copy of his script and many insights into his work.

Jim Magnuson also shared insights and history on his work.

Many people from various theatres worked to assist in the development of this book: Beth Downing at La Jolla Playhouse, Jacques C. Lamarre at Hartford Stage (who provided me with information about and a copy of the program from their production of *Oedipus Rex*), Amy Richards at the Oregon Shakespeare Festival (who worked overtime to secure permission for *Darker Face of the Earth* photos), and Brian and Marjorie Gill who gathered material for me at the Kennedy Center

The casts of productions at Bates College and the University of Pittsburgh also deserve thanks for their hard work.

As always, the family keeps one connected to a larger community, and I extend my thanks to mine: Kevin Sr., Eleanor, Lisa, John, Sean, Tom, Eileen, Toni, Myles, Forest, Mike, Faith, Daniel, and Maxine.

My companion, my best friend, my harshest critic and my biggest fan remains my wife Maura Chwastyk, without whom none of this would have been possible.

To my many students who have also taught me, thank you. There are many others who deserve mention, and I hope they forgive me for not being able to list all those who have been of assistance while this book was written. Any mistakes are, alas, my own.

Table of Contents

Introduction: Greek Tragedy and the African Diaspora

Caelum non animum mutant qui trans mare current.
(They change their sky but not their soul who cross the ocean.)

Horace

Modern man associates himself with the ancient world not in order to reflect it like a mirror, but to capture its spirit and apply it in a modern way.

Andrea Palladio (1508–1580)

Goree Island is located in the Atlantic Ocean, just off the coast of Senegal. On Goree sits a structure, a fortress, called "The House of Slaves." The fortress was one of the primary markets for the Euro-American slave trade. Tens of thousands, if not hundreds of thousands, were kept in narrow, confining holding pens in the House of Slaves, awaiting embarkation on slave ships that would take them to a life of servitude in the Americas, if they survived the journey. Goree Island was the last African soil many of the men, women, and children taken across the Atlantic on the Middle Passage stood upon. In fact, the "Door of No Return," as it was called, connected the house to the gangplank which the slaves would cross to enter the hold of the slave ship, allowing for no escape but into the ocean.[1]

The House of Slaves still stands on Goree Island, a reminder of the slave trade and African genocide, as well as a reminder that Africans themselves willingly participated in the selling of other Africans to the Europeans. Likewise, the island serves as a bridge between New World and Motherland—a reminder of the link between the Americas and Africa. It is a reminder of the hubris of the slave trade, of the epic journey of Africans across the sea to the New World.

The creation of the United States of America and the so-called "discovery" of the New World shaped African history and the perception of Africa by Europe as much as it shaped Europe and the Americas. James W. Loewen, in his excellent *Lies My Teacher Told Me*, notes that "From the beginning America was perceived as an 'opposite' to Europe in ways that Africa had never been."[2] Loewen's argument is that the discovery of the Americas profoundly transformed European identity. He argues that before 1492 there was no "white" in the sense of race, and that identity was based on locality: Tuscan, Spanish, Flemish, French, etc. It was the enslavement of the indigenous peoples of the New World, followed by the Africans that required Europe to distinguish racial difference: "With the transatlantic slave trade, first Indian, then African, Europeans increasingly saw 'white' as a race and race as an important human characteristic."[3] Before 1492 Europe perceived Africa as different and exotic, but not necessarily inferior. Colonialism and slavery are the causes of racism, far more than the product of it. In order for the former to occur, Europeans needed the latter to justify their behavior towards other human beings.

Without the New World, Africa may have been colonized, but the presence of colonies on the other side of the Atlantic Ocean are obviously required for a "transatlantic" slave trade. An estimated ten to twelve million Africans were brought to the Americas to serve as slaves. After several centuries of servitude they were eventually freed as slavery was abolished, but the act of emancipation does not necessarily bring with it the cultural, economic, and political equality that would allow people of African descent to live as equals with people of European descent in the New World. As J. McIver Weatherford observes, "Africa thus became victims of the discovery of America as surely as did the American Indians."[4]

In describing the African experience in the New World, many authors, playwrights, poets, historians, etc. use images, metaphors, and references from and to Greek tragedy, myth and epic. For example, in her study of African American theatre entering the mainstream of American culture, Holly Hill compares August Wilson's 1984 Broadway debut as "Athena, springing from the head of Zeus," indicating that Wilson seemingly appeared "fully-formed" without having developed anywhere (a gross and inaccurate exaggeration which gives the lie to Wilson's decades of work as a writer, but it is the metaphor used that is important for our purposes, not its accuracy).[5]

Hill goes on to state that white critics and audiences respond to Wilson because "the size and shape of his vision remind us...of the beginnings of western drama in Greece."[6] Hill privileges European culture and argues that Wilson's plays appeal because they remind white audiences of the best white plays. While intending to compliment Wilson, Hill has actually offered a backhanded insult—"Your plays are as good as white people's." There exists a complicated relationship between ancient Greek tragedy and modern African American theatre. It is a relationship that is compromised by colonialism, slavery, imperialism and racism. It is a relationship that is problematized by the assumption of Greek cultural superiority by Eurocentrists and the assumption of an underlying African origin by Afrocentrists. It is a relationship that is primarily rooted in America, far more than in Greece or Africa. In fact, it is America where the relationship between ancient Greece and ancient Africa is explored, debated, and fought over the most.

In *Greek Fire*, Oliver Taplin argues that "Greece is the geology underlying the mental landscape of Western civilization."[7] The title of his work refers to the legendary Greek fire that could stay alight even under water. Taplin argues that the culture of "ancient Greece can stay alight submerged in alien cultures."[8] Taplin, and many other authors like him, see ancient Athens and its many cultural products (philosophy, democracy, tragedy, etc.) as unique, important, and at the center of western civilization. What's more, the creations of Greek culture "can stay alight submerged in alien cultures:" they are universal.

We must remain wary of the idea that Greek tragedy is somehow "universal." It is the product of a culture that itself resulted from many different influences. Universality is a western conceit that would place western culture at the center and above all others. Greek tragedy has proven, however, to be a procrustean bed. Procrustus was a mythic figure in Greece who placed travelers in his bed. If too tall, he cut off their legs, if too short he stretched them. Thus all people were made to fit the bed. Perhaps this is a suitable metaphor for Greek tragedy, as "universality" can only be achieved through violent change, either to the tragedy or to the culture to which the tragedy is being adapted. Adaptation, in one sense, is a form of violence. In another sense, it is a kind of transformation that allows the audience to perceive something new in something old.

Greek tragedy has been adapted to African diasporan contexts for a variety of purposes and ends. Sometimes the purpose is metaphoric, sometimes it is to reclaim a "stolen legacy," and sometimes it is done in order to say that which cannot or will not be listened to if stated directly. Anthony Tatlow, in his survey of intercultural work in East Asia, observes that, "sometimes the only way of engaging with one's own cultural past lies in its alienation not just by but through the foreign."[9] The past is another country and the legacy of Africans in America is a legacy of oppression, suffering, racism, etc. Playwrights and theatre artists use Greek tragedy because it is distant enough to say things that audiences would not be as comfortable hearing and seeing directly. Race in America is a controversial subject to begin with, and the theatre has often been at the forefront of exploring these "hot button" issues. But sometimes one needs distance to see clearly. Tatlow, speaking of Brecht's *Life of Galileo* in a 1979 production in China, observed that, "in psychological terms the alienatingly unfamiliar eases the painful process of self examination."[10] Ultimately, all adaptation of Greek tragedy is about the culture that adapted it, not about the Greeks. Adaptation of Greek tragedy into African American settings is always about America, never about ancient Greece.

Afro-Greek tragedy can be subversive and resistant, or it can support the hegemony of European culture. This study is set to examine the different ways in which Greek culture has been used to engage African culture in the New World.

Plays do not mean, they generate meaning. The meaning is generated by a combination of content (the play itself—characters, plot, themes, etc.) and context (the audience, when and where the play is read/performed, the social, political, economic, religious, and cultural milieus, etc.). It is for this reason that the Medea Project of Rhodessa Jones is empowering when it posits a black woman as "Medea Jackson"—decades of feminist criticism have developed a sympathetic portrait of Medea. Likewise the performers and audience of *Women Are Waiting: The Tragedy of Medea Jackson* are incarcerated women performing in a prison. An understanding of the causes and nature of domestic violence have given us insight into the situation of Medea in Jones's play. Similarly, the play takes into account the political and economic reality of the performers and the audience—usually poor, undereducated women in prison, and reflects this reality in the characters and plot.

It is for this reason, conversely, that the editors of *Harper's Weekly* are disempowering and racist when they rename the lithograph of Thomas Satterwhite Noble's painting *Margaret Garner* as "The Modern Medea" in 1867. This new name posits Margaret Garner as Medea, who, in nineteenth century America, was viewed as an unruly and dangerous woman who murdered her children. To posit Garner as a Medea is to call her a vicious child-killer and sorceress, the embodiment of chaos and madness that supports the nineteenth century view of the character of Medea. Such a construction is in perfect agreement with white America's beliefs about women of color, thereby allowing stereotypes to continue and to use classical culture to dismiss the larger issues in the Garner case.

The purpose of this study, therefore, is to examine how Greek cultural material (Athenian tragedies, primarily) has been used by playwrights, directors, and others to present, represent, define, and explore African

American history and identity. The historian (and especially the theatre historian, dealing with a temporal, ephemeral art that starts with the beginning of the performance and ends with the final moment of the play) must examine the historical record—primary documents, eye-witness accounts, etc. In order to correlate the dramatic work (and by this I mean textual work—the script) to the larger cultural and historical contexts, it is sometimes necessary to rely upon other people's ethnographies and histories. I prefer to think of this as standing on the shoulders of giants in order to gain better insight into the context of a play or an adapted classic.

This study considers mostly dramatic literature, although attempts are made to engage the plays in performance and in the historical, cultural, and political contexts of their first productions and, in some cases, subsequent productions in which meaning has shifted. This study, however, remains rooted in the realm of theatrical adaptation and therefore, in comparative dramaturgies. A variety of methodologies are then called for: adaptation theory, postcolonial literary and performance theory, what Anthony Tatlow calls "textual anthropology"—"observing others and wrestling with ourselves in a self-distancing practice of interpretation," and others.[11] There is an absence of "fieldwork" because this is a literary and historical enterprise, although original contexts of the adaptation are always examined to help determine meanings.

This exploration is carried out under several assumptions. These must also be clearly enumerated:

African American theatre is not monolithic. The African American community is not monolithic. Paul Gilroy calls it "racial narcissism" to assume that the black community is homogeneous. He argues that differences based on class, ideologies, language, education, locality, gender, sexuality, sexual orientation, religious belief, and generation cause a very wide continuum in the black experience, and thus produce a highly diverse community.[12] A heterogeneous community develops a heterogeneous theatre. There exist a vast variety of African American theatre forms, genres, styles, and themes, as well as a continuum of performance related to or expropriating theatre.

African American theatre is intercultural theatre. As the product of more than one culture, created and performed by people of African descent in a European language, utilizing both Africanisms and elements of European and American dramaturgy and convention, African American theatre is by nature and by definition intercultural. When utilizing Greek material, another culture is simply added to an already intercultural mix.

The liberation struggles of African peoples on the continent and African peoples in the diaspora are similar and not yet over. People of African descent within the continent and in the New World have faced, and continue to face, a very similar struggle. All of them have been subjugated by European conquerors, have had their cultures attacked, languages subjugated, rights and property stolen, freedom taken, family members tortured and killed, all in the name of enriching people of European descent. The effects of colonization are felt in both New World and Motherland and the struggle to decolonize cultures and minds, even after emancipation and independence is a difficult one. Even today the psychological effects of colonization are still felt on peoples of African descent both within and without the continent. Scholars such as George M. Fredrickson have compared the parallel developments between Africans and African Americans in their struggles to overcome racism, legalized discrimination and segregation, economic exploitation, and domination by whites. The same ideologies in people of African descent, for example, gave rise to the "Black Power" movement in the United States at the same time that the "Black Consciousness" movement began to sweep South Africa.[13]

The related cultures of America, the Caribbean, and Africa therefore exist on a continuum. As will be explored in the second chapter, the African diapora has a variety of cultural survivals from the Motherland, and the development of African American theatre has paralleled the development of modern African theatre.

Yet different issues also affect the nature of African and African American theatre. Ngugi wa Thiongo can choose to write in Gikuyu and then translate his work into English for an international audience. August Wilson, Suzan-Lori Parks, Adrienne Kennedy, and Silas Jones do not have this option. While texts can be written in dialect or even "Ebonics," the dominant language is still English. Thus, for the African American playwright, the language issue is similar to the problems faced by the African writer, but with some important differences.

African diasporan cultures are subject to the highly unequal structures of global capital and the legacy of imperialism. Artists are subject to use the materials that they have been exposed to as a result of the educational system in their nations and cultures, etc. They can seek out others and a great deal of progress has been made on this front, particularly because of the development of Afrocentric curricula for primary, secondary and university education. Yet most students will most likely be more familiar with the epics of Homer than the Epic of Sun-Jata Keyta, more likely to know Greek mythology than Dogon cosmology.

"Slavery's twin legacies to the present," writes James Loewen, "are the social and economic inferiority it conferred on blacks and the cultural racism it instilled in whites. Both continue to haunt our society."[14] We must be aware of how the former legacy has shaped the theatre of African Americans and we must be wary of how the latter legacy has sharpened America's admiration for all things Greek.

The classics can and have been used as weapons of cultural imperialism, forced upon persons of African descent as the model of culture, and used to supplant indigenous literature (see the following assumption, however).

Lastly, artists are, in some ways, financially dependant on the very institutions that they seek to overthrow or transform or removed from the clutches of institutionalized racism. August Wilson might object to mainstream (read: white) theatre, but those very theatres and audiences are the ones that have popularized his work and, in the process, given him the financial and cultural clout to write as he sees fit.

Historically and ideologically speaking, Greek tragedy is not necessarily European culture. In recent years the controversy about the Afroasiatic origins of Greek culture has grown. Martin Bernal's opus *Black Athena* and numerous other authors and their works have raised the possibility that Greek culture developed out of Egyptian, and therefore African culture. Therefore, when a playwright uses Greek material it is not the result of cultural imperialism privileging European classics but a retaking of what was once African. This concept will be explored in the first two chapters.

This study has fallen into the trap of much postcolonial theatre research written in the West. It is textocentric. Dramatic literature is privileged, primarily because the topic is the transformation of Greek tragedy into African American tragedy, mostly through writing. Whenever possible, performance has been engaged, and productions of the plays considered. Likewise, some performance history is involved when examining how non-traditional casting shapes what otherwise would be a standard, mainstream (read: white) production. Audience and critical response, when possible and appropriate, is engaged, in order to understand how the performances of these texts were received. Nevertheless, my focus has been on dramatic literature, which, admittedly, is a Western preoccupation.

All Greek material is fair game. As a theatre historian, tragedy remains my focus, but Greek tragedy is intertextually linked to Greek myth and the epics of Homer. Epic and myth serve as a source material for Greek tragedy and all three form the images of ancient Greece that exist in the popular imagination. For the purposes of this study, the adaptation of Greek epic and myth, when applicable, will also be considered.

Adaptations are not copies of the originals, they are works of art in and of themselves. At a recent conference the author attended, a classicist announced to the audience that Greek tragedy should not be adapted because the original tragedians knew what they were doing when they created original works and playwrights today should simply write their own plays. Yet Aeschylus, Sophocles, and Euripides were not only adapting myth, they were also making direct reference to each other's works. One cannot encounter the *Electra* of Euripides without knowing that he is actively engaging his audience's knowledge of Aeschylus's and Sophocles's previous treatments of the legend, yet no one, not even the above-mentioned classicist, would say that Euripides's play is unoriginal or is simply another version of Aeschylus's. Each dramatic work builds on the ones before it and relies on the audience's knowledge of them. The Greeks invented tragedy. They also invented adaptation.

Shakespeare's *Hamlet* is not Thomas Kyd's, or Saxo Grammaticus's history of Denmark, although those were the original sources known to his audience when he wrote his play. *The Gospel at Colonus* is not *Oedipus at Colonus*. *Pecong* is not *Medea*. Nor are they mere copies of the originals, dressing them in borrowed robes, but reinterpretations as legitimate for their cultures as the Greek originals were in Athens.

Adaptation is a two-step process. First comes a textual transformation in which the text is removed from its original context and textual codes and transculturated. The codes are rewritten by the playwright into the new codes, as will be discussed in chapter three, and the work is placed into a new context. Not only is the language and the textual codes transculturated, however, performance codes must also be addressed. A text is merely a blueprint for performance. While the focus of this study is textual transformation, the reader should bear in mind that the second step of adaptation is the new performance codes that are indicated in the writing, but do not actually occur until the play is performed in front of an audience.

In some cases, the first step is skipped altogether, and, instead of writing a new adaptation, a director or group of actors will move the text to a new mise-en-scene, so that although two productions might use the same translation, their meanings are radically different, not because of a change in the text, but because of a change in the visual and performative aspects of the play.

Adaptations work on more than one level, and are perceived differently based on the audience and their experiences

and knowledge. Many of these adaptations are produced at colleges and universities, or by theatre companies in large urban areas. The audience base that attends the productions of the latter are usually well-educated, economically well-off, and interested in the arts. The former, however, might have both the well-educated audience members and those who have never been exposed to Greek tragedy or even necessarily to live theatre. There is no guarantee that the audience will be familiar with or even have been exposed to the original, especially with a less-studied play such as *Oedipus at Colonus* or Euripides' *Orestes*. Plays that therefore rely on the audience's foreknowledge of the story, situation, characters, or mythic origins will not be readily accessible to everyone in the audience. One should note, however, that those who do encounter such adaptations with the previous experience of the originals therefore perceive the production on more levels than those who are encountering the material for the first time. Additional levels of meaning are open and available to the former.

Likewise, experience with the original tragedies is not the only shaping knowledge that many of these plays require. Knowledge of American history, especially African American history, shapes the experience of these plays and the levels of meaning open to the audience. The greatest, most complex or most sublime references in the world are rendered insignificant if the audience member does not know to what is being referred. Plays like *Darker Face of the Earth* and *American Medea* rely upon the audience knowing something of African American history during the antebellum period and during the American revolution, respectively. One can still understand, appreciate, and enjoy these plays without that knowledge, but with it the plays have many more levels of meaning. This variety of audience foreknowledge and experience shapes the experience of the production differently for each audience member. The canny theatre artist is aware of this fact and attempts to open the doors as wide as possible. It is important to note, however, that no foreknowledge is guaranteed.

The plays in this study do not enjoy a vast popular exposure. Contemporary American theatre audiences are usually well-educated, middle to upper class and, unless the theatre organization actively cultivates a multi-ethnic, or ethno-specific audience, tend to be overwhelmingly European American. Audiences tend to be self-selecting, so the plays considered here are usually seen by a very small percentage of the population that has sought it out. Unlike television, film, or even long-running Broadway plays, many of the dramas discussed in this book have limited runs in one region of the country before small, selective audiences. Subsequent productions may expose additional areas or populations to the drama. If the text is published (and not all of them are), more accessibility to the work is gained, albeit in a different media. Nevertheless, the actual audience for these works is arguably rather small, and this fact can and will effect the impact and meaning of the drama.

This study is aimed at a variety of different constituencies, all of whom might bring different perspectives, viewpoints, and ideologies. It is my hope that this work will be of interest to scholars, students, and aficionados in the fields of Africana studies, theatre history, and classical studies both Afrocentric and traditional (Eurocentric), as well as theatre artists interested in these dramas. As a result, I have tried to balance out the needs of this perceived audience, and in some areas the analysis might become rather simple or state things commonly known in one field listed above, but relatively unknown in another, in the interests of ensuring equal understanding and accessibility.

In the interests of full and honest disclosure, the author of this study is a professor of theatre history and a professional theatre artist, a male of European (specifically Anglo-Irish) descent. I have studied and taught African, Caribbean, and African American theatre, have done research in the United States, the Caribbean, and Africa, and been a member of several multi-ethnic or predominantly African American theatre companies. As a theatre student at Bates College, I attended a lecture by Douglas Turner Ward, actor, playwright, director, and founder and artistic director of the Negro Ensemble Company. During the question and answer session, I asked him if and how a Euro-American director can work in African American theatre. He responded that of course Euro-Americans can work in and direct (and arguably even write) African American theatre, but there are necessary prerequisites. Such a director must always be self-aware, be respectful, and do the research into the subject matter. He or she must be humble and "go into the belly of the beast," without thinking that he or she knows anything about the black experience, or that they will ever experience what it is to "be black."[15] While not giving into the identity fallacy (that one can only truly understand something by being it), the director (and, presumably, the scholar) must also distinguish between understanding through experience and understanding through outside study.

The author has attempted to follow Douglas Turner Ward's advice in both his artistic and scholarly activities. By citing myself and my identity, I hope to be able to engage African American theatre and African American use of Greek material on their own terms, rather than arbitrary or Eurocentric ones. This book is the result of several years of research and performance, and should serve as both a continuation of the work I began in my previous book, *The American Sun in an African Sky: Modern African Adap-*

tations of Classical Greek Tragedy (McFarland, 2002), as well as a contribution to the analysis of both intercultural theatre and the theatre of people of African descent living in the new world.

The first chapter, "*Black Athena* meets *Black Orpheus*: Three Models of the Afro-Greek Connection," presents three different paradigms of the manner in which things African are presented through the lens of Greek myth, epic, and tragedy. "Black Orpheus" is a Eurocentric formulation of equivalence, rendering the African or African American in terms of the European. Such a use is metaphoric, arguing that the subject of the work is the black or African equivalent of the Greek paradigm. "Black Athena," however, is an Afrocentric formulation of reappropriation. This model assumes the Afro-Asiatic origins of Greek culture and represents and re-presents them as being African derived. Such a use is reclaimative, arguing that Greek culture comes from African culture, and therefore the work is corrective, not metaphoric. A third model, "Black Dionysus," recognizes the "Black Orpheus" model—using Greek material metaphorically, but presents the material in a counter-hegemonic, subversive manner. Rather than using a Greek metaphor to explain things African, such works reject the dominant notions of ethnicity and culture and seek, usually in a post-Afrocentric manner, to critique the dominant culture using its own material.

The second chapter, "Afro(American)centric Classicism and African American Theatre," explores the relationship between Afrocentric classicism and theatre history, and posits that the vast majority of those arguing that Greek culture is derived from African culture are actually American, not indigenous African. By positing Greek culture, including tragedy, as African-derived, such scholars revise theatre history to make Africa the originating point of theatre and drama.

The third chapter, "Ancient Plays, New World" first offers a brief history of Greek tragedy on the American stage and then examines issues of non-traditional casting and how actors of color shape productions of Greek tragedy. A consideration of how plays are transculturated from their original Greek context to an African American context follows, including cultural similarities and dramatic themes that link the African diaspora to ancient Athens and its drama. Finally, three adapters of Greek tragedy who move the plays into an African American context are considered: Adrienne Kennedy, who has adapted *Electra*, *Orestes*, and *Oedipus Rex*, Lee Breuer, whose *Gospel at Colonus* resets Sophocles' *Oedipus at Colonus* in an African American Pentecostal church, and Rita Dove's *The Darker Face of the Earth*, placing *Oedipus Rex* in antebellum South Carolina.

The fourth chapter considers the dominant position of Medea in African diaspora theatre. "Black Medeas," as it is called, explores productions of *Medea* in which Medea is played by and presented as a woman of color. Beginning with the historical case of Margaret Garner, which served as inspiration for the painting *The Modern Medea* and Toni Morrison's Pulitzer Prize–winning novel *Beloved*, and continuing through modern productions, the chapter considers the changing presentation of Medea as woman of color, from dangerous, violent child killer to admirable and justified protofeminist warrior. Next, several adaptations which relocate the play to Africa, New Orleans, antebellum Virginia, the Caribbean, and urban San Francisco are considered, the last being part of a larger enterprise entitled "The Medea Project," a branch of theatre company Cultural Odyssey that works with incarcerated women to develop theatre pieces.

The final chapter considers Greek tragedy in the Caribbean and the relationship between Caribbean Greek tragedy and African American Greek tragedy. Of particular interest is the work of Nobel Prize winning poet and playwright Derek Walcott, who frequently mines Greek cultural material in his presentation of Caribbean culture.

Unless otherwise indicated, all quotations from the original Greek tragedies are taken from *The Complete Greek Tragedies*, edited and (for the most part) translated by David Grene and Richmond Lattimore. Quotations from Greek tragedies are always cited by line number, not page number.

Lastly, all attempts have been made to ensure accuracy of spellings of African, Caribbean, and African American names, terms, and quotations, particularly when in indigenous languages. The absence of any diacritic marks is an indication of the limitations of the author's word processing program and should not be perceived as an attempt to anglicize or denigrate any language or culture. In cases where numerous variant spellings exist, such as *voodoo* (*vodou*, *vodu*, etc.) I have attempted to use either the most historically accurate or the most popular.

> *Omnia mutantur, nihil interit.*
> (Everything changes, but nothing is truly lost.)

1

Black Athena Meets Black Orpheus: Three Models of the Afro-Greek Connection

> Yep, you done taken my blues and gone.
> You also took my spirituals and gone.
> You put me in *Macbeth* and *Carmen Jones*
> And in all kinds of *Swing Mikados*
> And in everything but what's about me...
>
> Langston Hughes
> "Note on Commercial Theatre"

> In a debate about whether or not Homer had ever existed, I threw into their white faces the theory that Homer only symbolized how white Europeans kidnapped black Africans, then blinded them so that they could never get back to their own people (Homer and Omar and Moor, you see are related terms; it's like saying Peter, Pedro and Petra, all three of which mean rock). These blinded Moors the Europeans taught to sing about the European's glorious accomplishments.... "Aesop" was only the Greek name for an Ethiopian.
>
> Malcolm X
> *The Autobiography of Malcolm X*

In *The Souls of Black Folk*, W.E.B. DuBois, writing of the history of African American people compares cotton to the Golden Fleece, the hide of the golden ram that rescued Phrixus and Helle and was sought by Jason and the Argonauts in Greek myth. Writing of the cotton fields of the American South, he states, "I have sometimes half-suspected that here the winged

13

ram Chrysomallus left that fleece after which Jason and his Argonauts went vaguely wandering into the shadowy East three thousand years ago...."[1] DuBois is one of many who have used Greek myth, epic, and tragedy to convey a sense of the past, to evoke a sense of myth or mystery, or metaphorically to illuminate some aspect of African or African American culture.

There are many different ways in which Greek culture intersects with the African diaspora. Most obviously (and the focus of this study) is the adaptation of Greek tragedy into African American or Caribbean contexts. Similarly, artists of color working in or on a production of Greek tragedy that has not been transculturated into Afrocentric contexts nevertheless can bring an Afrocentric perspective to their work and shape the meaning of the presentation. There are literary uses of Greek myths, epics, and tragedies that serve as inspiration or point of reference for novels, poems, etc. There also exist all manner of material culture—paintings, essays, articles, etc.—that link ancient Greek culture to modern or ancient African diaspora culture.

Many of the works considered in this study rely upon an intertextuality between Greek material and African material, creating meaning on several levels. The recontextualization of Greek tragedy can often be viewed as a "parallel" or "overlay" (in Oliver Taplin's terminology) of the original narrative into a new cultural context.[2] Yet the level of adaptation can vary. Sometimes there is exact one-to-one correspondence between original and new text. In other cases, individual characters, plot, specific dramaturgies, and events are borrowed and moved from one context to another. Sometimes the use of Greek material is limited to allusions and references, or quotations from the originals. Sometimes only a title is kept, the rest being the playwright's free invention based on and, as it is often termed, "inspired by" the original.

The three things that must be considered when examining drama that transculturates Greek tragedy to the African diaspora is the type of adaptation (how faithful to the original, what is changed, etc.), the purpose of the adaptation (why did the playwright choose to adapt a tragedy rather than create an original work, and to what end) and the intended audience and historical context of the initial production and, occasionally, of subsequent productions.

There are three models of interaction between ancient Greek cultural material and contemporary African diasporan culture. The first, "Black Orpheus" is a model that is rooted in parallel and overlay. The works in this category tend to be "straightforward" adaptations with direct, one-to-one correspondences, or not even adaptations, but referential works, pieces that use Greek culture as a metaphor for African culture. "Black Orpheus" is a model of equation; the African material is the equivalent of this aspect of Greek culture.

The second model, "Black Athena" is a reappropriation of material that is already African in origin. Under this model, the Greeks received their myths, their religion, their culture, etc. from the Egyptians. Therefore, all Greek material is really all African in the first place. The use of Greek material is not cultural colonialism and an expression of western superiority, but rather a corrective, returning the culture to its rightful African context.

The third paradigm is "Black Dionysus," which considers adaptation of Greek tragedy within the context of the African diaspora as a creative and constructive system of complex intertextuality designed to critique the very cultures that prioritize ancient Greek culture. It seeks to uncover the historical reality behind both Greek and African cultures, respecting both within their own contexts.

Black Orpheus: Greek Tragedy, Myth, and Epic as Metaphor

Several authors, playwrights, filmmakers, poets, and cultures have used Greek cultural material in African diasporan settings. Many of these are titled using "Black" or "African" as an adjective to be followed by a name from Greek mythology, tragedy, or epic, or their Roman equivalents. For example: "Black Odyssey," "African Medea," or "Black Venus."

"Black _____" is first and foremost a metaphor: it explains the unfamiliar in terms of the familiar. The unstated assumption in that statement is for whom are these elements familiar and unfamiliar? The answer is, of course, the Eurocentric west, where, by and large, most educational systems will ensure that the citizens learn Greek mythology and read at least some Greek drama. The Greeks, after all, are the "fathers of Western Civilization," and therefore worthy of study. African culture, orature, literature, mythology, etc. is what is unfamiliar. The citizens of Nigeria do not need to be told who Eshu or Shango are. Nor, for that matter, do they need to be told who Orpheus is, as the educational system left in place by more than a century of British colonial occupation ensures that the Nigerian student will be as familiar with Greek material as he or she is with indigenous culture. The name *Black Orpheus* is a metaphor for non-Africans (read: Westerners). It presents a model for understanding, for translation, for rendering the unfamiliar into the familiar. We shall examine the metaphoric use of Greek tragedy, epic, and myth (and sometimes their Roman equivalents) by both Westerners and people of African descent to "explain" or "understand" African and African American culture. Here follows Black Orpheuses, Black Odysseys and Black Ulysses, Black Apollo, African Oresteias, and Black Venuses.

In 1948, Jean-Paul Sartre was asked by Léopold Sédar Senghor to write the preface to *Anthologie de la nouvelle poésie nègre et malgache de langue française*, an anthology of Francophone poetry by writers of African descent that Senghor had edited. Sartre's essay, "Orphée Noir" ("Black Orpheus") became a significant (and controversial) work in its own right, and the first work (but certainly not the last) to use the name "Black Orpheus."

Sartre's essay explored the poems in the anthology as examples of Negritude, which he saw as the negative side of a Hegelian dialectic. Negritude, according to Sartre, was an "anti-racist racism," a black response to white racism that would eventually give way to the synthesis of universality.[3] He saw the emblematic poet of Africa and the African diaspora as a "Black Orpheus" for whom Negritude was "Eurydice," something that was loved and pursued, but eventually to be abandoned:

> Thus Negritude is for destroying itself, it is a passage and not an outcome, a means and not an ultimate end. At the moment that every black Orpheus most tightly embrace this Eurydice they feel her vanish from between their arms.[4]

Sartre followed the European notion of Africa being in a stage of development similar to the Greeks of twenty-five centuries before. For Sartre, the difference between African poetry and European poetry was that the Africans still believed in their myths:

> The blacks of Africa, on the contrary, are still in the great period of mythical fecundity and French-language black poets are not just using their myths as a form of diversion as we use our epic poems; they allow themselves to be spellbound by them so that at the end of the incantation negritude—magnificently evoked—may surge forth.[5]

Sartre's formulations are problematic not least of which because behind them is a benign racism and a patronizing Othering of things African. His use of pronouns indicates the distance he feels from "them" and "their myths."

Sartre ultimately posited that African poets owed a debt to Western forms, beginning with ancient classical poetry: "...the dawn of Greek and Mediterranean culture—snatched from the sacrosanct Homeric poems by a black thief," he wrote of African epic.[6] For Sartre, Homer was "sacrosanct," whose works were stolen by the African who used Homer as a model to develop his own forms. This charge is the exact opposite as the one leveled against European culture by Martin Bernal, Edward Jones, Chiek Anta Diop, and especially George G.M. James, whose very title *Stolen Legacy* suggests that it was a white thief who snatched African culture. The idea of the stolen legacy will be explored below.

Sartre's essay has been critiqued and criticized by a number of authors, not least of which are Franz Fanon and Senghor himself. Fanon, in *Black Skin White Masks*, rejects Sartre's model, noting, "Help had been sought from a friend of the colored people, and that friend had found no better response than to point out the relativity of what they were doing."[7] The poets might represent a "Black Orpheus," but for Sartre, a Black Orpheus is a pale imitation of the Greek original.

Sartre, in 1948, provided the first model for an Afro-Greek connection: that African culture could be explained via a metaphor of Greek culture. His audience knew who Orpheus and Eurydice were, therefore he could explain African poetry in terms of European myth. "Black Orpheus" is the model of defining the African in terms of the European. Rather than African appropriation of Greek culture, it is the use of Greek culture to render the African Other into a European Self. Greek myth, epic, and tragedy, argues Sartre by example, can be used as a metaphor to explain Africa to both Westerners and Africans.

Since Sartre, the title "Black Orpheus" has been used several times for different cultural products that attempted to site the African diaspora within European culture. There is a Black Orpheus Press in Washington, D.C. Saadi A. Simawe edited a book entitled *Black Orpheus: Music in African American Fiction from the Harlem Renaissance to Toni Morrison* which references the musical aspect of Orpheus's character to frame the agency of sound and lyric in fiction by black American authors. Noting the "orphic" quality of many of the works of fiction discussed in the book, Simawe argues that:

> the term crosses nationalities and historic periods to highlight an essentially human urge—that is, self-realization, which seems to find, according to many iconoclastic writers, its full expression in the medium of music and poetry.[8]

In other words, the book on one level erases difference and posits the figure of Orpheus as the embodiment of the "human" urge of self-realization. African American writing is thus analyzed from the humanistic ideal of Greek myth. The danger in Simawe's formulation is that it locates the "human urge" in a fundamentally western cultural construction and uses that as the measure by which writers of the African diaspora will be weighed. Although no doubt unintentional, the framing of the black writers in terms of European myth posits European culture in a superior position. No doubt the author felt that "Black Orpheus" worked better than "American Griot," or some other title that suggested African culture as a baseline, but which would not have had the name recognition in America or in the academy that Orpheus does.

The two best known examples of the use of the title "Black Orpheus" in the West, after Sartre, are arguably the African journal founded and edited by Ulli Beier and the 1959 film set in Brazil during Carnival.

The journal *Black Orpheus* was a regularly published collection of essays and creative writing founded by a German expatriate living in Nigeria named Ulli Beier. The first series was edited by Beier and began publication in September of 1957, nine years after Sartre coined the term. The journal then went through a second editorial series under J.P. Clark and Abiola Irele.

Peter Benson notes that *Black Orpheus* and a fellow publication, *Transition* were "at the center of much that happened—intellectually and culturally—in anglophone black Africa during the period from the late fifties to the late seventies."[9] The journal was begun with the express aim of translating Francophone authors into English, such as those published in Senghor's anthology in which Sartre's essay appeared, and with giving a forum for Nigerian writing in English. Aside from the reference to Sartre's by that point well-known essay, the title *Black Orpheus* is meant to imply "cultural self-definition."[10]

The irony, of course, is that a European metaphor is being used to encourage African "cultural self-definition." In other words, the self-definition is not a self-definition at all, but a definition of African culture in terms of European myth, privileging the latter as a metaphor by which the former might be better understood by all, including the Africans. Sartre "compared the African poet's search for identity to Orpheus's descent into hell," as Benson puts it, and the magazine sought to frame the African search for a literary identity in the same context.[11] The problem with Sartre's (and thus Beier's) formulation is that Orpheus did not go to hell in search of himself or in search of an identity. He went in search of someone else—Eurydice.

Orpheus's quest was for something he had lost, granted, but that something was not similar to a pre-colonial identity, as Sartre posits. Orpheus lost his wife—another person, someone completely separate from him and his self. Orpheus, it must also be remembered, failed in his attempt to bring his wife back from hell. Is failure really the model that is desired for the "search for identity" by African writers?

The content of the first issue, notes Benson, "was further indicative of the magazine's simple goals of establishing links between anglophone West Africa and the black diaspora, educating Africans about their traditional culture, and promoting new writers and artists."[12] During the course of its decades long run, the journal stayed committed to these goals, publishing works by established African writers such as Wole Soyinka, but also offering opportunities for new writers of African descent; Adrienne Kennedy had her first published work in *Black Orpheus*, for example. Again, the problematic metaphor created by the name creates a journal with a European name that "educate[s] Africans about their traditional culture." While the journal relies on name recognition in order to gain a following, the name centers Europe at the expense of Africa and uses Greek myth as the model by which to understand African culture. The *Black Orpheus* name would be used again in books edited by Beier reprinting the best articles, fiction, and poetry from the journal, such as *Black Orpheus: An Anthology of New African and Afro-American Stories* in 1964 and *Political Spider: An Anthology of Stories from Black Orpheus* in 1969, both of which rely upon the same metaphoric construction as the journal.

The film *Orfeu Negro* (*Black Orpheus*), directed by Marcel Camus and written by Jacques Voit, was based on the stage play *Orfeu da Conceicao* by Vinicius de Moraes. As with Ulli Beier, the European who creates African diasporan culture from within Africa, *Orfeu Negro* was a joint French and Italian production, made in Brazil. Like Beier's journal, the intentions might have been good, including a desire to celebrate indigenous culture, but there remains behind the intent a kind of cultural colonialism that frames the former colony's culture in terms of European culture.

Set during Carnival, *Orfeu Negro* tells the story of Orpheus, a streetcar conductor in Rio who is engaged to be married to a woman named Mira. During Carnival, however, he meets a young woman from the country named Eurydice, who is fleeing from a man dressed in a Carnival skeleton costume and whom she is convinced is trying to kill her.

Orpheus is a musician and after recovering his guitar from the store where he had pawned it, he teaches neighborhood children to play. Written on his guitar is "Orfeu is my master." Like his mythological namesake, he is a master musician. He tells the boys who come to hear him play that his music "makes the sun come up." When the mythic Orpheus played, water stopped flowing, wild beasts sat calmly at his feet, mountains moved, and everything under the sun would stop to listen. His music controlled the world.

Unlike many other adaptations of Greek material to new settings, the characters in *Orfeu Negro* are self aware of their mythic connection and their namesakes. "You see, there was an Orpheus before me," Orpheus tells the neighborhood children, "Perhaps there will be another one after." When Orpheus and Mira apply for their wedding license, after hearing Orpheus's name, the clerk jokes that Mira's name must be Eurydice. Mira does not know to what he is referring and grows indignant, assuming Orpheus is cheating on her. The clerk reassures her, "It's old history. It's a joke!" yet when Orpheus and Eurydice do meet, the names prove to be prophetic and fateful. Eurydice, who, like Mira, does not know the story, learns of the myth from Orpheus who assures her, "Everybody knows Orpheus loves Eurydice."

The figure dressed as death begins to stalk Eurydice in Rio, and when confronted by Orpheus, tells him, "Look after her. I'm in no hurry. We'll see each other soon. Quite soon." The mythic Eurydice dies on her wedding day, bitten by a venomous serpent. The cinematic Eurydice goes to Carnival the day after she sleeps with Orpheus for the first time, and chased by Mira, she runs into the arms of death. A kindly colleague of Orpheus's, a fellow conductor named Hermes, tells her to go to the streetcar depot and he'll fetch Orpheus.

Death waits for Eurydice at the depot, and, as she climbs atop a streetcar to escape from him, she grabs a power line for the streetcars to steady her balance. Unaware of her location, Orpheus throws the switch that turns on both the lights and the streetcar powerlines. Like the serpent in the myth, the line electrocutes Eurydice, killing her. "Now she is mine," death tells him.

As his mythic forebear, Orpheus does not accept the death of his love. While seeking for his lost love in the missing persons department, a janitor leads him down to a yard past a barking German Shepard named "Cerebus," after the dog that guards the underworld in Greek mythology. At a *Candomblé* ceremony taking place inside the temple in the yard, women dance, sing, and summon the *orisha*, who possess the dancers. *Candomblé* is an Afro-Brazilian religion that developed, much like *voudon* or *obeah* in the Caribbean, out of the religions of West Africa, syncretically linked to Catholicism. As in its Caribbean equivalents, *Candomblé* involves the possession of its practitioners by spirits and gods. At the ritual, Orpheus hears Eurydice's voice behind him. She warns him not to turn around or he'll lose her forever, just as in the Greek myth. "Do you love me enough to hear without seeing?" she asks. "You killed me," she tells him. When he turns in shock and horror he sees that the voice comes not from Eurydice, but from a possessed old woman who has been taken over by the spirit of Eurydice. "You've lost me forever," she tells Orpheus.

Recovering her body from the morgue, Orpheus wanders back to his home on the cliffs that look down on Rio. Mira, in revenge, has set fire to his house and pelts him with stones as he returns. Struck on the head by one, Orpheus falls from the cliff with Eurydice's body. Their dead bodies are then seen intertwined in the garden at the foot of the cliff. The two young boys who learned guitar from Orpheus get his instrument and play to make the sun rise, as he taught them. A little girl dances and tells the boy playing guitar, "You are Orpheus now," showing the cycle of myth continuing on with the next generation as Orpheus predicted.

The film transculturates the Greek narrative in a manner similar to how playwrights transculturate Greek tragedy into African environments, by deconstructing the Greek story and rewriting the cultural and performative codes—a lengthy process of substitution: a guitar for a lyre, power lines for a serpent, a streetcar for the winged feet of Hermes, etc. The characters are aware of the Greek culture with which they engage. It is, as the clerk says, "old history" that, according to Orpheus himself, "everybody knows."

As with Beier's magazine, the film *Orfeu Negro* uses Greek mythology as the metaphor by which the events that took place at this Carnival might be read. No attempt is made to interrogate the primacy of the Greek material. No attempt is made to consider the colonialist implications of the privileging of European culture. It is presented as a story "everybody knows." *Orfeu Negro* recreates the story of Orpheus and Eurydice with an Afro-Brazilian cast, no more, no less. It was made by Europeans and privileges Greek culture over Afro-Brazilian. The film follows the same model as Sartre's essay and Beier's journal: Greek material can be used as a metaphor to familiarize the Other that is the cultures of the African diaspora.

Like "Black Orpheus," "Black Odyssey" has been used as the title of no less than half a dozen books linking things African to Homer's narrative of the journey home of Odysseus. There are many ways to view Homer's poem, but the names *Odyssey* and Odysseus are used in a "Black Orpheus" manner to suggest three different types of narrative: epic journey (real or metaphorical), biography of the main character, and naval or seafaring story. Some of the narratives are fictional, others are scholarly, biographical, or historical works which use the Greek metaphor in the title (and sometimes as an organizing principle) in order to define the African person, event, or activity.

Two different, early, seminal volumes used the title "Black Odyssey" to suggest journey of people of African descent to the New World and their subsequent development there. Both Nathan Irvin Huggins and Roi Ottley present the history of African peoples in America as a metaphoric journey after a very real one.

Ottley's book was arguably the first to employ the Greek metaphor, and it's full title is *Black Odyssey: The Story of the Negro in America*. Ottley wrote his volume in the immediate post–World War II years, noting that, "This book might well be named 'The Negro's Adventure in America.' For it is a detailed story of his experiences in this country from 1619 to 1945" [sic].[13] Ottley's book is a straightforward narrative of the history of people of African descent in America during the years cited. He discusses racism, slavery, and the continuation of prejudice and oppression even up to and including the war years.

Citing a lack of books and writings by Africans in America, he laments of the early Negro in America, "His dreams, his aspirations, and his condition, expressed in his own words and from his own point of view, remain a closed book."[14] Ottley, unfortunately, is a Homer telling the story of an Odysseus who has not been allowed to tell his own story. The European American must tell the story of the African American, as the European epic must stand as a metaphor for the experiences of African peoples.

"Odyssey" is used by Ottley as a metaphor for a journey/history. It is a long voyage home full of suffering, travails, and enforced labor. Eventually, however, the resourceful, cunning, and clever hero will return home and restore his house, family, and self to glory. In chapter five, concerning Caribbean Greek adaptation, this meaning of Odyssey is frequently evoked, particularly by Derek Walcott.

Similarly, Nathan Irvin Huggins subtitled his *Black Odyssey* "The African American Ordeal in Slavery." Huggins, like Ottley, presents the history of Africans in America as a tragedy that ends, as many tragedies do, with the promise of a better future for the community at the expense of the tragic hero. In this case, protagonist and community are both African-America. He begins his narration with conditions in Africa at the beginning of the slave trade and traces the history of African people in the New World until 1850.

Huggins' thesis is that the slave experience shaped the individual and communal African American identity, but that this shaping is ultimately one of triumph, despite the conditions of slavery. He argues that this period sees the "self-creation of the African American people," a time when Africans were forced to develop a new identity in a new land.[15] Whereas African society was a "seamless web," the rupture of the individual African from the communal collective and the reduction of him or her into a marketable object whose culture and social ties were attacked by the slave masters required a remaking of African identity in the New World.[16] Huggins sees the refusal of slaves, individually and collectively, to compromise their humanity and the commitment to preserving aspects of their African cultures while developing a new communal culture within America as the triumph of the "tragic hero" of the African slave community.

Huggins asserts the tragic conditions of slavery. In allowing an economy built on slavery to develop, he asserts, "the United States became something other than a free society," further observing that, "the liberty of some Americans rested on the unfreedom of others."[17] Huggins book is a critique of American (read: white American) society and a celebration of African American achievement in the face of this oppression. Yet he uses a European metaphor to do so. Let us not fault Huggins, however, as the culture in which he lived privileged Greek epic and myth and ignored African culture. Huggins' work, however, is not "Black Dionysus," as he does not use the Greek metaphor to critique European culture. He only uses it as a metaphor by which the struggles of African Americans might be understood.

The Odyssey might also be seen as a sort of biography of Odysseus. The focus of the tale is this single individual, as opposed to *The Iliad*, which, while focusing on the wrath of Achilles also details the deaths of Hector and Patroclus and the calamities that befall the Greeks in the ninth year of the Trojan War. *The Odyssey* is very much Odysseus's story. Once he arrives back to Ithaca, the story is not over—how he regains his family, position, and power is also then detailed. In his invocation at the beginning of the epic, Homer asks the muse to "tell the story of that man skilled in all ways of contending, the wanderer."[18] It is this conception of *The Odyssey*, as the narrative of a clever man, that Randall Bennet Woods attempts to evoke in his book *A Black Odyssey: John Lewis Waller and the Promise of American Life, 1878–1900.*

John Lewis Waller (1850–1907) was born into slavery just before the Civil War. He migrated to Kansas in the late 1870s and became a leader in the black community and in the Republican Party of the time. He became a lawyer, a journalist, a politician, and eventually a diplomat, serving as the U.S. Consul to Madagascar under President Benjamin Harrison from 1891 to 1894. He attempted to start a black empire while in Africa and was imprisoned by the French and deported to America. He was, as Woods argues, "an ambitious, resourceful black American."[19]

In this case it is not the epic narrative of a journey (although Waller certainly had both an amazing life's journey and a journey to Africa and back) that the author seeks to evoke by employing the Greek title. Instead, it is the comparison between Waller and Odysseus that drives the metaphor: Waller is a clever, resourceful man who can rally other men around him.

He went on an amazing journey, but the interest of the reader is not primarily in the journey, but in the man who journeyed and who made it so interesting. By comparing Waller to Odysseus, Woods hopes to demonstrate that Waller, too is a "man skilled in all ways of contending" and a "wanderer," in short, that Waller is the equivalent of a mythic hero who survives by his cleverness and talents. The reader's focus is as much, if not more so on the man than the journey.

Mary Cable combines the epic journey narrative and naval narrative in her 1971 book *Black Odyssey: The Case of the Slave Ship Amistad.* Straightforward and fairly uncritical, Cable presents the story of the *Amistad*, the Spanish ship aboard which the fifty-three Africans destined for slavery in the New World (49 men, 3 girls and 1 boy) revolted and took over in July, 1839. Ten Africans, the Spanish captain and cook were killed in the uprising. Joseph Cinque, or Singbe, the leader of the mutiny, instructed the two Spaniards who had purchased the Africans to pilot the craft back to Africa. By day the sailors went east towards Africa, but at night sailed northwest to America, finally landing on Long Island, New York. The Africans were placed on trial for piracy and murder. Although initially found guilty, the U.S. Supreme Court ruled on 9 March 1841 that President Martin van Buren could not return the Africans to Cuba as they had been kidnapped under international law and therefore were not slaves. Granted their freedom, thirty-five of the original fifty-three survived to be returned to Sierra Leone in 1842.

The story became part of the popular consciousness after it was the subject of a 1997 film by Steven Spielberg. Cable's book, however, over two decades before, by its title, compares Cinque and his compatriots with Odysseus—fighting those who would imprison them or take them from home and overcoming tremendous difficulties to return there. While the metaphor fits the *Amistad* story better than most, it is still an example of the "Black Orpheus" model of Afro-Greek connection. By using the reference to *The Odyssey,* Cable links what was at the time of her writing a little known episode in the history of the slave trade to the better-known myth of Odysseus and the idea of Odyssey—a long, epic journey home.

Another *Black Odyssey* that deals with African Americans and naval culture is James Baker Farr's *Black Odyssey: The Seafaring Traditions of Afro-Americans.* Farr's history studies the wide variety of ways in which African Americans have been a part of American seafaring. Beginning in the early colonial period, Farr traces the black presence on whaling ships, merchant ships, warships, privateer fleets, and vessels of exploration and then continues into the modern period when the United States Navy was segregated until the Second World War saw the commissioning of the first black officers and the end of racial separation in the ranks. Slave sailors and free sailors of color served on all types of vessels and in all capacities throughout American history, argues Farr, and the African American community is responsible for many contributions.

In titling his book *Black Odyssey*, Farr seeks to connect to the maritime associations of Homer's epic. The story of a ten year journey, mostly undertaken on sailing and rowing vessels across many waters serves as a metaphor for the wide variety of maritime experiences of sailors of African descent. The idea of a journey home, or of an epic narrative, or of the cleverness of an individual are irrelevant to Farr. His title is meant to evoke Scylla and Charybdis, storms, and sirens. The title refers to the first twelve books of *The Odyssey*, which recount Odyssey's adventures on the sea, as opposed to the last twelve books, which mainly deal with land adventure. As with the other works discussed in the section, the metaphoric title is not always apt, but does serve as a referential metaphor by which the reader can understand things African via a classical allusion.

Part naval narrative, part biography, part epic journey, Daniel Panger based his 1982 novel *Black Ulysses* on the historical narrative of Estevan, a Moor from North Africa who accompanied a Spanish voyage to the Caribbean and Florida coast in the third decade of the sixteenth century. Although a slave, Estevan was known for his courage and his cleverness, and was one of only four out of three hundred men who survived the journey.

The book is told from the point of view of Estevan, and shares the events of the eight years that he spent with his Spanish masters trying to reach a Spanish settlement in the New World after losing contact with his ship. Three hundred men set off with the Governor for the New World, with the intention of finding gold, becoming wealthy and then returning to Spain. After a storm in the Caribbean sinks some of the ships, the rest land in Florida and the company embarks to explore the interior. Disease, accidents, storms, wild animals and attacks by the indigenous people eventually reduce the number of the company to four, who eventually are enslaved by an Indian tribe. Upon escaping, the four find themselves captured and enslaved again. After another escape, the four become physicians among the Native Americans and slowly work their way across the American Gulf coast and then down through present day Texas and across Mexico to Mexico City. The journey from Spain to Mexico City took eight years. The Afterword informs the reader that Estevan ended his days as a slave in the household of the Viceroy of Mexico. Sent as a guide for an expedition to the North, Estevan was captured by the Zuni and tortured to death in 1539.

The book is presented as a revisionist view of early exploration of America. The paperback edition boasts a back-cover endorsement from Dr. Martin Luther King's widow, Coretta Scott King, who calls the book "fascinating and valuable," noting that, "It dramatizes the little-known role of a Black man in the early exploration of America in a way that is both entertaining and enlightening." High praise indeed for a novel, following the "Black Orpheus" model, that uses its Greco-Roman name metaphorically to suggest the similarity between its African hero and a Greek one.

By basing his novel on a real historic episode, Panger has chosen to limit himself to the facts of history as best as they are known. But by calling the novel *Black Ulysses*, he links the historical Estevan with the mythical Ulysses (the Roman name for Odysseus), and, in doing so, establishes Ulysses as a metaphor for understanding Estevan.

Admittedly, there are similarities in the characters as presented. Both are known for being proud, clever, and able warriors. Both undertook lengthy journeys. Both only wanted to return home; Ulysses to Ithaca and Estevan to Africa. The journey narratives are told in an epic fashion with time variances: in both Homer's poem and Panger's novel a year can pass in a single sentence, but pages are spent describing the activity and thoughts of a single minute.

The differences between Estevan and his novel's metaphoric namesake, however, are significant. Ulysses returns home and, even though he served as a slave at various points in his journey, arrives in Ithaca not only as a free man, but also as the king. Estevan never returns to Africa—he dies a slave in the New World, working as a guide for an expedition to colonize and conquer the indigenous people of the Southwest. He was a slave forced to aid in the effort to enslave others. His journey never ended.

Panger's novel serves as a meditation on two things: slavery and the true nature of Christianity. Estevan, a Moor from North Africa, had been a slave since his capture in battle by the Spanish several years earlier, but, for his cleverness in helping the Spanish officers, is freed from his state of slavery. He is then, with those officers, captured and enslaved by Indians. They escape, but are captured by another group and enslaved again. Escaping again, they reach "Christian" Mexico City where the Viceroy, after giving Estevan a gold statue of the Virgin Mary, declares Estevan his new household slave. The experience of slavery is treated indifferently in the novel. Though Estevan hates being a slave, he loves some of the Spanish officers as brothers, and instructs them in how to be a slave once they have been reduced to his condition by the Indians.

Estevan was also converted to Christianity, a religion he embraces and follows readily. As a result of the hardships and experiences in captivity, the Spanish officers, who were accompanied on their voyage by a member of the Spanish Inquisition and who, as Christians, believe themselves superior to pagans, learn how to live in a Christian manner. They leave honor behind and learn to forgive. By novel's end they no longer care about gold but about healing and caring for others. It is Estevan, the black slave who teaches them first how to be good slaves and then how to be better Christians.

These two constructions: that slaves are better Christians, and the Moor, being used to slavery, accepts it more willingly, and that Estevan, the proud Moor would not only embrace Christianity but would embody it and become the model of its practice, are problematic. It is only by giving up his freedom, his religion, his name, and his cultural identity that Estevan can become a Ulysses-like figure. It is only by denying his very Africanness that Estevan can survive in the New World and willingly helps his Spanish masters to do the same. Panger has not written anything along the lines of the Amistad story, there is no revolution here—only an African who, by accepting Christianity and slavery survives to remain a slave at the end of his journey. The title suggests that this is comparable to the journey of Ulysses. Perhaps not so. Nevertheless, Panger's novel remains a strong example of the "Black Orpheus" model of linking black narrative to Greek cultural material for metaphor purposes only.

As with Randall Bennet Woods's biography of John Walker Lewis, Kenneth Wilson evokes a figure from Greek mythology to summarize the life and achievements of an African American. In *Black Apollo of Science: The Life of Ernest Everett Just*, Wilson narrates the life of the Howard University biologist by comparing him in the title to Apollo, god of medicine, music, the arts, learning, and reason. Just originally majored in Greek, ironically, at Dartmouth before switching to biology. He then went on to complete a doctorate in biology at the University of Chicago. Racism kept Just from employment at a white institution despite the fact that he was one of the greatest biologists of his generation. By using the title *Black Apollo of Science*, the author attempts to rescue Just from the racism he faced in life by metaphorically indicating his superiority in his field. Just was, says the title, a god of science, and therefore worthy of our respect.

Interestingly, Frank R. Lillie, Just's European American mentor, eulogized Just after his death in the journal *Science*, also locating Just in the world of Greek culture: "...an element of tragedy ran through Just's scientific career due to the limitations imposed by being a Negro in America."[20] Lillie's remarks seem to evoke the idea of a "tragic flaw," that Just would have had a brilliant career if he had not had the "flaw" of being black in America.

In both cases, Greek cultural material is used to generate the meaning of Just's life. Manning sees him as a mythic figure, a god who can be reclaimed from a racist society and given the admiration he deserves. Conversely, Lillie sees Just as tragic, limited by fate and tragic flaw to lesser role than he otherwise might have had. Both writers use Greek material to construct very different portraits of Ernest Everett Just, their frames of reference result in a "Black Orpheus" paradigm for the life of Just, neither of which may be entirely accurate.

In 1970, Italian filmmaker Pier Paolo Pasolini released *Appunti per un Orestiade Africana*, translated into English as "Notes for an African Orestes," but perhaps better translated as "Notes for an African *Oresteia*," as it is Aeschylus' version of the story of Orestes that Pasolini wanted to film in Africa.

Pasolini already had experience in adapting Greek tragedy to the media of cinema. In 1967 he filmed *Edipo Re* (*Oedipus Rex*—but actually a combination of *Oedipus Rex* and elements from *Oedipus at Colonus*) in Morocco, an African nation, and set in a relatively modern period. The music and settings firmly locate the film in third world North Africa, although the characters are played by Italian actors.[21] In 1971 he would film *Medea* with Maria Callas, set and shot in Turkey. In both of these films Passolini used the images of the third world cultures to connect to the idea of ancient Greece. Naomi Greene observes of the two films, "Here, striking third world landscapes suggest the physical presence of archaic and sacred civilizations, of mythic layers of time."[22] In doing so, Pasolini hopes to project to modern Western audiences a sense of the timeless mythic past of Europe. By using Morocco and Turkey, however, he constructs these nations in the same way that the Cambridge anthropologists did at the turn of the century, seeing civilization as an evolutionary development in which the third world nations of today are where Europe was during the age of Greece. It is a way of privileging Europe and denigrating the cultures and civilizations of African and Middle Eastern nations. Although a Marxist who feels a sense of community with the proletariat of Africa, Pasolini still sees Africans as "primitive and savage," and thus the equivalent of mythic Greeks.[23] Thus, his ideology creates a sense of benevolent racism that manifests itself in his *Notes for an African Oresteia* and how he frames developing Africa in terms of Greek tragedy.

The voiceover at the beginning of the film shares that it is "not a documentary and not a feature picture." Pasolini has actually made a film about the film he wants to make. The African *Oresteia* was never made, but the filmed "notes" were edited and released as this piece that narrates the story of modern Africa's development through the myth of Orestes. The narrator, who is assumed to be Pasolini, states that he wants to film the story of Orestes, "to be shot in the Africa of today, in modern Africa." He then summarizes the story while the film shows images of Africans engaged in various activities on city streets.

The filmmaker then begins showing close-ups of individuals and commenting on the appropriateness of using them as characters in the tragedy. The comments reveal both Pasolini's assumptions about Greek tragedy and his (rather racist) attitudes towards Africans. Showing one woman he states, "This can't be Cassandra, who was young and beautiful." Showing a group of girls the narrator states that "Electra is hardest to find," because African girls "don't know how to do anything but laugh and accept life as a kind of holiday." They cannot be serious or "haughty," he intones, as the character of Electra must be.

Pasolini's Africa is a poor one that is grateful to Europe for the advances it offers. The narrator states that the characters and settings must be "as real, as true as possible," without ever defining the nature of "real" or "true." The "real" Africa of Pasolini is not the "real" Africa of his subjects. At one point he shows a market and announces that it is a "poor, abandoned" area, yet dozens of people are visible in the shot. He shows a factory, claiming that the industrialized areas are "the modern part of the continent," positing the rural, poor, abandoned area as "traditional Africa" and factories as "modern Africa." In showing a classroom, the narrator informs the viewer that, "African students look on the knowledge that is offered them with obedience, passive and humble," a construction of the only recently independent African nations as full of happy, obedient, humble citizens who are grateful for the gifts of the West.

It is only a third of the way through the film that Pasolini introduces his thesis as to why Greek tragedy transculturates well into an African setting:

> I feel I can recognize some analogies between the situation of the *Oresteia* and the situation of Africa today, especially concerning the transformation of the Furies, the Eurynes, into the Eumenides. In other words, I mean that the tribal civilization seems to resemble archaic Greek civilization, and Orestes' discovery of democracy, carrying it then into his country which could be Argos in the tragedy and Africa in my film, is in a sense the discovery of democracy that Africa has also made in the last few years.

At the risk of seeming unscholarly, how many levels of wrong is this statement? Orestes did not "discover" democracy in the *Oresteia*, nor did African nations "discover" it. Orestes did not bring democracy to Argos but, depending on which myth or tragedy one consults, either ascends the throne of Argos to rule it as a king, or married Hermione, daughter of Helen and Menelaus, and subsequently had Apollo convince the Argives to accept him as their king. In other words, Orestes never discovered or practiced democracy, he only benefited from the Athenian legal system, using it to his advantage to gain his freedom and return to a life of wealth and power.

Pasolini's understanding of African history is even more inaccurate than his understanding of Greek tragedy. Under Pasolini's formulation, the centuries of European imperialism are erased, leaving only a period when western nations led African "tribal civilizations" to discover democracy, which had apparently been available to them all along, had they chosen to look for it. Such a construction ignores the reality of colonialism, oppression, and the manner in which the West controlled Africa politically, economically, and culturally for centuries. Such a construction posits "tribal" Africa as culturally and politically backwards until taught democracy by the West, which is patently untrue.

In the next scene, Pasolini gathers a group of young African men, whom he never identifies in any way, and asks them about his idea that Africa can be explained via the metaphor of Greek tragedy. They immediately begin to resist his ideas and the manner in which he phrases the questions and state the flaws with the formulation from their point of view. When he asks if Africa is like ancient Athens, one man remarks, "Africa is a continent, not a nation." Pasolini responds by asking him which African nation "best represents" the continent. The man replies, "I have not seen all of Africa." Pasolini, the European, wants to paint all of Africa with the same brush and generalize about his culture. The Africans he questions resist such reductivist thinking and try to offer him a new paradigm, which he cannot see.

He tells them the story of Orestes and asks if they see it as a metaphor for their own nation's development. A man responds, "I don't know much about your movie, but I don't see the connection." "Do any of you see my connection?" a frustrated and condescending Pasolini asks the group. No one answers him.

Pasolini's misunderstanding and false constructions of both Greek tragedy and Africa continue. For the furies he shows trees and a lioness on the savanna, arguing that, "the furies are destined to disappear. And in my film, a part of ancient Africa is destined to disappear with them." Yet the furies do not "disappear," they become the Eumenides, the "kindly ones" who protect the city. Pasolini never specifies what part of "ancient Africa" is destined to disappear, but the images on the screen at that point in the narration are of wildlife on the savanna. Perhaps he means to indicate that endangered species of Africa are fated to die off as the continent modernizes, a disturbing prediction, and seemingly unrelated to the transformation of the furies.

Pasolini then announces his intention to use actual footage from the Biafran War to suggest the Trojan war, which is over before the story of Orestes truly begins. Showing unidentified African soldier after unidentified African soldier, he reads from Aeschylus, positing that the individual shown could be a particular functionary in Greek tragedy: "These could be palace guards in Argos," "This man could be then messenger who comes to tell of Agamemnon's return," etc.

Suddenly and inexplicably, Pasolini shows an American jazz band performing in a club in urban Africa. The narrator states that the *Oresteia* could be sung jazz style to approximate original Greek tragic performance. He links the African struggle to the African American struggle in Marxist terms: "It would be well to clarify to all in fact, that twenty million black members of the American subproletariat are the leaders of any revolutionary movement in the third world." One might ask why Africa cannot produce any revolutionary leaders of its own in Passolini's assumption (when it already clearly had), or why Africa needed African Americans to lead it to revolution? Ironically, the first musician to receive a close-up is a Euro-American saxophonist who is clearly white. Pasolini seems to indicate that it is the United States that must lead Africa into a modern, Marxist existence, which does not even make sense, but does again privilege the West over Africa.

Pasolini then returns to rural Africa to film a sequence from the *Libation Bearers*, which he narrates to assure that the viewer understands his concept. He has a father and a daughter demonstrate traditional graveside ceremonies for their ancestors. Pasolini never identifies to which ethnic nation the individuals belong or what kind of ritual they carry out. They are "African," according to the narrator, carrying out "traditional" rituals. He films a young man walking through the bush, stating that "This is the moment when Orestes arrives at his father's grave." The furies arrive as angry jazz is played on the soundtrack while the film shows trees shaking as a violent storm rocks them.

Pasolini then announces that Kampala, Uganda will serve as Athens in his film, although he never explains the choice. The University of Dar el Salaam will be the Temple of Apollo at which Orestes will undergo his trial (again, Passolini confuses his Greek tragedy—the trial was in the temple of Athena in Athens, Apollo's temple opens the *Eumenides*, but that is in Delphi, not Athens!)

Finally, as the film winds down to its conclusion, Pasolini returns to the group of young men he was questioning earlier in the film. "Do you feel a little bit like Orestes?" he asks. They do not. He asks them how to show the Furies becoming the Eumenides, and is told that he must synthesize modern, traditional, western, and indigenous cultures and images. Passolini seems incapable of thinking along those intercultural terms, however, as he is only interested in showing what he perceives as the "real" Africa.

Leaving aside the racism, the pejorative and condescending constructions, and the ignorance, Pasolini follows the same model as *Orfeu Negro*: constructing a film using narrative and dramaturgy from ancient Greece set in an African context. Unlike *Orfeu Negro*, however, that transculturated the story for purposes of entertainment, Pasolini seeks to use the *Oresteia* to explain the transition of modern Africa from tribal civilization to modern democracy. The Greek tragedy is a metaphor for the history of Africa. More than *Orfeu Negro*, Pasolini's film uses Greek tragedy as a metaphor to understand things African. While claiming to represent the "real" Africa, however, Pasolini's rather racist constructions posit an Africa that is inferior to the West and in need of guidance. The film represents the "Black Orpheus" paradigm at its most pejorative.

Pasolini had definitive ideas about what the *Oresteia* is and sets out to find equivalents in "modern Africa" to frame the story. In seeking to construct the *Oresteia* in terms of Africa, he ultimately constructs Africa in terms of the *Oresteia*. Pasolini interprets Africa in terms of the Greek mythic and tragic material and through his racist commentary demonstrates not only the privileging of Western and European culture, but also a prejudicial, pejorative, and limited view of African culture.

The Roman version of the Greek goddess of love, Aphrodite, is Venus. It is in this guise that she has been used in a "Black Orpheus" paradigm by several authors and for a historical person, making "Black Venus" almost as popular as "Black Orpheus" and "Black Odyssey" as a metaphor for explaining Africa in terms of classical culture.

Award winning British author Angela Carter has a short story entitled "Black Venus's Tale." In the story a woman of color becomes a muse of sorts, involuntarily. The story was inspired by the relationship of Charles Baudelaire and his mistress Jeanne Duval, and explores issues of negritude, colonialism, art, romanticism, and gender.

T. Denean Sharpley-Whiting also used the phrase to title the book *Black Venus: Sexualized Savages, Primal Fears, and Primitive Narratives in French*. Sharpley-Whiting argues that the Roman deity was used in two ways. Venus was the protector of prostitutes and the embodiment of sexuality as well as the goddess of beauty. In her former sphere of influence: "The projection of the Venus image, of prostitute proclivities, onto black female bodies allows the French writer to maintain a position of moral, sexual, and racial superiority."[24] In other words, French writers use the idea of Venus to eroticize, exoticize, and sexualize black women. In her role as the goddess of beauty, Venus is also a metaphor for what is considered beautiful. Thus, "Black Venus" refers to African standards of beauty, which it was assumed were different (read: inferior to) European standards of beauty.

Sander Gilman notes in his study of nineteenth-century art that black females are always "more primitive, and therefore more sexually intensive."[25] The presence of black servants in a painting from this period indicates a sense of sexuality. Black women are exotic Other, particularly under the gaze of white males. In both Europe and America the black woman was first and foremost a sexual object. What Sharpley-Whiting states of the French is also true of Americans: "the black female must always be black female in relation to white males."[26] White Europeans and European Americans both desire and fear black bodies, both desire and fear being "fueled by sexual myths of black women and men," in the words of Cornell West.[27]

A strong stereotype of women of color that emerges in this period is the "Jezebel," the seductive temptress that craves sexual satisfaction from all men.[28] Black women are perceived as "an object of sexual pleasure," but are constructed in contradistinction to the ideology of white female beauty. White women are perceived as pure and beautiful, women of color are objects on which white men may slake their lust. At the same time, however, black sexuality "is a form of black power over which whites have little control."[29] In other words, black women have a powerful allure, which leads to the myth that white men can't control themselves around black women, and blame the women for being objects of sexual desire. Thus, the Black Venus, like the original Venus, is a figure who creates in men the need for sexual intercourse. The Black Venus is a result of the view of whites of black women as the exotic Other: "closer to nature (removed from intelligence and control) and more prone to be guided by base pleasure and biological impulses."[30]

There was also an historic figure, Saartjee Baartman (anglicized to "Sarah Barthman"), a South African woman who was known as "The Hottentot Venus." Baartman was placed on public display because of her unique physical characteristics, and three times has been on stage. The first was when she herself was the object of public display. Before she had even died, she was the subject of a French melodrama, *La Vénus hottentote, ou haine aux Françaises* (The Hottentot Venus, or Hatred of Frenchwomen) in 1814. In 1996, African American playwright returned to Baartman's story in *Venus*.

All three performative events use the metaphor of Venus to contextualize Saartjee Baartman.

Baartman was an African woman who was placed on public display because of her enormous buttocks and enlarged genitalia, which were seen as common in African women and emblematic of African female sexuality by Europeans at the time. She was displayed in 1810 in London until an inquiry was held to determine whether or not she was being held against her will (England had abolished the slave trade in 1807, although slavery was still in existence in the nation in 1810). She was later sold to an animal trainer and put on display in Paris. Upon her death in 1816 she was dissected and her genitalia, skeleton, and organs preserved in a French museum.

Baartman was placed on public display under the name "The Hottentot Venus," suggesting that she was an example of African standards of beauty. She was also regarded as a sexual object. People were allowed to examine her buttocks and genitalia. By naming her "The Hottentot Venus," those who were exploiting her hoped that the above-mentioned connotations of beauty and unmitigated sexuality would prove a selling point. It eroticized Baartman, explaining her person in terms of the metaphor of Venus.

While Baartman was still alive and on display in Paris in 1814, the Théâtre de Vaudeville produced the one-act by Théaulon, Dartois, and Brasier, *La Vénus hottentote, ou haine aux Françaises*.[31] Played by a white actress, a character representing Baartman exhibits "beauté effrayante [frightening beauty]" "savagery." The melodrama was a way of ridiculing Baartman and her public sexuality as "a reaffirmation of Frenchwomen as erotic objects of the white male gaze."[32] As the subtitle suggests, men who find the "Hottentot Venus" sexually appealing are demonstrating "hatred of Frenchwomen."

In the play a male character insists that Baartman is "a Venus," she is "more than a women," she is "the mythic goddess of beauty and sexuality."[33] He stands for all Frenchmen who find the idea of the Hottentot Venus titillating and appealing. He has, however, not yet seen the complete woman—he is only entranced with the idea of oversized buttocks and genitalia. At play's end, when Baartman's face is finally revealed, the same character cries out, "With such a face/she cannot be a Venus!"[34] Sharpley-Whiting concludes, "She is certainly not representative of the mythic Greek goddess of beauty and sexuality, and thus her billing as the Hottentot Venus is a misnomer."[35]

More than a misnomer, in this play the name is used ironically and pejoratively. The "Hottentot Venus" is not beautiful, according to the play.

When compared with European (specifically French) women, Baartman is to be considered hideous, says the play. The authors reject the "Hottentot Venus" title, not because of how it represents (and demeans) Baartman, but rather how it represents (and demeans) Frenchwomen, whom the authors believe far more beautiful than African women. "Hottentot Venus" is an insult, says the play, not to African women, but to Frenchwomen. The ironic use of the term also mocks supposed African standards of beauty: "Look at what the Africans believe is Venus-like, see the black standard of beauty and how far below ours it is," is the message given by the play.

It is this attitude that is framed in Suzan Lori-Parks play of 1996, simply entitled *Venus*. An eclectic and anarchic telling of the Baartman story, the narrating ringmaster of the play, a character called "the Negro Ressurectionist," informs the audience:

> With an intensely ugly figure, distorted beyond all European notions of beauty, she was said to possess the kind of shape which is most admired among her countrymen, the Hottentots.[36]

It is this construction of Baartman, as embodiment of the inversion of notions of beauty, that makes the 'Black Venus" label a pejorative one. Everything that is ugly in Europe is found beautiful in Africa, according to this construction, emphasizing difference and Othering the African in a manner that is not accurate.

Venus was directed by Richard Foreman in a co-production by the Yale Repertory Theatre and the New York Public Theatre/New York Shakespeare Festival and presented in 1996. The text was subsequently published in *Theatre Forum* later that year and in script form by Theatre Communications Group a year later.

Parks presents a series of incidents in the life of Baartman relying upon her technique of 'repetition and revision."[37] Tom Sellar sees the play as "a resurrection of Sartjee Baartman on stage."[38] In addition to the Negro Ressurectionist and the Venus herself, the play features a group of individuals who serve as five different choruses, including a chorus in a play within the play, a fictitious melodrama (though rooted in *La Vænus hottentote*) entitled "For the Love of the Venus," that attacks Park's Venus even as the French melodrama did the historic Baartman.

Set at the turn of the nineteenth century, but rooted in a contemporary sensibility, the play focuses on the public investigation of 1810, called by the English king to determine if "Venus" was being held against her will. It also deals with the "Venus craze that swept England at the time."[39] Parks rescues Venus from being the object of European gaze and derivation, and instead focuses on why this figure was so fascinating to westerners at the

Susan Lori-Parks's *Venus*, as performed in 1996 at the Yale Repertory Theatre. Photograph © T. Charles Erickson.

time. The play deconstructs the ideas of gender, sexuality, and performance, so that one questions the construction of the identity of the "Black Venus." Parks is the only interaction with Baartman that approaches a "Black Dionysus" paradigm, as described below.

Saartjee Baartman's skeleton and internal organs were finally turned over to South African officials on 29 April 2002. Thuthukile Edy Skweyiya, the South African ambassador to France, said at the ceremony that Baartman is "the symbol of a nation's need to confront and acknowledge its past, and of a nation's overwhelming desire to restore and reaffirm dignity and honor to all its people."[40] France finally gave up the body of the Hottentot Venus so that her remains might be returned to Africa and buried. Baartman thus finally lost the Greco-Roman metaphor that defined her existence in terms of European expectations and again became African in her own right.

In all of these cases—*Black Orpheus*, *Black Odyssey*, *Black Apollo*, *African Oresetia*, and *Black Venus*, the model is the same. The word "Black" or

"African" is placed in front of a name from Greek myth, epic, or tragedy, and used to explain or identify things African in terms of European culture. The "Black Orpheus" paradigm, as I have termed it, is a model of interaction between Greek and African diasporan culture that uses the Athenian material (or its Roman equivalent) to understand the African. It is a Eurocentric metaphor that makes the Other of African culture into a familiar Self.

Black Athena: Reclaiming the Stolen Legacy

The name for the second model of ancient Greek/African diasporan linkage comes from a series of books by Martin Bernal and taken up by his critics to argue against his model. The term "Black Athena" is readily identifiable in classical studies for a school of thought that the Greeks stole their culture from Egypt and Africa and, to a lesser extent, Asia.

In 1987, Martin Bernal published the first volume of his extended work *Black Athena*, subtitled *The Afroasiatic Roots of Classical Civilization, Volume I: The Fabrication of Ancient Greece 1785–1985*. This book was followed in 1991 by the second volume, subtitled *Volume II: The Archeological and Documentary Evidence*. The third volume is forthcoming as of this writing. Bernal, following in the footsteps of such Afrocentric classicists as Edward Jones, Cheikh Anta Diop, John Henrik Clark, Yosef Ben-Jochannan, Joel Rogers, and George G.M. James, theorizes that Greek culture was profoundly shaped and developed by Egyptian and Near-Eastern influences.

Bernal proposes two models—the "Ancient Model," in which the Greeks acknowledged their cultural debt to Africa and the Levant, and the "Aryan Model," developed by later, racist Europeans who "were concerned to keep black Africans as far as possible from European civilization," and so attempted to erase any evidence of African influence in Greek culture, arguing that Greek culture is purely European.[41] Bernal then proposes the "Revised Ancient Model," which re-emphasizes African influence in Greek culture.

Although not original, Bernal's construction of the Afroasiatic origins of Greek civilization popularized the ideas in a manner that they had not been before, and a controversy arose quickly over his theories. Mary Lefkowitz emerged as a key opponent of Afrocentric classicism, writing *Not out of Africa* and co-editing *Black Athena Revisited* (with Guy MacLean Rogers), using Bernal's title as both a reference to Bernal's book and as a metaphor for Afrocentric classicism. *Arethusa*, a journal published by the

American Philological Association, devoted an entire special issue to "The Challenge of 'Black Athena'," again using the title to refer to the concept, and including articles from Martin Bernal, Sarah Morris, and Frank M. Snowden, Jr. Bernal fired back on his critics with *Black Athena Writes Back* and the forthcoming *Debating Black Athena*. Other scholars analyze the debate and attempt to frame it in the contexts of classical studies, the academic world, Africana studies, and American culture. Jacques Berlinerblau's *Heresy in the University*, for example, identifies Bernal as a heretic within the American academy, in the original Greek sense. By this, Berlinerblau means that Bernal has chosen to believe and express something that runs counter to orthodoxy, and as such is singled out for inquisition, as all heretics eventually are.[42] Orthodoxy does not always handle dissent well and must move to reassert itself.

The controversy does not use Bernal's name, but is centered around the title of his opus, which suggests that the Greek gods, Athena being the model of them, indeed the deity after whom the city of Athens was named, were African, if not black. The larger reality suggested by *Black Athena* is that Greek culture is derived from African culture, specifically Egyptian culture. This debate will be explored in more depth in the next chapter, but the terminology is useful in establishing the second paradigm of Afro-Greek material.

The "Black Athena" paradigm, like the book and debate after which it is named, posits Africa as the source of classical civilization. Artists and writers who follow this model use Greek culture because they perceive it as African or African-inspired, and use the material to reestablish the primacy of Egypt and Africa.

Before Bernal wrote his volumes Edward Jones wrote *Black Zeus: African Mythology and History*. Jones, like Bernal, argues that the Greeks took their religion and culture from the Africans. Jones's three main premises are:

> ...that Egypt was Africa; that the origin of the gods was Africa; and that since the gods were started by Africans, and named by them, then the gods were surely black like them.[43]

Jones argues that Greek mythology is derived from Egyptian mythology. Egyptians were black Africans, and if the Greeks worshipped the Egyptian gods then the Greek gods were black, hence the name *Black Zeus*.

For Jones, as well as other Afrocentrists, including Bernal, racist Europeans who could not accept that the cornerstone of their civilization had been created by black Africans deny the African origins of Greek culture and claim that the gods and mythical heroes were white. For Jones, exploring the connection between Greece and Africa is not colonialist culture, it is the reappropriation of a stolen culture—one the Europeans stole from Africa.

Jones argues that the Greeks were descended from Egyptian colonists, and that they, and the people in their myths, were all black. He notes that, for example, "all of the people in the house of Oedipus were Black for real" (sic).[44] Jones's writing is an example of the "Black Athena" paradigm: the use of Greek cultural material based on the assumption that it is actually African cultural material that is being used. The Greeks received it (or stole it) from Africa, but later European cultures covered up this cultural debt. Theatre artists who use Greek tragedy, therefore, are actually using African cultural material, which means that the use of Greek tragedy is not colonialist, but sited well within the realm of Afrocentrism.

A theatrical example of the "Black Athena" paradigm of the intertextuality of Greek culture and contemporary African American theatre is the writings of playwright Ifa Bayeza (born Wanda Celeste Williams, and sister of Ntozake Shange). Bayeza's first major work, *Homer G. And the Rhapsodies in The Fall of Detroit* is a musical satire of American and African American culture based on *The Iliad* and *The Odyssey*. The play received a Kennedy Center Fund for New American Plays Grant and was performed first in February of 1996 at the Lorraine Hansberry Theatre in San Francisco. According to John Williams, who reviewed the initial production for *American Theatre* in an article entitled "Hip Hop Homer," the play is "a hybrid of African American storytelling and traditional European forms."[45] The play tells the story of a "discordant wedding" between "the radical daughter of the most influential black congressman in America" and "the international playboy son of the despot king of Benin."[46] The action moves through Europe, America, and Africa, all the while questioning notions of culture and identity, and, in particular, questions the origins of Greek culture, which the West claims, but playwright Bayeza sees as an African legacy.

The chorus consists of three doo-wop singing African American men called "The Rhapsodies." Their leader is Homer G., "a griot turned rapper."[47] This titular character embodies several levels of reference that demonstrate how the play links African and ancient Greek culture. "Homer" refers to both the Greek poet and "Homie," an slang term, short for "Home Boy" meaning both friend and someone from the streets. "G," in this case, is short for both "griot," the storytelling figure in many African cultures who also serves as historian, lawgiver, teacher, entertainer, and repository of community knowledge, and is a street term, short for "gangster," again indicating friendship or that someone possesses street credibility and is "real." "G" might even be short for "Greek." Homer G. is thus

"Homer the Griot," linking Africa and Greece and "Homer the Gangsta," a streetwise rapper linking Greece and African-America, suggesting Greek poet, African storyteller, and gangster rapper embodied in one individual.[48]

Bayeza states that the bride, Thetis (also the name of a Greek sea deity, wife of Peleus, and, prophesied to give birth to a son who would be greater than his father, subsequently was mother of Achilles) and her maids "represent lots of ancient goddesses, both Greek and African, and they are composites of my classmates and peers."[49] Bayeza links her own friends with Greek and African goddesses, and links those two sets of goddesses with each other. Other classical references via character names include a drug runner named Paris and "Professor Aphrodite," who shares a name with the Greek goddess of love.

Clinton Turner Davis, the director of the premiere production, argues that, "This is the first play I've encountered where African American characters are allowed through myth to visit all of their origins, no matter who claimed them."[50] Homer G., he says, is not merely "a black Homer," meant to suggest the Greek original—he is the Greek original: "Homer was black."[51] According to Davis, like the epigram from Malcolm X that opened this chapter, Homer, historically, was African, a black man, whom the Europeans have taken and claimed as their own. Greek culture, he argues, was stolen from Africa. The play suggests, through the journeys of its characters, that the Western classical heritage of Greece and Rome is, in fact, based upon, built upon, and stolen from African culture. By claiming Greek culture as part of Africa's legacy, and therefore part of African American cultural origins, Bayeza and Davis dismiss the possible colonialist nature of Greek culture. Instead, they view themselves as reclaiming a culture that was taken from them. Using ancient Greek culture is a not an appropriation but a reappropriation that corrects colonialism.

Such a formulation creates a larger problem for postcolonial critics who would see the use of Greek material as perpetuating the centrality of the West. In postcolonial formulations, the West has dominated other cultures through imperialism, imposed their own culture over non-western cultures, privileging European art over indigenous, and at the cornerstone of western civilization is ancient Greece. Critics such as Rustom Bharucha, for example, would argue that Greek tragedy dominates intercultural theatre because of the colonialist efforts to place it at the apex of cultural superiority. Calling for an "ethics of representation in theatre," Bharucha expects the West to stop "Othering" non-western cultures on stage, beginning with Greek representations of others and Others.[52] Under the "Black Athena" paradigm, however, a more complex model of interaction and postcolonial culture emerges.

Tejumola Olaniyan, for example, critiques Derek Walcott for his continual use of western culture to inform his poetry and drama. Although such a choice is not inherently negative, and is one of many, Olaniyan argues that, as opposed to Walcott's assumptions, "the choice is not natural, self-evident or automatic but thoroughly ideological."[53] Olaniyan is correct in that the choice of material is always ideologically-based. But he does not take into account the formulation of Greek culture as being African-derived as some Afrocentric classicists such as Edward L. Jones or Martin Bernal would propose. Under this formulation, the choice is still thoroughly ideological, but not in the manner Olaniyan suggests. Many ideologies can inform the choice of Greek source material to develop new postcolonial texts. In the case of Silas Jones or Ifa Bayeza, for example, the playwright chooses to use Greek material based on the ideology that he or she is actually using African material and correcting the (European-created) historical falsehood that it is not. The choice of Greek material is therefore rooted in a very Afrocentric (as opposed to Olaniyan's assumed Eurocentric) ideology.

In a situation where the playwright believes Greek culture is African, the playwright is under an obligation to use Greek material to combat the colonialist creation of Greek culture as European. Decolonization would not result from not performing Greek tragedy, but rather from reconnecting it to its African roots. Rather than avoiding Greek drama, as August Wilson or Olaniyan might suggest, the Afrocentric theatre artist is free to draw upon it as part of his or her cultural heritage, and indeed must do so in order to fight the lie (widely believed) that Greek culture is European culture.

Under the "Black Athena" paradigm, there is no metaphor, as there is in "Black Orpheus." Instead there is the re-establishment of the historic connection between ancient Athens and ancient Africa. Rather than seeing African culture in terms of European culture, the "Black Athena" paradigm sees Greek culture as African-derived and sets out to formally and publicly establish that fact through drama. As "Black Orpheus" is a Eurocentric way of viewing the Afro-Greek connection, "Black Athena" is an Afrocentric way of reclaiming the stolen legacy of Greece's African connection.

Is There Another Option?: Black Dionysus

One model of the link between Greece and things African posits Greek models as metaphors for understanding Africa and African Americans.

The second model of the link between Greece and Africa posits that it is actually the Greeks who derived their culture from Africans, and thus Greek material is actually African material and must be reclaimed from the Europeans. Is a third model possible?

Several factors come into play when considering a third option. First, for some, the origins of Greek culture are irrelevant. More important than Eurocentric cultural imperialism is the condition of living directly under an oppressive political and economic (which admittedly, always carry with them cultural) colonial rule that does not allow for dissent or critique. South Africa under apartheid perhaps being the best example. When the government actively works to suppress theatre that is actively resistant or openly opposes apartheid, the theatre becomes much more difficult to perform. The government was happy to allow productions of Greek tragedy, perceiving its production by blacks as an acceptance of European colonial hegemony.

Such productions, however, serve to disguise their own resistance and oppression. *Antigone in 71*, for example, performed by students involved in the Theatre Council of Natal in 1971 is an example of the use of Greek text being used to gain permission from the government to perform, and then using the Greek material to critique the government. The play opened with a black man being hung, and instead of a set used projections of the slums of South Africa to draw a direct connection between the injustices of Creon in the Greek play and those suffered daily under the apartheid regime.[54] The change in title, to *Antigone in 71* suggests that the play is set in the (then) present day, and that the issues are relevant to the black audience. Antigone's defiance of Creon thus becomes a model of behavior that actively stands up to the very regime that allowed the drama to be performed. In a case such as this, adapting not only is not cultural colonialism, the Greek text becomes the means to an act of resistance.

In the Clark Lecture given at Trinity College Cambridge (and subsequently published as *Exposed by the Mask*), British director Peter Hall concludes "The Greek stage itself ... is a mask."[55] Hall argues that the Greek mask exposes as it contains, reveals more by hiding the human face behind it. The stage of the Greek tragic theatre functioned in the same way—by leaving the extreme violence off stage it must be imagined, rather than seen, which paradoxically makes it more real. To see a death on stage, for example, is to know that one is watching a special effect. To hear a dying scream offstage and then be shown a bloody body allows the mind to envision a very real death that is not a special effect. The mask, likewise, takes basic human emotions and hides it, allowing the imagination of the audience to take over and, again paradoxically, make it more real.

In this sense, Greek tragedy, when adapted for use in other contexts is a mask. It serves as a disguise to distance the audience from the actual issues and themes being addressed. One can use Greek theatre as a tool to critique and resist Western imperialism, European drama, society, colonial culture, or even Greek theatre itself. The tragic texts are means to an end, not the end in and of themselves. The canny adapter can literally use European literature to attack and critique European culture, including European literature. Context cannot be ignored.

The danger in opposing ancient Greek culture across the board as imperialist is that one then creates a binary construction of Greek/non-western that is inaccurate to begin with and risks excluding those artists of color who wish to work with Greek tragedy regardless.

Kobena Mercer argues, as a "cultural critic whose interests lie in the visual arts of the black diaspora," that the black artist can become burdened with "exceptionalism" just as much from racial and social ideology as from inherent racist attitudes in the white population. "Black artists are never allowed to be ordinary," he notes, "but have to visibly embody a prescribed difference."[56] The problem, therefore, is that the black artist is always a *black* artist and never "an artist": "the aesthetic dimension of their work is made subservient to its sociological context," which is limiting not just to the artist, but ultimately to the ethnic group, as "it perpetuates the ideological condensation characteristic of racist discourse."[57] Many cultural critics would argue that the artist has no choice, it is a racist society with unequal distribution of capital and cultural clout that subserviates the aesthetic dimension of their work to the sociological context. Yet Mercer's point still remains, that in limiting an artist of color to his or her color regardless of whether or not society or the cultural critic does so limits the artist, who, after all is an individual, not an ethnic group, and therefore capable of individual choice not always shaped by racist social and economic forces.

Another difficulty with the binary construction of Africa and the West is that such a division into Eurocentrism *or* Afrocentrism and white *or* non-white "tend[s] to ignore everyone who does not fit into them," or, conversely link together completely unrelated groups on the basis of a single characteristic.[58] A black/white binary not only ignores gender, sexual orientation, class, environment, and education, as well as a wide variety of other ethnic groups (the various Asian, Latin American, indigenous American, Arctic, indigenous Australian, and South Pacific ethnicities, to name a few), but also those who have more than one ethnic background: the bi-racial or people of mixed race descent literally fall between a black/white binary.

A third model, therefore, must seek to transcend ethnicity while keeping the subversive and oppositional qualities of Greek adaptation. Intelligent, informed adaptation, the product of an individual artist's choice, but not expressing the African in terms of the Western is the basis for a third model.

This third model manifests a self-aware intertextuality. Derek Walcott, whose work is analyzed in chapter five, for example, denies that his work follows the parallel or overlay that a "Black Orpheus" text entails. The danger, indeed, of my proposed models is that individual works vary greatly in their complexity and degree of parallel with Greek models and originals. Both "Black Orpheus" and "Black Athena" recontextualize Greek cultural material, but there is a third paradigm, let us term it "Black Dionysus," which sees Greek material as the original tragedians saw myth—a convenient and familiar vehicle by which one might critique society.

In other words, in addition to Eurocentric formulations of equivalence ("Black Orpheus") and Afrocentric formulations of reappropriation ("Black Athena"), there is the Post-Afrocentric formulation of drama that is counter-hegemonic, self-aware, refuses to enforce dominant notions of ethnicity and culture, and uses ancient Greek material to inscribe a new discourse that empowers and critiques all cultures, even as it identifies the colonizer's power and the colonized's powerlessness.

The difficulty with such a discourse, of course, is the unequal nature of global capital and the unequal nature of global culture, and the complex issues that one must navigate in developing a work of art that acknowledges possible cultural colonialism involved in its creation, even as it critiques that culture. Rita Dove's *Darker Face of the Earth* and the adaptations of *Medea* by Jim Magnuson and Ernest Ferlita fall into this third category.

The "Black Dionysus" paradigm returns to the original use of Greek tragedy while serving the needs of a postmodern, postcolonial, post-Afrocentric, post cultural audience. Marianne McDonald argues that Greek tragedy "unmasks" the Homeric heroes, and demonstrates that the true heroes are "women, slaves, and children."[59]

"Black Dionysus" adaptations present to the elite of society, as the original tragedians of Athens did, a celebration that "unmasks" the heroes and demonstrates the reality behind societal myths. Is it any wonder that there are more adaptations of *Medea* than any other play? Medea is the great outsider—a woman with no family, *apolis*, *barbaroi*, and unwanted by her husband or adopted city. Yet she takes control of her situation, unmasks the hypocrisy of husband and king, enacts revenge for her wrongs, and escapes unpunished.

The key in the adaptations is to ask, as Rustom Bharucha's theorizes (as summarized by Patrice Pavis): "does [the] artist use a foreign country as an experimental ground for his own theatre experience or is he in a position to interact meaningfully with its historical context?"[60] In the "Black Dionysus" paradigm, the foreign (whether cultural or historical) is not a mirror for the reflection of the Self or an object for Othering. Rather, it is recognized and valued in and of itself. Familiarity is celebrated, but not used to erase difference. Greek tragedy becomes a means by which diverse communities might be encountered in public space and the historical forces that have shaped them might be exposed.

Like its namesake, "Black Dionysus" drama is a force that threatens to overwhelm the very things that have created it. As Dionysus first seemingly submits to Pentheus, only to rise up and destroy him, Greek adaptations after this paradigm use the Greek culture to threaten the cultural forces that privilege Greek tragedy.

All three models of the connection between ancient Greek cultural material and the African diaspora will be used to consider how various African diasporan adaptations of Greek tragedy use the material and to what end. Initially, however, Afrocentric classicism and the role it plays in shaping our understanding of theatre history is a necessary digression.

2

Afro(American)centric Classicism and African American Theatre

They are the scatterlings of Africa,
each uprooted one,
on the road to Phelamanga
where the world began.
I love the scatterlings of Africa,
each and every one,
in their hearts a burning hunger
beneath the copper sun.

Scatterlings of Africa
Johnny Clegg and Savuka

In the chapter on Roman theatre in their college-level theatre history textbook *Living Theatre: A History*, Edward Wilson and Alvin Goldfarb ask, in "Debates in Theatre History" (a section included in each chapter), "Was Terence the First Black Playwright?"[1] They summarize the description given in Suetonius, noting the remark that he was "dark-complected" and that his name "Afer" indicates a person of African origin. Wilson and Goldfarb then go on to note that, "This interpretation has become more prominent in recent years, as historians try to identify Afrocentric rather than Euro-centric origins of cultural achievements," followed by a definition of "Afro-centric approach."[2] They then state, after Walter E. Forehart, that "there is little evidence that Terrence was a black slave from Africa," as "many biographers of the time embellished their subjects' life stories to make them more interesting literary figures," and that Terence most likely came from Libya or Carthage, and therefore was not black.[3]

46

In the guise of presenting a "debate in theatre history," Wilson and Goldfarb have privileged the Eurocentric approach. Other than Suetonius they present no evidence from the position that Terence was black. Furthermore, they state the debate as being about whether or not Terence was black, instead of whether or not he was African—which he clearly was. They further rely on a type of evidence that, when used by Afrocentrists, is called into question: possibility rather than probability. Mary Lefkowitz, for example, objects to Afrocentric claims about ancient Greece based on inference from possibility—it was possible, she notes, for Socrates to have had African ancestors, but it is not probable.[4] In this case, just because "many biographers of the time embellished their subject's life stories," there is no indication that Suetonius did so in the specific case of Terence. There is no evidence that Suetonius embellished the details of Terence's ethnicity or his history as a slave. As Lefkowitz argues, one cannot argue a fact based on possibility, or even necessarily probability. The argument cuts both ways—if Afrocentric claims are to be held to rigorous academic standards (which they should be), then so must Eurocentric claims such as the possibility that Suetonius exaggerated about Terence. Absence of evidence is not evidence of absence, and we must always read ancient historians critically, and not simply accept their statements on faith, but Forehand (and Wilson and Goldfarb by singling out this sole quote from his work) are presuming that the possibility that the information may not be entirely factual allows the reader to dismiss the possibility that Terence was a black African. Possibility does not make it so, or even make it probably so. We must dismiss all of Suetonius's writing, therefore, by the standard that Forehart arbitrarily evokes for determining whether or not Terence was actually "dark-complected."

While ostensibly presenting a "debate" in theatre history, the text privileges the European position and makes one wonder what the debate is about if there is "little evidence" to support one side of it. There is a need to combat theatre histories such as this one, especially as the same volume has a single chapter on classical Asian theatre, no single chapter on African theatre (although there are sidebars on Wole Soyinka and African theatre is referred to in other chapters on modern theatre). Students might be tempted to think that precious little performance happens outside of the West, and that theatre which does occur is all "traditional" theatre.

A debate has raged for the past fifty or so years, growing in volume and in the seriousness of the charges leveled by each side at the other. Greece has been presented as being self-developed. While influenced by surrounding communities, ancient Athens and the other Greek city-states are often presented as springing fully formed out of the tribes of the

Peloponnesus, as Athena came from the head of Zeus. Afrocentric classicists have argued, and offered evidence that they believe proves, that Greek culture is derived from African, specifically Egyptian culture.

Just as the African American community is not monolithic, nor is the Afrocentric classicism community. At one end are those who are interested in uncovering not only the African but also the Asiatic influences on ancient Greece. Martin Bernal, whose *Black Athena* has made him the poster boy for the Afrocentric classicism movement, has "aligned [himself] on historical issues with more moderate historians," among whom he numbers W.E.B. DuBois and George Washington Williams.[5] By this he means that he sees Greek culture as developing out of numerous Afroasiatic influences during the Bronze Age.

At the other end of the Afrocentric spectrum are the "extreme Afrocentrists," as Bernal terms them, scholars who ignore Asiatic influence and argue for the primacy of Africa as the source of all Greek (and hence all European) civilization. "Nilocentric scholars," who focus on Egypt as the primary, if not the sole, influence on ancient Greece include such figures as George G.M. James, Chiekh Anta Diop, Theophile Obenga, Chancellor Williams, Ivan van Sertima, Yosef Ben Jochannan, Joel Rogers, and John Henrik Clark. To many of these scholars, Bernal is not even on their side, but exemplar of the problem. Not only does Bernal dilute the influence of Africa by combining it with Asiatic influence, he has stolen and "popularized" (read: brought to the white mainstream) ideas that he stole from black Afrocentrists. Nilocentrists argue that Greek culture is a "stolen legacy," as it is described in the title of George G.M. James's book, taken from Africa and glorified as European.

Bernal argues that he and the extreme Afrocentrists agree on two points: "It is useful to see ancient Egypt as an African civilization," and "that Egypt played a central role in the formation of ancient Greece."[6] He disagrees with James's formulation, however, seeing the legacy of Egypt as not "stolen" but "appropriated," because it implies further developments by the new owners."[7] Bernal seeks to evoke "the image of a new civilization growing up at the intersection of Europe and the Middle East as a thoroughly mixed and eclectic culture."[8] In other words, ancient Greece was the original multicultural society, influenced by numerous cultures and societies from Europe, Asia, and Africa. For too long, he argues, the West has ignored the African and Asian contributions, focusing solely on the European origins of Greek culture.

The debate around Afrocentric classicism focuses on two key questions: what were the Egyptian contributions to Greek culture, and were the ancient Egyptians "black" in the modern sense. A third question that is also raised are the related issues of the extent to which racists in Europe and America have conspired to hide the African origins of western civilization, and the extent to which the Greeks (as Europeans) "stole" African culture and claimed it as their own. In other words, the (evil) European Greeks took Egyptian culture and, claiming it as their own, re-named in Greek, and when (evil) European nations discovered the society they viewed as the cornerstone of Western civilization had stolen the culture of Africans, they moved to hide the facts, and work today to keep the lie of Greek culture's origins in place in order to continue to promote European superiority.

The first major work to promote this idea as George G.M James's *Stolen Legacy*, first published in 1954, at the beginning of the modern civil rights era in America. "The aim of this book," wrote James, "is to establish better race relations in the world by revealing a fundamental truth concerning the contribution of the African continent to civilization."[9] With chapter titles such as "Greek Philosophy is Stolen Egyptian Philosophy" (chapter one), "So-called Greek Philosophy was Alien to the Greeks and Their Conditions of Life" (chapter two), and "The Egyptians Educated the Greeks" (chapter four), James sets out to prove that ancient Athens could not have created its religion, philosophy, and culture and, instead took that of Egypt.

Many Afrocentrists followed James, finding that Greek philosophy, science, mathematics, religion, language, and indeed every aspect of culture was snatched from the Egyptians by the ancient Greeks.[10] Molefi Kete Asante, one of the most important figures in the Afrocentric movement, writes that Africalogy, a "liberating discipline," takes as its basic premise:

> The foundation of all African speculation in religion, art, ethics, moral customs, and aesthetics are derived from systems of knowledge found in ancient Egypt. To some extent it is this foundation, rather than the Greeks, that has made a lasting impact on the Western world.[11]

Asante asserts Egypt as the cornerstone of the ancient world, in the place of Greece, which would imply that all western civilization is rooted in Egyptian Africa, not Greece. Asante writes from an African-centered perspective, which he offers as a corrective to the Eurocentric perspective that informs almost every aspect of western culture.

Going one step further than Asante and Bernal are Afrocentric theorists who argue that in actuality Greece was also African, in culture and color if not in geography, and that most Greek gods, heroes, and rulers were black. Edward L. Jones, whose *Black Zeus* was discussed in the previous chapter, has written extensively about "Black Greece." In *Profiles in*

Black Heritage he writes, "My purpose in writing this book is to continue the research into our African past and to reclaim the black heroes whom the whites have portrayed as members of their race."[12] Among those who Jones argues were black and have been represented as white are Alexander the Great ("His father, king Philip claimed direct descent from Heracles and Heracles was black."[13]), Heracles, Zeus (here called Zeus-Ammon, after the Egyptian god in which he is rooted), and ten historic personages from Africa.

In *The Black Diaspora: Colonization of Colored People*, Jones argues that a vast number of mythic and historic personages were, in fact, black. "I found that the French Revolution was started in 1789 when the Bastille was stormed by *colored* people, who then ran the *colored* royalty out of France [emphasis Jones's]."[14] (One is tempted to ask that if all parties involved were colored, where is the racial oppression then in the colored nation of France colonizing colored Africa?) Jones asserts that Shakespeare, Robespierre, Napoleon, Josephine, Pushkin, Peter the Great, Beethoven, Mozart, and President Warren G. Harding were all black or of black descent. In ancient Greece, Socrates and Alexander the Great were both black, here the evidence offered for the ethnicity of Alexander is that he was "son of Nectanebus, the last African Egyptian king" instead of the previous descent from Heracles through Philip.[15] Heracles, however, is present. Called "The Black God" here, Jones places Heracles in the Egyptian section of the book and offers as the only evidence for his blackness a painting in the National Museum of Archeology in Naples, Italy, in which Heracles has a darker shade of skin than the Amazon queen in the same painting.[16] For Jones, it is not enough to claim Egypt, he must claim Greece, France, and much of Russia as black or of African descent.

Jones represents the extreme of a movement, most of whose more moderate members are interested in the origins of Greek culture and its relationship to Egypt, not in proving that the Greeks themselves were "black." Jones's premises are rooted in a modern understanding of race, not one that either the ancient Egyptians or the ancient Greeks had. Frank M. Snowden has argued convincingly that skin color or the modern notion of race is "not an issue" for the Greeks.[17] He finds an absence of prejudice in regards to color and race, noting that the Greeks define people by one quality: were they Greek. Rather than black and white, or European and African, the ancient Greeks identified people by where they were from and whether or not they spoke Greek. European tribes and African nations were both *barbaroi*, non-speakers of Greek, and therefore equal in Greek eyes.

Greeks have lived in Egypt from the seventh century B.C.E. on. In

331 BC, Alexander the Great, historically regarded as Macedonian, not African, established the city that bears his name in Egypt. He died before it was completed, but after his death Ptolemy ruled and maintained a strong Afro-Greek connection. Greek merchants and mercenaries spread Greek culture in North Africa, even as Egyptians and Africans brought their cultures to Egypt. There can be no doubt that there was a continued cultural engagement between Greece and northern Africa, and that culture flowed both ways. The larger questions of the actual influence of Egypt over Greece and the ethnicity of Egypt remain unanswered.

In a backlash against Afrocentric classicism, several authors have argued against the Egyptian origins of African culture. As Bernal serves as the popular representative for the Afrocentrists, Mary Lefkowitz has emerged as the popular representative for traditional classicists. Indeed, in each of their more recent publications the two of them have singled each other out, making the debate between the two sides into a far more personal one. Lefkowitz and those like her object to Afrocentric classicism on the grounds of writing out of context, use of selective facts, arguing from possibility, and for failing to distinguish between ancient and modern understandings of race. Lefkowitz also objects to the motivation of practitioners of Afrocentric classicism that she perceives as rooted in "rigid ethnic categories that have little demonstrative connection to practical reality."[18] The charge that is leveled against traditional classicists in return is that they have a vested interest in maintaining and promoting a Eurocentric understanding of the ancient world, that they maintain a system founded in and continually perpetrating racism.

That Greece has been influenced by Egypt seems a safe assumption, and we can leave it to the classicists, both Afrocentric and Eurocentric to debate the exact amount. But Afrocentric classicism is also rooted in the belief that Egypt is not only African geographically, but that it is a "black" nation—meaning it is part of the African diaspora that links sub-Saharan Africa to the New World. As noted above one of the two key questions about Afrocentric classicism is whether or not Egypt is "black." One might ask why is "blackness" even an issue, since Egypt is clearly in Africa, and therefore African.

Indeed, Ann Macy Roth, an Egyptologist, has written an open letter to her "Egyptological Colleagues" about Afrocentrism and Egypt. She argues that Afrocentrism is "less a scholarly field than a political and educational movement."[19] She sees four contentions between practitioners of Afrocentric Egyptology and those of "Traditional Egyptology." The first is that the former see ancient Egyptians as being "black" in the modern racial sense. Second, that the former believe that Ancient Egypt is superior to all other ancient civilizations, especially Greece, which derived all of its culture from Egypt. Third, the former believe that Egyptian culture had tremendous influence on later African and European cultures beyond what the latter believe is possible. Lastly, the former believe that there is a vast racist conspiracy to hide all of this, especially from African Americans.[20]

Roth counters that Egyptians saw themselves as "darker than Asiatics" and "lighter than Nubians," but actual skin color is irrelevant, as first and foremost they saw themselves as "Egyptian," just as the Greeks saw themselves not as "white," but Greek.[21] Roth does admit (after Bruce Williams), however, that no Egyptian, ancient or modern, "would be able to get a meal at a white lunch counter in the American South during the 1950s."[22] In which case, might it not be argued that even if the Egyptians are not "black Africans," they are certainly African, geographically speaking, and they are certainly not "white" or "European."

Roth locates the Afrocentric claims on Egypt as being rooted in a direct response to Eurocentrism. Claims on Greece and Egypt are made because they are known and because they are civilizations highly respected in the West. Nubia, Axum, Ghana, Mali, Ife, Benin, and Zimbabwe are all ancient African empires that are easily the equal of anything in Europe, but they are not taught in the universities and high schools, they are not commonly known.[23]

Roth, although obviously a traditional Egyptologist, is not alone in the idea that the focus should move to sub-Saharan Africa as a source of cultural study and cultural pride for people in the African diaspora. In his essay "Rethinking black history," Harvard sociologist Orlando Patterson notes three "conceptions of history" present among New World peoples of African descent. First is the "catastrophic" conception of history, a view that the Middle Passage was nothing but destructive and disastrous for people of color who were acculturated and assimilated into a Eurocentric society. All links to Africa and all elements of African culture were lost. Second is the "survivalist" conception, which takes the point of view that the transported African "maintained his African roots," despite the ravages of the Middle Passage and slavery.[24] Third is the "contributionalism" conception of history, which can take several forms.

Contributionalism focuses on "the black man's contributions to 'civilization'," whatever "civilization" may mean.[25] For some historians, use of this conceptualizing frame entails examining the contributions made to American art, history, culture, politics, etc. by African-Americas. Patterson, however, argues that the larger history of humanity has recently become the province of contributionalist historians. America, they argue, is recent, racist, and ultimately insignificant. Egypt, Nubia, Carthage, and the other kingdoms of North Africa is where civilization and human history began. Patterson terms this the "Three Ps" approach to history: "princes, pyramids and pageantry."[26] Why focus on small contributions to a racist society when your ancestors created civilization, not contributed to it, goes the argument.

Interestingly, Patterson himself rejects this approach to black history. In Greece, Rome, ancient North Africa, and the Near East, he argues, contribution by "black Africans" is "marginal," as "they were predominantly an exploited and largely enslaved minority."[27] It is this statement that demonstrates the points of contention and shapes the entire discourse of Afrocentric classicism: first, were the Ancient Egyptians "Black" in the modern sense, and second, how much did they contribute to ancient Greece and therefore the shaping of Western civilization? For the purposes of this study, we must add a third: how much influence did Africa have on the creation and development of drama in general and Greek tragedy in particular? Rather than "contributionalism," we might term such an approach "creationalism"—the idea that Africans did not contribute to civilization, they created it.

Patterson points out the difficulty of the extreme contributionalist conception: it is still rooted in the black/white binary. Why lay African claims to the Mediterranean? Those who do so are setting European civilization as the pinnacle and the standard by which others might be measured. Why try to measure up to Europe when sub-Saharan Africa has legacies, empires and civilizations of its own to claim and acclaim?

The answer is simple. The glaring exceptions of Cheikh Anta Diop and Theophile Obenga, and a handful of others aside, much of Afrocentric classical writing and theorizing is not being done in African by Africans, but rather by African Americans in the United States. Afrocentric classicism is primarily the project of writers, teachers, artists and scholars in the United States. Bernal is British, but lives and teaches in the United States. Yosef ben Jochannan, George G.M. James, Edward L. Jones, Chancellor Williams, etc. are all American. These scholars live, work, and write in the United States. By and large, the enterprise of linking ancient Egypt and ancient Greece is an American one.

Partly Afrocentric classicism is part of a larger response to the Eurocentric culture of the United States. Asante writes from an African perspective to place Africa and things African at the center of the discourse. "Europe is insinuated into every aspect of black existence," he writes.[28] Afrocentric classicism, at its best, shifts the focus from western civilization as the measure by which all things are weighed to African civilization, and Egypt is an African civilization. Afrocentric classicism is a response to the dominance of Greece in Eurothought, ignoring all other races and achievements by those people. Afrocentric classicism is a methodology of combating that dominance by proving that the ancient world was a much more multicultural one, rooted in African and Asian cultures, not merely European. Afrocentric classicism is a response to hundreds of years of racism that was justified through the example of Greece.

Afrocentric classicism emerges in partial response to the use of ancient sources to justify modern slavery. Joseph Roach reports that, "Nineteenth century historians of slavery traced the performance genealogy of the slave market to the ancient world, in which they profess to find detailed precedents for contemporary practice."[29] Roach provides an example from W.O. Blake's 1857 work, *History of Slavery*, in which Blake describes the slave market of ancient Athens comparatively to that of the antebellum South: "The sales seem to have been conducted precisely like those of the present day in Richmond, Charleston, New Orleans, and other cities of the South."[30] In fact, the full title of Blake's opus is *The History of Slavery and the Slave Trade, Ancient and Modern. The Forms of Slavery That Prevailed in Ancient Nations, Particularly in Greece and Rome. The African Slave Trade and the Political History of Slavery in the United States. Complied from Authentic Materials by W.O. Blake.*[31]

Molefi Kete Asante argues that in white Southern society "neo-Greek orientation" and Christianity provided justification and a referent point in Western civilization to justify the enslavement of people of color.[32] Yet slavery in the ancient world, while similar in practice to American slavery in its effects had the distinction of not being rooted in ethnicity.

Ancient Athens and ancient Rome both relied on institutional slavery to support the privileged class of citizens. Like the pre-Civil War United States, the economy of these societies depended on the use of slave labor. The slaves came from conquered peoples, including those of Africa (exclusively African, in the case of the New World). The slaves brought with them, in all three cases, their culture and their resistance to oppression. As Anthony Tatlow states, "The slaves in Rome were a source of both culture and rebellion."[33] As African slaves brought African culture to the New World, so slaves owned by Greeks or Romans brought their cultures to Greece and Rome. As the white southerners feared slave rebellion more than anything (witness the repressive measures against African Americans after John Brown's raid on Harper's Ferry or during the Civil War—slaveowners feared slave uprisings in the face of these military actions against slavery), slave rebellions in Rome and Greece were greatly feared and when they did occur were responded to in the harshest possible terms. Witness the story of Spartacus.

Paul Cartledge writes:

Slavery, arguably, was both the principle material basis of society and the governing paradigm of human worth in classical Greek antiquity, affecting not only economics and politics, but also, more subtly, the ideological representations of, and interpersonal relations between, the sexes. At the limit of degradation, ancient slavery meant the total deracination and depersonalization, the social death, involved in chattel slavery experienced by the untree in Athens and elsewhere. At best, it consigned hundreds of thousands of human beings to a vague limbo status 'between slavery and freedom' such as the Helots of Sparta enjoyed (or suffered).[34]

Thus, ancient slavery had much in common with American slavery. Unlike American slavery, however, it was not directed at one particular group. Blackness in America until 1865 was a marker of slavery. No such condition existed in ancient Greece. "Greeks and Romans did not establish color as an obstacle to integration in society," Snowden reports.[35] Africans were accepted as members of society in ancient cultures, slavery was a condition created either by birth or by capture during battle. Race, in the modern sense, played no significant role in ancient slavery.

The ancient world, particularly ancient Rome, often represented slavery in the theatre. Slave characters abound in the tragedies and comedies of ancient Greece and Rome. But, if the depiction of slavery were enough, then there should be dozens of African American adaptations of Plautus, whose plays feature more slave characters than any other ancient dramatist. Yet there are none. The use of slavery in these plays is uncritical and accepted. The slaves may be clever, they may solve the problems of the wealthy elite protagonists, as in Plautus' The Pot of Gold, but they neither question nor resist their slavery.

Playwrights who use Greek tragedy to examine the African American experience do not use such an uncritical presentation of slavery. Instead, they chose material that can be used to critique slavery, or the continued presence of institutionalized racism. Taking an Afrocentric point of view causes one to even question the role Africa has played in the ancient development of theatre. Much like the problem with the "debate" of the ethnicity of Terence at the beginning of this chapter, the Eurocentric view has always been that theatre developed in Greece. Afrocentric classicism, however, can and has caused artists to ask how Africa has therefore influenced the theatre and how might this influence be brought to light in the theatre itself.

Playwrights such as Silas Jones and Ifa Bayeza use the theatre to argue that Greek culture is rooted in Egyptian culture, and indict not only western civilization but also western theatre in their dramas. "That's your version, Jason, the Greek tragic version," Jones's Medea tells her husband in *American Medea*, "You've had your plays; this is Medea's tragedy."[36]

Afrocentric historians and theatre historians look to ancient Egypt to see the possible origins of theatre and drama. Cheikh Anta Diop, in a chapter entitled "Egyptian and Greek Theatre" locates the origins of theatre in the Mysteries of Osiris, whom he associates with the Greek Dionysus.[37] Paul Carter Harrison sees Greek tragedy as the earliest example of "Nommo Drama," African word-based drama, as it developed out of Egyptian culture.[38] Bernal, as well, parallels the Festival of Dionysus with the Abydos Passion Play, a ritual re-enactment of the death of Osiris.[39] Oscar Brockett's popular theatre history textbook, *History of the Theatre* posits the roots of theatre in the Egyptian rituals such as the Abydos Passion Play and the Memphite dramas. In earlier editions, while Brockett observed that Herodotus went to Egypt and claimed Dionysus was another version of Osiris, he also noted that there is "no direct connection has yet been established between the Egyptian and Greek theatrical traditions."[40] Within two decades the revised textbook acknowledged Egypt's "considerable" influence over Greece, but cited one "important difference": Egypt "never developed theatrically beyond ritualized performances, repeating the same ceremonies year after year for centuries."[41] As a result, Brockett concludes, Greece developed drama, whereas Egypt had no "autonomous theatre." Thus, while the origins of theatre are Egyptian, the Greeks developed the form into an autonomous one, separate and distinctive from ritual.

Even Brockett's acknowledgement of the Egyptian origins of theatre, however, remains too Eurocentric for some historians. Carleton W. and Barbara J. Molette critique the notion of progress—that the Greeks built on and improved what the Egyptians had created. In *Black Theatre: Premise and Presentation*, an Afrocentric theatre history, they argue that "the Eurocentric aesthetic ideal places a greater value on the presentation of new content [rather] than [on] the continuation of traditional values through ritual" as Egyptian ritual did.[42] They ask, "To what extent did the secular competitive nature of Greek drama reduce its effectiveness in instilling the values of truth justice, and righteousness in its audience?"[43] The assumption behind their question, however, is that the purpose of Greek drama was to "instill the values of truth, justice and righteousness," which is arguable. Certainly part of the purpose of the Dionysiac festival was instructive, and certainly part of the purpose was to instill the values of the community in the audience. Yet the main purposes seemed to be the patriotic celebration of the Athenian city-state, the worship of Dionysus through drama, and the creation of original works of drama that competed for public acclaim and prizes.

Another assumption lurking behind the Molettes' argument is that the purpose of drama is the achievement of perfection in the performance of traditional ritual that continues traditional values, rather than the creation of a variety of new and original texts to perform. The Egyptians valued performing the same text at every festival for 2500 years, ensuring a cultural continuity. The Greeks valued a variety of dramatic texts resulting in a variety of theatrical performances, encouraged by the competitive nature of the City Dionysia. Carrying the Molettes' valuation to its logical conclusion, the Afrocentric approach to contemporary drama would entail only a single play (or a small number of texts) which were performed over and over again. Yet they also celebrate the variety of the African American theatre, which is rooted in a mixture of the two models: new content originating in traditional forms.

Egyptian "theatre" remained more or less unchanged for 2500 years. The Greeks, working from the model of ritual drama that the Egyptians provided, created a form that required new content and engaged the community on a variety of issues that were topically relevant, rather than simply celebrating tradition. It is the Greek model that resulted in the development of drama. This is not to say that Egyptian ritual is not theatre, or that there is a "progression" from Egyptian to Greek, marking a movement upward. The Egyptians created performative theatre; the Greeks, however, created drama—the texts written by playwrights, that often serves as the basis for performed theatre, and is the origin of western drama, which is the dominant model for contemporary theatre practice.

Asante also privileges the African origins of theatre, noting that Egyptian ritual unified performer and spectator—all were involved. He argues that one must begin any theatre history with Egypt and must also privilege the African tradition: "A cultural analyst who begins with Sophocles rather than with African ritual drama can only end with the separation of actors and audience."[44] The assumption behind his assertion is that the separation of actors and audience is, in some way, inferior to or lesser than a "unified performance" in which no distinction is drawn between spectator and performer, a seemingly arbitrary assertion. It begs the question, what is theatre? Does the definition of theatre include performer/spectator separation? If so, then "ending with the separation of actors and audience" is not a problem—it is, in fact, what is required to distinguish theatre from ritual or other activity. If, on the other hand, the definition of theatre expands to include activity in which no distinction is made between performer and spectator, a hierarchy is not necessarily established that indicates that that form of performance is preferable. Asante's point that one must begin theatre histories with Egypt is correct; his assertion that Egyptian forms are superior to Greek is arbitrary, and possibly inaccurate.

Paul Carter Harrison, a prominent activist, artist, and scholar in establishing an African-centered understanding of theatre, takes a different approach than Asante and the Molettes. Where they assert the superiority of Egyptian forms over Greek, which they see as limited, according to an Afrocentric value system, Harrison sees evidence in Greek tragedy of African cultural survivals. Harrison, like Bernal and Diop, posits Greek tragedy as offering proof of Egyptian influence. The *Oresteia*, he argues:

> points to the remnants of African influence on the moral structure of ancient Greece which, by this time, had been overcome by the values of nomadic Aryans.[45]

Whereas the Aryan system valued the male and asserted a patriarchal system, "in the more stable black communities [of Egypt] mother-rights are advanced without challenge."[46] Aeschylus' play, asserts Harrison, is a celebration of how European patriarchy killed African matriarchy in Greece.

Bernal argues that the "hidden narrative" of Aeschylus' *Suppliants* is the story of the colonizing of Greece and the origins of the city of Athens by Egyptians.[47] Bernal relies on linguistic and referential arguments from the plays of Euripides and Aeschylus to support his theories. Greek tragedy contains the evidence, he argues, that the Greeks themselves accepted the idea that they were descended, culturally if not literally, from Egypt.

Perhaps the most important thing to note about Afrocentic classicism is that even if one does not accept its tenets and beliefs, one must still acknowledge its presence and power as a force within the theatre community and especially within the African American theatre community. Those who acknowledge an African-centered view of theatre find their work informed by this point of view. The theatre that these individuals produce serves to cause others to question their assumptions about ethnicity, history, identity, and even theatre itself. Afrocentric classicism forces even those who disagree with it to defend the traditional Eurocentric classicism, and in doing so, explore what beliefs they hold and advocate and why. Afrocentric classicism is a presence in the modern theatre whose influence will continue to grow.

For theatrical purposes, the suggestions of Patterson and Roth to focus on other ancient African civilizations leaves theatre artists with new subject matter to explore, but as the Western theatre tradition (which through colonialism has become the contemporary world theatre tradition) emerged out of Greece and Egypt. Those who wish to engage the theatrical past must do so with the rituals of Egypt and the dramas of Greece. The performative traditions of ancient African civilizations have either been lost or are known only to a few. The (seemingly) unbroken line from Egypt and Greece provides a direct link to theatre history from which we modern theatre artists trace our descent.

As part of the "Black Athena" paradigm of Greek theatre, Afrocentric classicism challenges the identity of "black theatre." If Greek theatre is African in origin, then Greek tragedy and comedy is, in one sense, "black theatre." While Terence is a classical playwright whose African origins are not in dispute, his plays are still not widely produced by Afrocentric theatre companies, many of which simply reject all plays written before the advent of African American theatre in the late eighteenth and early nineteenth century. Yet the possibility exists that the larger challenge brought to African American theatre by Afrocentric classicism will be the place of ancient plays in the black canon. The adaptation of Greek plays by playwrights of any ethnicity, so long as they transculturate the plays into an African American context, also demonstrates the issues surrounding the identification of "black drama" and "African American theatre."

The larger question raised, especially in relation to African American classical theatre and black adaptations of European classics, is what elements essentially constitute "black drama"? The ethnicity of the playwright? The ethnicity of the characters? The ethnicity of the performers, or the artistic staff, or the director? The subject matter or source material? The intention and commitment of the artists? The ethnicity of the audience? If an all-black cast presents *Hamlet* for an all-black audience, is it black theatre, or not?

For example, *The Gospel at Colonus* requires an all-African American cast, is rooted in a traditional black dramatic form (the gospel musical), and, during its original run, had some of the highest figures of African American audiences on Broadway. It was, however, created, developed, and directed by Lee Breuer and Bob Telson, two European Americans who were accused by one reviewer of being "two white guys colonizing the gospel."[48] Conversely, Derek Walcott's *The Odyssey* was written by a Caribbean playwright of African descent, and demonstrates the influence of Caribbean culture and performance styles. The original production, however, had been commissioned by the Royal Shakespeare Company, directed by Trevor Nunn, featured an almost all-white cast (including Ron Cook as Odysseus—the main character), and was performed before European audiences. Which of these two productions is "black theatre"? Which is "more black" or "more Afrocentric?" Black theatre may not be as cut and dried as August Wilson would have it.

Does ethnicity travel and does ethnicity carry meaning in different cultural contexts? As argued previously, plays do not mean in and of themselves; they generate meaning. Meaning is generated through the implicit meanings in the text, the choices of the performers and the artistic staff, and the context in which the meanings are received. The "meaning" of ethnicity, therefore, is rooted in context in drama. Plays "mean" differently when they are performed outside of their original ethnic contexts.

Fences has been performed in China with an all-Chinese cast, transforming the meaning created when an African American cast performs the play in America. Another extreme example would be the Tokyo production of Tony Kushner's *Angels in America* which featured an all-Japanese cast. Joe Pitt, a white Mormon, Louis Ironson, a New York Jew, Belize, a black drag queen, and Prior Walter, a WASP, were all played by Japanese actors. External notions of ethnic difference and characteristics were erased in production as all the performers were of the same ethnicity. Thus, mannerisms, costumes, and direct reference were the ways in which characters established "ethnicity."

The larger implications for African American theatre posed by Greek tragic adaptations and Afrocentric classicism is the challenge that is leveled at any theatre rooted in ethnicity and representation. Who controls the representation? Who is being represented? To whom are they being represented? For what purpose are they being represented? Who gets to decide whether a piece of theatre is "black" enough to qualify as "African American theatre"?

Rustom Bharucha has correctly pointed out that all theatre, like all politics, is local, not only because it is a live art form that is available only to the people in the geographic area of the theatre, but also because it is always about the audience for which it is performed.[49] *Dionysus in 69* is more about New York in 1969 than about ancient Athens. Ferlita's *Black Medea* is just as much about New Orleans in 1976 as it is about New Orleans in 1810 (its setting) or Athens in 431 B.C.E. (when the original was first performed). Silas Jones's *American Medea* ultimately concerns itself with America in 1995 than the colonial setting or the Greek original.

For that matter, Afrocentric classicism, rooted as it is in the American academy far more than in the African academy, is ultimately about the identity (historic and cultural) of African Americans first and foremost, only then is it about Egyptians and Greeks. All identity, like all politics and all theatre, is local, even if one chooses to identify with a people three thousand years and several thousand miles distant. Afrocentric classicism is a methodology that engages the classical world from an African (American) perspective.

Bharucha further argues, again correctly, that, "the strongest resistance to cultural domination lies in creative work."[50] It is the role of the theatre under Black Dionysus to combat imperialism, engage the myths of culture and history, and create an ethical, accurate representation. As such, the plays considered in this book represent a wide variety of theatrical experiments that engage the link between Athens, Africa, and America. It is through the theatre that Afrocentric classicism can make its arguments in a lively and compelling way that at the very least offers a challenge to racism, Eurocentrism, and cultural domination. This resistance begins by offering an opening for dialogue about national and cultural identity that will lead to a better understanding of both past and present, of our classical cornerstones of Egypt and Greece, and of ourselves.

3

Ancient Plays in a
New World:
Multicultural Currents

Jean-Pierre Vernant calls attention to the dichotomous property of Greek tragedy that he terms "historicity and transhistoricity."[1] The nature of art is paradoxical, argues Vernant, after Marx, in that:

> If it is true that works of art, like any other social products, are connected with a specific historical context and that their genesis, structure and meaning can only be understood within and through that context, how is it that they remain alive and continue to communicate with us when the forms of that social life have been transformed at every level and the conditions necessary for their production have disappeared?[2]

In other words, every dramatic text from the Greeks developed out of a specific cultural, geographical, historical, social, political context, and yet these plays still serve as scripts for performance, even millennia after the manner and means of production (*City Dionysia*, masks, *skene*, *machine*, etc.) have ceased to be.

In other words, Greek tragedy has historicity—the specific place and time it occurred, when and where it developed, the cultural forces that created it, springing from fifth-century BCE Athens. Greek tragedy also has transhistoricity—the plays are cultural artifacts that continue to be read, performed, and analyzed nearly two and a half millennia later. Yet, as Vernant and Marx have observed, the original conditions of performance no longer exist, and the original purposes and meanings are no longer culturally relevant. Does it really matter to modern audiences whether or not the war between Athens and Sparta continues, now that is has been over for twenty-four centuries? The answer is in the re-historicization of Greek tragedy. Modern production and adaptation creates a new historicity for contemporary production of Greek tragedy.

J. Michael Walton argues, correctly, that while the source material of Greek tragedy is myth, the theme and ultimate subject is actually contemporary social and political issues: "...the central issues of Greek tragedy are immediate, dealing with the process of living in fifth century Athens. Although the heroic figures seem prehistoric, the treatment, through them, of contemporary issues is of immediate concern."[3] The repetition of the word "immediate" is not accidental and of extreme importance for the purposes of this study. Modern production and modern adaptation of Greek tragedy must make the text "immediate" again—literally relevant to this exact moment to this exact audience. The plays, while set in the prehistoric past, concern only the now.

Vernant argues that the specific context of the plays, i.e. the myths, come from "the Greeks' shared knowledge" of their mythologized past.[4] The dramatist, however, takes the legend shared by the audience and reworks it, using what Vernant calls "tragic vision," i.e. a way of viewing contemporary problems through myth, which is unique to tragedy.[5] In the reworking of the collective past, the hero is no longer a model as he was in the works of Homer, but "now he has become a problem."[6] The hero is then used to explore a particular ethical dilemma or political issue. The ultimate consequence of this debate is to "implicate the fifth-century spectator, the citizen of democratic Athens."[7]

To state this process in a different way, the tragic dramatist adapts the myth in such a way as to transform the narrative into a debate on moral, political, religious, ethical, or social issues (frequently more than one of these, or all at once) of import to the audience, which is comprised of the elite citizens of the *polis* and their households. Myth is used because the primary requirement for tragic vision is distance; one must be emotionally detached from what is depicted on stage. Tragic vision requires that the spectator experience the events at a distance so that they may be understood as deeper truth. It is this very process that makes Greek tragedy amenable to transhistoric production. The truth that is created "by tragedy's refusing to place itself on the level of contemporary events and current political life" is a truth that, while about the topical, transcends the contemporary (which is still addressed, regardless), and creates archetypes that can cross cultural and historical boundaries.[8]

The adaptations and productions considered in this book reflect the attempt by American playwrights, directors, and theatre artists to develop a "new historicity." Rather than making claims for the "universality" of

Greek cultural material (which simply is not the case, and is, rather, an example of Eurocentric notions of cultural superiority), this study will examine how the plays are not "universal" but *always* culturally specific. The theatre artists who create modern Greek tragedy use Greek tragedy in the same manner that the tragedians used myth—it is a distancing device that allows one to comment indirectly on contemporary society and indict the spectator for his or her role in maintaining and perpetuating the society. Modern Greek tragedy in America is aimed at a modern, American audience, addresses issues of import in modern America, and ultimately represents American society on stage as the originals did Athenian society. In speaking of Peter Sellars' *Ajax*, Marianne McDonald finds that, "Ajax makes the familiar world strange. He shows it to us as a foreign land and creates a fresh perspective."[9] This description summarizes the process of tragic vision, making the familiar strange so that one might better understand the familiar. The use of Greek material provides necessary distance, as the use of Greek myth provided necessary distance in Athens.

The productions and adaptations that will be evaluated in this work revalue Greek tragedy. They rescue it from being either the province solely of specialist scholars who would have us sit alone, quietly reading the original works in their original tongue and never approach production or translation, or from being, in the words of Walton, a set of "convenient pegs on which a new writer or director can hang his own ideas."[10] They take Greek tragedy and invest it with a new historicity that renders the play relevant and meaningful for contemporary audiences.

Greek Plays on the American Stage

Greek tragedy began being "exported" from Athens almost immediately after its origins in the fifth century B.C.E. The *Persae* of Aeschylus was revived in Syracuse for Heron I by its author. Archelaus invited Euripides and Agathon to Macedonia to stage their works. During the fourth century B.C.E. travelling companies began performing all over the Mediterranean and theatre buildings quickly sprung up in other areas of Greece, Rome, and even Africa.[11]

Rome was the first culture to begin adapting Greek plays for its own culture. Plautus and Terence used Menander and the other New Comedians as source material, adapting their plays for Roman audiences. Likewise, Seneca turned to Greek tragedy to develop his own dramas. The Romans identified four types of drama, two of which were derived from Greek models: *fabula palliata* (comedies based on Greek models) and *fabula crepidata* (tragedies based on Greek models).

The Renaissance in Europe marked a rebirth of classical culture, including its theatre. Newly found and translated Greek tragedies influenced the theatres of France, Italy, and England. One can examine Goffe's *Orestes* (England, 1623), Racine's *Phaedre* (France, 1677) or the experiment of opera in Italy, itself an attempt to recreate Greek theatre, to see a rebirth of Greek tragedy, not in the form of translation, but in the form of adaptation.

The latter half of the twentieth century saw a worldwide growth of performance of Greek originals in translation and in the original Greek, as well as numerous adaptations by Europeans, Africans, Asians—almost every culture in the world.[12] Suzuki Tadashi, Ariane Mnouchkine, Robert Wilson, Wole Soyinka, and John Barton, to name but a few, are international artists who have returned to Greek tragedy more than once to create works of intercultural theatre.

Americans have wanted to rewrite the classics from the beginning of the nation, using the Greeks in school, performing tragedies in the original Greek at colleges and universities in the nineteenth and early twentieth centuries. Eugene O'Neill, one of the greatest American dramatists of the twentieth century and a worldwide influence on theatre was awarded the Nobel Prize for Literature, not least of which for his *Mourning Becomes Electra*, which transculturated the *Oresteia* to the American Civil War. More recently, in 2000, the Denver Center for the Performing Arts spend a great deal of time and money to develop *Tantalus* by John Barton, who had already developed a theatrical event called *The Greeks* using the better known Greek tragedies. For *Tantalus*, Barton adapted Greek myth and elements of several Greek tragedies into ten plays and a dramatic epilogue that collectively tell the story of the Trojan War, presented with a mixed-race cast of British and American actors and directed by Sir Peter Hall and his son Edward Hall.

Kalista V. Hartigan provides a fascinating summary and survey of Greek tragedy in American theatre entitled *Greek Tragedy on the American Stage*. She divides the twentieth century into six periods during which Greek theatre grew in popularity and influence, finally "achieving status" and serving as a cultural arena in which the issues of the day could be debated over. According to Hartigan, Greek tragedy "came of age" between 1915 and 1935, becoming a means by which the theatre might "respond to war, drugs, and flower children" in the sixties, and serving as a forum for self-reflection and reevaluation in the seventies, eighties and nineties. Whereas in the first half of the century the performance of translations dominated the stage, from the sixties on adaptations began to grow in number and importance.[13] American Greek tragedy in one sense is almost always adaptation, as translation itself is a form of adaptation: adapting the narrative from not only one language to another, but from one culture to another. As Amy S. Green writes, "Classical revival has always meant revision."[14] The plays are also problematic, given that the predominant acting tradition in America is realism, and Greek tragedy is anything but. Richard Beacham, writing of Barton's *The Greeks*, concedes that "experience seems to indicate that they [Greek tragedies] are virtually unplayable."[15] The ideal production of Greek tragedy in America, according to Beacham is "a production as true as possible to the form and meaning of the original, but cast in a mode which is accessible to a contemporary audience."[16]

The issue of fidelity is a difficult and debated one. Beacham favors linguistic fidelity, but how can one be faithful to language in a translated performance text? Likewise, a contemporary audience may not understand references in the text or the use of idiom, so the translator, director, and actors might work together to find a comparable expression on the stage.

Modern production and adaptation must also take into account the original production conventions versus the requirements of modern staging. Most modern productions and adaptations are performed in modern theatres, with electric lights and contemporary costumes, in the evening, not in an outdoor theatre beginning at dawn. Thus, the modern adapter of Greek tragedy, whether playwright or director must recreate the Greek theatre experience with modern production techniques and conventions, some of which only approximate or parallel the original conventions.

One might argue the need for paralleling original convention, as the Greeks themselves were writing adaptations of their own myths. They developed the tragic form and its conventions in order to explore their own contemporary society. Modern adapters of Greek tragedy, like their forebears, must be faithful to their own audiences first and foremost. In order to parallel the original conventions, it is sometimes necessary to give a modern audience the modern equivalent of tragic convention. The two conventions that seem to require the most consideration for modern production and adaptation are masks and the chorus.

The original Greek theatre relied upon masks, and some significant productions have attempted to use masks to remain faithful to the Greek tradition. *Tantalus* begins with an unmasked group of modern characters that slowly don masks as the story of the Trojan War begins to be told. Ariane Mnouchkine used the makeup and masks of East Asian theatres to approximate the distance that Greek mask use created. In other cases, however, actual masks are not used, but a substitute is introduced that functions in the same way.

In his productions of *Ajax* (1986) and *The Persians* (1993), director Peter Sellars used microphones to function as masks. In both plays, characters sit or stand literally behind microphones to deliver many of their lines. In addition to the practical benefit of ensuring that the lines are projected to the audience to hear, this practice, Sellars argues, is the equivalent of a modern mask:

> I felt a microphone was very important for the masks; I replaced masks with microphones because the microphone is an amplifier, but also a cover. It enlarged the human figure, but it also creates distance and also is deceptive. It is the mask of our society, as it were.[17]

For Sellars, the microphone was far more effective than a mask would have been, as a contemporary audience is more familiar with the use of microphones than with masks, but are also savvy enough to recognize the masking function that a microphone provides.

The chorus, likewise, can be problematic in modern production, as the contemporary American theatre is not one of communal voice, but rather one of individual voices. The adapter of Greek tragedy must find a way to incorporate the chorus that is both logical and effective. *The Gospel at Colonus* has a literal chorus—a Pentecostal Gospel Choir. As communal singing is a natural part of the service, Sophocles' chorus transculturates very easily into such a new format. The communal singing of slaves is also used as a chorus in *Darker Face of the Earth*. The playwrights of both plays agree that the call-and-response nature of African American music, derived from African sources and significantly different than European and American music, lends itself to Greek tragedy well, as the polyphonic response to a single voice is already a part of the African American culture.

On the American stage, African Americans were performing Greek tragedies in the universities before the turn of the century. It was not until the Great Depression, however, that Greek tragedy began to be performed by all-black companies in earnest. The Federal Theatre Project's Negro Theatre Units were the first major professional producing organization to present African American Greek tragedy in adaptation. Not by choice of the performers were the plays adapted, however. The first African American adaptations were by white playwright/directors who adapted the plays for racist reasons. Amy S. Green reports:

> The Negro units in particular presented a direct challenge to tradition. Black actors, professionals who had been denied opportunities to perform

major classical roles in the commercial theatre were eager to prove their mettle. The white heads of the units, apparently unwilling to stage the plays straight with black casts, devised production schemes to accommodate the skills and cultural backgrounds of their companies.[18]

The most famous example of which was Orson Welles' "Voodoo *Macbeth*," setting Shakespeare's play in Haiti during the slave revolution. Other companies performed Greek plays setting them in Africa, for example the Seattle unit's production of *Lysistrata*, adapted by Theodore R. Browne, set in "Ebonia."[19]

Although born out of the prejudice of white directors who would now perform "straight" versions of the classics with black actors, African American adaptation would develop out of these racist origins to form a type of theatre fairly common by the sixties. Joseph Papp, the creator of New York's "Shakespeare in Central Park" planned in the sixties to develop an "emerging third world repertory classical acting company" that would perform western classics, especially Shakespeare and the Greeks with minority actors.[20] But by the sixties there had been a change in attitudes and the emergent black theatre community began to reject Western drama. The controversy over so-called colorblind casting continues to the present day, suggesting as it does the universality (and therefore superiority) of European culture.

Universalism, Colorblind Casting, and Black Classical Actors

In his seminal study of black performers of Shakespeare, *Shakespeare in Sable*, Errol Hill surveys and champions the performance of western classics by actors of color. Hill himself, an actor, director, playwright, author, professor at Dartmouth College, and native Trinidandian, actively engaged Greek tragedy from an Afrocentric perspective while a student at London University. In 1951 Hill directed *Oedipus Rex* at the Hans Crescent International Student Center, following it with a production of *Antigone* in which Hill played Creon and fellow Caribbean theatre artist Errol John played Haemon. According to Hill, *Antigone* was "staged in a West African tribal setting with the actors wearing authentic Ghanaian kinti clothes borrowed from African fellow students at the center."[21]

Although Hill's book deals mostly with productions of Shakespeare, he remains a staunch defender of people of African descent playing any role in the Western classical canon. He deals with the controversy of the idea that acting in Western plays displays a "growing cultural imperialism," a perpetuation of colonialist mentalities and the promotion of Western superiority, arguing that he prefers a "big tent" approach. Hill urges more producers, actors, and directors of color to engage Western classical theatre and make it their own. He is not alone in this belief, nor is he without adversaries who completely disagree about the place of Western classics in the theatre of the African diaspora. Colorblind or color-conscious casting is perhaps the first way in which modern production of Greek tragedy engages the African American community, and there is not a clear consensus on the legitimacy of it.

For the purposes of this study there are two models of casting non-white actors in classical plays: colorblind casting, in which the ethnicity of the actor is considered unimportant, and conceptual casting of ethnicity, in which the race or color of the actor is what generates the meaning of the production, or, as Angela C. Pao puts it: "The desired impact can only be achieved if the spectators not only notice the color of the actors but simultaneously activate their consciousness of the social, historical, political, and cultural implications of racial difference."[22] For purposes of illustration of these types of casting which place actors of color in Greek plays, let us consider three productions of Greek tragedies in which African American actors took lead roles to very different ends: *Prometheus Bound*, staged at Bates College in 1989, directed by the author, Peter Sellars' *Ajax*, staged at the Kennedy Center, the La Jolla Playhouse and several European theatre festivals in 1986, and an adaptation of *Phaedra*, staged at the University of Pittsburgh in 1995.

Prometheus is a mythic figure who was transformed by tragic vision. He is not of great significance in the writings of Hesiod. He is an object of laughter in plays by Epichamus and Lucian, the latter writing a satiric dialogue entitled *You Are a Verbal Prometheus*. Even Aeschylus used Prometheus to comic effect in his satyr play *Prometheus the Fire Bringer*. However, in *Prometheus Bound*, as C. John Herrington notes, "Aeschylus is freely inventing."[23] Durant argues that it is amazing that Aeschylus was able to get away with the heresies in the play, as he was blaspheming at a religious festival and critiquing the tyranny of the state at a state-sponsored festival.[24] Aeschylus dramatizes the Prometheus myth into a conflict between an older order that would show mercy to humanity (the Titans) and the new regime of Zeus that crushes those who oppose it.

The play begins with Kratos and Bia entering, bringing Prometheus as captive. He is to be chained to a rock at the end of the world for defying Zeus and giving fire to humankind. Hephaistos, blacksmith of the gods, oversees the chaining, binding and nailing of Prometheus and the three exit. Prometheus speaks for the first time, deploring his fate, but still defiant.

The chorus enters and engages in Prometheus in a lengthy discussion about his situation, his fight with Zeus, and his gifts to humankind. Oceanus, the titan, enters and suggests that Prometheus bow to authority, which Prometheus, secure in the knowledge that someday he will be free, refuses to do. Io, a maiden given cow horns by Hera for sleeping with Zeus, pursued across Asia and Africa by a stinging gadfly also sent by Hera, enters and commiserates with Prometheus, both of them victims of the gods.

Lastly, after Io's departure, Hermes, messenger of the gods, arrives and demands to be told the secret that Prometheus carries: the knowledge that one will be born who will free Prometheus and overthrow Zeus, ostensibly Heracles. Prometheus refuses to divulge the information and, after threats and torture, Hermes calls down an earthquake. The play ends with Prometheus still screaming his defiance.

After reading the play and encountering the writings of Donald Woods and the film *Cry Freedom*, this author directed a production of the play in March of 1989 set in South Africa in 1977. Arvelle C. "Ozzie" Jones, Jr., an African American actor played Prometheus, meant to suggest Steve Biko, the young South African student leader who was killed while in police custody. C. John Herrington, in his introduction to the translation by himself and James Scully, argues that the play translates very easily to reflect the reality of the twentieth-century political prisoner. "We see here," he writes, "a political offender whose will must be broken by the rægime at all costs, by isolation from all fellow beings, by torture, by chaining, and even by psychological means..."[25] The production, using the Scully and Herrington translation, without changing a word, set about to evoke the legacy of Steve Biko and draw attention to the conflict that was underway at that time in South Africa under the apartheid system.

The needs of Aeschylus' text were met by reproducing a South African prison cell on stage. A cell wall made of cinder blocks was literally constructed on stage, with chains hanging from it, which were attached to Prometheus' hands, legs, and waist at the beginning of the play. The audience, sitting in thrust, created the other three walls of the cell. Prometheus was beaten, slapped and kicked by the guards/gods and then chained to the wall. At the end of the play, in reference to the mythic bird that would return daily to tear out his liver, Prometheus was tortured by Hermes with an electric cattle prod stabbed into his abdomen until he screamed his final lines and collapsed on the wall as the lights faded.

In the cast, gods were white, played by Euro-American actors, and the

Titans, with one exception, were black, suggesting the supplantation of the gods where the titans once ruled, and the need of the gods to suppress and oppress the titans in order to maintain the legitimacy of their rule. Herrington further observes that in a modern production Kratos and Bia (Power and Violence) "might appropriately be clothed in neat black uniforms and jackboots..."[26] In this production, Kratos (Power), Bia (Violence), and Hephaistos were all dressed in the military uniforms of the South African Defense Force. Hermes appeared dressed in the uniform/suit of a high-ranking police officer, sent by the regime to question and silence. Io, the "beautiful young girl horned like a heifer," was instead represented as a colored woman (under South African law, the child of mixed race parentage was considered "coloured" and was highly problematical, as miscegenation had been outlawed).[27] Io had to flee, never having a home(land), constantly under attack by the stinging horsefly simply because, according to Prometheus, "Zeus was hot for her/Now she's hated by Hera" (873–74). By having this character played as a person of mixed race parentage, Io becomes a metaphor for how the illogical and unjust South African legal system created and then sought to eliminate the class of "coloured" people.

The sole non-black African titan was Ocean, in this case played by a Euro-American actor and meant to suggest those white South Africans who were sympathetic to the plight of their non-white countrymen, and who would oppose apartheid, but for fear that they, too, would become victimized by the system. Although he supports Prometheus and his actions "my heart goes out to you," he insists, "for there's no one,/no one I respect more than you. You can believe that" (444, 446–7). Yet he also warns Prometheus, attempting to silence him for his own sake:

> You don't keep your profile
> low enough, you don't
> give in to torture: you insist
> on more of the same!
> Let *me* be your teacher, and you won't
> stick your neck out,
> not when there's a hard Chief-of-State
> in power, accountable to no one. (474–481)

The language suggests apartheid South Africa: a regime that in the face of worldwide condemnation carried on its policies as if it were "accountable to no one." After praising Prometheus, Ocean suggests Prometheus not endanger himself by being socially and politically active. By having the role played by a Euro-American, suggesting support, but not in the face of oppression, the impression of an ineffective liberal white sympathizer was presented.

The chorus, identified in the text as "Daughters of Ocean," were played by a small group of African American women, representing those who had descended from the African titans, but were at a distance from the recent events. They were interested in what was happening to Prometheus and why it was happening, and ultimately were sympathetic to him to the point of becoming, in the words of Hermes, the "girls who cry over his pains" (1619).

In his conversations with the chorus, Prometheus reveals the two gifts he gave to humankind—hope and fire. Under the production concept, hope remained hope—the possibility for a change for the better, which in South Africa Steve Biko seemed to represent and embody. Fire, however, became a metaphor for Black Consciousness—that which would make the oppressed black Africans the equal of the "gods"—white South Africans. Prometheus tells the chorus:

> PROMETHEUS: Humans used to foresee their own deaths. I ended that.
> CHORUS: What cure did you find for such a disease?
> PROMETHEUS: Blind hopes. I sent blind hopes to settle their hearts?
> CHORUS: What a wonderful gift you helped mankind with!
> PROMETHEUS: What's more, I gave them fire. (374–78)

Prometheus, as a Biko-figure (or, perhaps Biko, as a Promethean figure) brought hope to those who saw only suffering and death in their future. He brought fire, which transformed men and allowed them to realize they could equal the gods, just as the Black Consciousness movement was a decolonization movement designed to create unity, pride, and political action against the apartheid regime. "The first aim of Black Consciousness," writes Hilda Bernstein, "was to conquer feelings of black inferiority, to incubate black pride. Black Consciousness was declared a way of life, an attitude of mind."[28] As Prometheus brought fire to humankind and, as a result, was arrested and tortured, so, too, Steve Biko "brought" Black Consciousness to the oppressed people of South Africa, and was arrested and tortured until he died.

Similarly, Prometheus is tortured throughout his final speech, until he screams the last lines of the play:

> see how I suffer,
> how unjust this is
> ESORAIS M'HOS EKDIKA PASKHO! (1668–70)

The play then ends with a tremendous earthquake, in production the sounds of a bulldozer, troop transports, thunder and gunfire. In other words, the sounds of a black township being destroyed by the South African Police, with the thunder to suggest the power of Zeus. Underscoring the silence after the build of the destructive noises, however, was the sound of schoolchildren singing a defiant freedom song. Like Prometheus, even in the face of violent oppression there are those who will stand up and resist.

Without changing a word of the text, using only the modern translation of the Greek, the production presented a narrative that reflected both the narrative of Prometheus and the history of Steve Biko and apartheid South Africa. By purposefully casting African American actors in key roles, and creating a mise-en-scene that was suggestive of South Africa, the play generated a meaning completely alien to the original Greek context, but completely faithful to the audience and the text. The use of the *Prometheus Bound* text provided tragic distance from which to consider the situation in South Africa. The playing of Greek characters by African American actors projected this new meaning to the audience.

Such productions are by no means limited to colleges and universities, nor are they limited to straightforward translations. Peter Sellars, who would go on to direct a *Merchant of Venice* in which all Jewish characters were played by/as African Americans in order to force audiences to rethink race and prejudice as presented in that play, has directed several Greek tragedies, usually in adaptation by Robert Auletta, aiming them at American audiences and re-historicizing the plays as critiques of the American nation, even as the originals critiqued the Athenian nation. Sellars directed Sophocles' *Ajax* in 1986 at the American National Theatre at the Kennedy Center in Washington, D.C. (arguably the "American Athens"—not a state in and of itself, but a city-state of sorts, and certainly the seat of power of the United States), where it was not very successful, nor very well received. The production was then performed at the La Jolla Playhouse and toured to several European festivals to great acclaim and with far greater success than in Washington.[30]

In Sophocles' original text, the action initially occurs in front of Ajax's tent, and then transfers to the ocean's edge. Odysseus and Athena confer on the behavior of Ajax, who has, in his madness, slaughtered sheep, believing them to be the Greek army. Ajax enters, still mad. He enters his tent, believing he has trapped Odysseus, his enemy who was awarded the armor of Achilles, inside. Athena then lifts the madness from him, and he realizes what he has done. Meeting first with his brother, then with his son, Ajax makes his way to the shore where he throws himself upon his sword. Menelaus and Agamemnon then enter and propose that Ajax be denied burial rites. The family of Ajax pleads for his burial and, eventually, Odysseus adds his voice to theirs. Ironically, it is by the argument of

Odysseus, the man who indirectly caused Ajax's death, that Ajax receives a hero's burial and thus has his heroism acknowledged by the Greeks, his own people.

Robert Auletta adapted the text for Sellars' production, setting the play in "America" in "the very near future."[31] Auletta and Sellars set the play in front of the loading dock of the Pentagon, the symbol of American military might, and replacement, in this case, for the Greek *skene*. Characters are dressed in contemporary American military uniforms: Menelaus and Agamemnon are both five star generals, for example.

Ajax, played by the deaf actor Howie Seago, is the grandson of a "Sioux chief, a warrior!"[32] Interestingly, during the debate about whether or not to bury Ajax, Agamemnon argues that he is descended from a family that has been in America for over two hundred years.[33] Agamemnon is thus the descendent of European imperialists, colonists who came and took the land from the indigenous people, the native Americans such as the Sioux from whom Ajax descends. Thus Sellars both asks the question what, exactly is "an American," and implicates European Americans in the colonial enterprise of building a nation at the expense of the indigenous population.

Odysseus, when introduced, is a "Kissenger-type figure."[34] He is associated in the text with the CIA and with both intelligence gathering and the dissemination of false information and counter-intelligence. He is the wily trickster who convinced the Greeks to give him Achilles' armor. He is a contemporary "spin doctor," stating only the "facts" which support the choice of action he favors. Sellars' Odysseus, while based on the Sophoclean original, differs substantially in his ultimate role in the play. J. Michael Walton states of the original, "It is Odysseus, initially the villain of the piece ... who turns into the savior."[35] No savior is he in Sellars' play: Odysseus always remains the man who twists the truth for his own ends.

Interestingly, Odysseus was played by an African American actor, which Sellars found provocative and significant. He states, "And, of course, in Washington, the fact that I could have five star generals played by black people was incredible. [These were the days before Colin Powell]."[36] The casting of actors of particular ethnicities in roles that they have yet to occupy in the real world is both indictment of the real world and a reminder of what is yet to come. After all, as Sellars himself pointed out, after Odysseus came Colin Powell.

When Ajax "enters," in this version of the play, he is actually unveiled, having been in a transparent plastic box, filled knee-deep with blood, and covered with a cloth. The box represents his madness, according to McDonald, but it also demonstrates how trapped Ajax is by the system in which he, a minority, fights the battles, and Menelaus, and Agamemnon, the Euro-American generals, are awarded and decorated.[37] The blood is soaked into his clothes, and he tracks it everywhere when freed from the box. The blood is reminder both of the slaughter of sheep which Ajax has just carried out and the blood already on Ajax's hands from carrying out the military campaigns on which the generals have sent him. Their uniforms are clean by contrast, his is blood-soaked, further distinguishing the two.

The play is constructed as a series of hearings. Initially, the hearings are to determine what to do with the mad Ajax. Then, after Ajax leaves the Pentagon and kills himself with a knife by a nearby stream, which runs over the stage, washing away the blood Ajax has tracked everywhere, the hearings continue, now to determine what to do with the body and how to publicly respond to these events.

Seago, a deaf actor, must sign his lines, many of which are also spoken by the chorus, a group of five camouflage-wearing actors, three of whom were African American. The chorus literally speaks for Ajax. Like him, they are soldiers. Like him, they are predominantly ethnic minorities, speaking out against the military leadership who are entirely Euro-American. Like him, the chorus is also in the service of the military industrial complex. They are both visible ally and active enemy to Ajax. The means of communication isolates and traps Ajax as much as the plastic box did.

Yet, the speaking of Ajax's lines by the chorus also gives voice to the silent man, and further legitimizes his arguments against the government who used him. In an interview with Arthur Bartow, Sellars argues:

> The chorus had to share his lines. Talk about that yin-tang thing, the idea that nothing is complete until it contains its opposite—the people arguing with him then had to translate his lines. So (the play) contained that awful thing of having to acknowledge your antagonist's argument. The Greek theatre had that collective quality.[38]

Sellars visually and aurally demonstrates that Ajax once had a place in the military order from which he has since been isolated in a number of ways. The military authority must acknowledge his contribution to their history. The blood and his presence are an embarrassing reminder of recent military campaigns. He is a true warrior in a land of Kissengers and clean five-star generals, a mad, deaf, Native American veteran, driven to suicide by a government and a military who no longer need him and do not wish to acknowledge his contributions to their maintaining power.

What makes *Ajax* significant in terms of its non-traditional casting ("crucial," according to one reviewer[39]), is that Athena was played by Aleta Mitchell, an African American actress. She was, literally, a Black Athena on stage. According to Sellars, having Athena played by an African American was "serendipitous."[40] And yet in having the goddess played by an actress of color, Sellars generates entire new levels of meaning that are reinforced by Auletta's translation/adaptation.

In the Greek original, Ajax has offended Athena by refusing her help in battle. Auletta adds the fact that Ajax has also raped Athena, which is, as McDonald notes, "more than just the violence of war; it is also sexist and racist."[41] Because Ajax is native American and not Euro-American, such a rape is not a metaphor for colonialism, but it does reflect the representation of woman of color as sexual object, and perpetuates in some ways the idea of black woman as the embodiment of uncontrolled sexuality, as will be explored below.[42] Athena is dressed in a form-fitting gold lamé dress and is barefoot in a room full of men in full dress military uniforms. She masturbates with a microphone as she watches Ajax. Unlike the Greek goddess, who remained fairly asexual in both myth and drama, Auletta and Sellars remind us of her femininity and sexuality, both visually and through the lines.

A messenger eventually recounts Athena's rape by Ajax:

> And then one day he decides to use her as a woman, as a wanton, as a soldier would use his slut, caressing her breasts and thighs. "Oh, Ajax," she cries, "Oh dear Ajax, treat me like the sister of your soul, and not like the soldier's whore, twisted in foul sheets." "Then go off and consort with General Odysseus," he says. "I'll have none of you.... But still she loves him, and one day comes to him in a field and rests her head upon his heart, and sweetly nuzzles his chest. But suddenly evil explodes within him like a bottle, and throwing her down upon the ground, he rips open her clothes with his dark shards, and then he rapes her.[43]

Thus, Sophocles' refusal of help by Ajax is transformed by Auletta and Sellars into a rape. The text was written without consideration of the ethnicities of the characters, but by casting African Americans as Athena and Odysseus, this dialogue reads very differently than it would were non-blacks in the roles. Athena is "a soldier's whore," a woman used for sexual purposes and thrown away. While Athena "loves" Ajax, and asks simply to be treated as "the sister of [his] soul," he uses her and then tells her to go to the black general and be his "consort." There is present in this dialogue, when spoken in this context, the same desire for and fear of black women that will be discussed in depth later. Of import for this discussion is the simple fact that by casting an African American actress as Athena and an African American actor as Odysseus, a play that demonstrates issues of gender suddenly also concerns issues of race and ethnicity. It is the ethnicity of the characters that generates meaning.

Such creation of meaning through casting is not limited to gender or ethnicity. Don Shewey argues that Howie Seago, as a deaf actor playing Ajax, "clearly recalled" Clarence Fountain, a blind Gospel singer, as Singing Oedipus in *The Gospel at Colonus*.[44] Although such a comment reveals as much about Shewey as it does about *Ajax*, nevertheless a connection is made between two production/adaptations that employ differently-abled performers to portray characters in a Greek tragedy in which the text is fundamentally altered to reflect seemingly new ways of communicating text (signing for *Ajax*, singing for *Oedipus*), but which reflect both the music and gesture which are at the heart of the original performance of Greek tragedy in Athens. Both productions also deal, at some level, with the relationship between Greek tragedy and African Americans or African American culture.

The presence of a black Athena as a character, however, is not necessarily indicative of a "Black Athena" mode of engagement of Greek culture. Neither *Ajax* nor *Prometheus Bound* can be termed "Black Athena" productions, but rather "Black Orpheus." Both productions employ Greek tragedy as a metaphor; one that implicates apartheid in the case of *Prometheus Bound* and Euro-American military abuses in *Ajax*, thus serving to counter official narratives, but still a metaphor that uses Greek tragedy to represent contemporary social and political realities in the African diaspora rather than root the dramatic experience in an Afrocentric idea of theatre.

Both plays are, however, examples of conceptual casting that purposefully place African American actors within Greek tragedy or adaptations (in the case of *Ajax*) of Greek tragedy in which the ethnicity of the actors matters and is significant precisely because of what is signified by the differences of race in context.

Conversely, a production such as the 1995 University of Pittsburgh production of Marina Tsvetaeva's adaptation of *Phaedra*, directed by Tim Golebiewsi, is an example of colorblind casting. *Phaedra* was the second play in an uncompleted trilogy entitled *Theseus*. Tsvetaeva, a Russian symbolist poet and Tsarist, living in exile after the Russian revolution, penned the play which blends elements of the previous versions of the story by Euripides, Seneca, and Racine.

Seneca and Racine both entitled their versions *Phaedra*. The Euripidean original, *Hippolytus*, produced in 428 B.C.E., however, focuses on the male character. Aphrodite, in the prologue, announces her intention of punishing Hippolytus, son of Theseus, as the only mortal in Troezen who does not worship her, preferring instead to remain celibate. She causes Hippolytus' stepmother Phaedra, Theseus' second wife, to fall in love with Hippolytus. Phaedra confesses her love to her nurse, who then informs

Hippolytus. Hippolytus rejects Phaedra and condemns both women. Shocked, Phaedra hangs herself, but leaves a letter accusing Hippolytus of rape. Theseus returns and learning of his wife's death and the ostensible reason banishes Hippolytus, calling upon Poseidon to punish him. A messenger arrives after a choral interlude, informing Theseus that his son was indeed punished by Poseidon and now lies dying. Artemis appears and tells Theseus of the machinations of Aphrodite. Theseus and the dying Hippolytus are reconciled. Seneca and Racine, as their titles indicate, both shift the focus from Hippolytus to Phaedra. She remains alive to be confronted by her false accusation before dying in these versions, and in Tsvetaeva's as well.

In the University of Pittsburgh production, Phaedra was played by Michelle Proctor, the Nurse by Kashi Johnson, and Theseus by Howard Williams, Jr., all three of whom are African American actors. The messenger (Shannon N. Murin), the chorus, and Hippolytus (Shawn B. Ebbert) were all played by Euro-American actors. The casting followed a principle of the best actors to the best roles. The fact that a black Theseus fathered a white Hippolytus, or that a black Phaedra was attracted to her white stepson did not mean anything any different than if the ethnicities were reversed, or even other ethnicities inserted. The actual races of the actors were insignificant.

Certainly, for much of the twentieth century, African American actors were initially kept from classical roles, and then slowly inserted into Greek plays without any special meaning given to their ethnicity. By mid-century, African Americans were appearing in key Greek roles in professional theatres all over the nation. Ruby Dee played Cassandra in *The Oresteia* in Ypsilanti, Michigan early in her career.[45] James Earl Jones appeared as Oedipus in *Oedipus Rex* directed by David Gild at the Cathedral of St. John the Divine in New York City.[46]

Of course, "non-traditional" and "color-blind" casting are celebrated by the mainstream theatre only comparatively recently. Greek tragedy (and other classical dramas) have been enacted by African American actors for over a century, traditionally at universities, and especially at historically black schools. As Glenda E. Gill observes, "Many historically black college theatre groups produced only plays by white playwrights until the early 1960s."[47] Thus, it was not unusual in the thirties, forties, and fifties to see all-black casts of plays by the Greek playwrights or Shakespeare.[48] Gill cites by means of example James T. Guines playing Creon in Jean Anouilh's adaptation of *Antigone* with Alabama A & M's Thespians in 1954.[49] Hill discusses Charles Winter World (1870–1953), a "great Negro tragedian" who was admitted to Beloit College in 1891, playing Heracles in *Alcestis* in

1893, and Oedipus in *Oedipus Rex*, which played both at the college and in Chicago. Wood would return to Beloit in three years, after graduating in 1895 with a degree in Greek, to play the title role in *Alcestis* when the student originally playing the role fell ill.[50] What the mainstream considers groundbreaking was, because of a Eurocentric culture that encouraged the production of Western plays at even historically black college campuses (often to the exclusion of African and African American plays), standard practice at such schools.

As a further consideration for the unevenness of casting practice and how it shapes our understanding of theatre, William H. Sun notes that color-blind casting is only one-way: no whites play in non-white roles.[51] This practice might be ascribed to the recent growth of "political correctness" and racial sensitivity in the American theatre; witness the debate that occurred after British actor Jonathan Pryce was cast as a Eurasian character in *Miss Saigon*. Yet the fact that such an unwritten rule exists also demonstrates the continued unequal opportunities in the arts for artists of color.

Still, the casting of non-white actors in classical Western plays can serve to highlight the issues confronting the nation, the theatre, the culture, and various ethnicities. Angela Pao argues that productions that engage in the practice of non-traditional casting "rely on a historical rather than a taxonomic conception of race."[52] In other words, the plays contextualize race, not in terms of biology but in terms of historic interaction between cultures created by different races and between individuals of different races. In doing so, such productions address a number of concerns related to race: social and economic inequality, political disenfranchisement, segregation, cultural imperialism, etc. Greek tragedy is about the history of people of color, not in a universal sense, but in a very real, historical sense by illustrating via the Greek text presented by a conceptually cast production that illustrates the historic reality of race and race relations.

Yet, even when not purposefully highlighting a racial issue in the play, the presence of black actors in a "white play" generates meanings different than were the actors of European descent. Sun, after August Wilson, argues that even in colorblind casting, the audience isn't colorblind—they observe and bring ideas.[53] So the above-described production of *Phaedra* still is about race inasmuch as race is always an issue when difference is displayed on stage.

It is for this reason, among others, that August Wilson is the most outspoken critic of non-traditional and colorblind casting, seeing the practice as assimilationist. His reading strictly follows the "Black Orpheus" paradigm. He believes African American performers are better off performing only in African American drama.

In his address to the 11th Biennial Theatre Communications Group National Conference, held at Princeton University, entitled "The Ground on Which I Stand," Wilson laid out his vision of the nature and purpose of black drama. While acknowledging that African Americans and European Americans "can meet on the common ground of theatre as a field of work and endeavor," he denies the possibility of meeting on "the common ground of experience."[54] Arguably this statement is accurate.

From here, however, Wilson moves to condemn non-traditional and colorblind casting:

> Colorblind casting is an aberrant idea that has never had any validity other than as a tool of the Cultural Imperialists who view their American culture, rooted in the icons of European culture, as beyond reproach in its perfection.... Their gods, their manner, their being, are the only true and correct representations of humankind.[55]

Wilson argues against the universality of Western culture, rightfully so. Western culture, and specifically Greek tragedy, is not universal. It is, as noted in the first section of this chapter, rooted in a specific cultural moment. However, Wilson assumes all production of Western plays is rooted in an assumption of universality, which may not be true. Following the "Black Athena" paradigm, Greek drama may not even be Western, but African, a possibility that Wilson discounts.

Wilson further argues:

> To mount an all-black production of ... any ... play conceived for white actors as an investigation of the human condition through the specifics of white culture is to deny us our own humanity, our own history, and the need to make our own investigations from the cultural ground on which we stand as black Americans.[56]

Wilson's supposition is that when actors of color appear in Western plays, they deny their African heritage and privilege Western culture. The argument lies upon the intent of the production—is it, as Wilson assumes, to frame the black experience in terms of the white experience, in which case Wilson is correct. But, as noted in the previous chapter, Wilson also allowed a production of *Fences* in China with an all-Chinese cast. Wilson, therefore recognizes that ethnicity is determined by context and that humanity is not necessarily automatically denied to any actors appearing in a play originally written for a different ethnicity.

The slippery slope of Wilson's argument leads one to conclude that he believes African Americans should only appear in "black theatre," whose definition is also fluid and not monolithic, as noted in the introduction and previous chapter. Wilson would not allow actors of color to appear in Greek tragedy in the name of developing African American theatre. What is one to do, then, with plays like *The Darker Face of the Earth* or *American Medea*, rooted as they are in Greek tragedy, but written by African Americans for American audiences and mixed-race casts. Wilson's concern is not as simple or as cut and dried as he might wish it.

Wilson further undercuts himself by arguing that "The common values of the American theatre that we can share are plot ... dialogue ... characterization ... design."[57] Technically, these "common" values are also European in origin. Aristotle observed that the elements of tragedy included plot, character, and dialogue, and these developed out of Greek tragedy. The idea of "drama" is arguably an inherently Western one. In fact, James V. Hatch cites a "severely circumscribed definition of theatre", meaning the activity is only theatre if actors memorize and perform a drama that has been written by a playwright—a very western conceit, as one of the "critical obstacles" to the study of black theatre history.[58] Design, equally, is much more of a western value than an African one, given the stylized performances of many African cultures. Wilson's plays arguably rely much more on Western dramaturgy than African, and yet he finds this to be "common ground."

Adaptation is one way around the problem of colorblind casting. Rather than allow the director to dictate race of the characters through casting and therefore possibly framing Western drama as universal, playwrights turn to adaptation because adaptation allows playwright to dictate ethnicity. In a play entitled "Black Medea," Medea's ethnicity is obviously much more predetermined than in a production of a translation of the Sophoclean original. In order to avoid the conflict of interest that Wilson argues against, playwrights, both African American and European American adapt the plays in order to make them into African American theatre. By adapting the play, focusing on issues of importance to the African American community, providing work for actors of color, and removing at least the first level of Western influence (present when using a simple translation) the Greek tragedy becomes African American drama, making it more acceptable, perhaps, to Wilson and those who share his view.

In order to adapt the play from the Greek original to an African American context it is necessary for the playwright to rewrite the cultural and performative codes embedded in the original, in order to make the text relevant to a contemporary audience.

Shifting Contexts and Cultural Codes

As I argued in *The Athenian Sun in an African Sky*, transculturation is the process by which playwrights and theatre artists take a text from the source culture and transform it for the target culture.[59] This transformation occurs in a series of steps outlined by Carl Weber. A "foreign" text is deconstructed and its original performative codes and cultural codes are removed from the narrative. The narrative (and perhaps the characters) are reinscribed in new codes taken from the target culture, in this case African American history and culture. The original model text disappears and the next text is a complete text in and of itself, though it can also be viewed intertextually.[60] Playwrights, drawing upon both similar situations between Greek tragedy and African American history and cultural similarities between ancient Greece and African America, deconstruct Greek tragedy and transculturate it into an African American context that is more relevant to a contemporary African American audience. When there is a strong enough similarity between the original Greek cultural codes in the tragedy and African American culture, (such as the magic of Medea and the historic practice of voodoo) the playwright is usually able to enact a successful adaptation. When a similarity does not exist between the two cultures through which an adaptation moves (such as in the Hartford Stage's attempt to link AIDS to the plague in *Oedipus Rex*), the text does not transculturate as well and the adaptation may be less successful.

One of the cultural traditions that serves as a useful code by which Greek tragedy can be rewritten into an African American context is religion. Two forms of African American religious practice in particular seem to parallel, to a certain extent, the Greek religious and cultural codes embedded in the tragedies: Afro-Christianity and the syncretic blend of African and Western religions alternately called voodoo, vodu, obeah, Santeria, etc. In both cases, it is the performed rituals (Greek theatre, after all, began as a ritual chant in praise of Dionysus and continued to incorporate religious elements into the individual tragedies) and the religious leaders who serve as the greater link between Africa, America, and Greek adaptation.

Just as Greek tragedy began as the danced and chanted worship of Dionysus, voodoo is a performed religion, called a "danced religion" by Gerdès Fleurant, in which the main form of worship is "a ritual dance designed to interact with the *loa* [voodoo gods] and control the cosmos."[61] Voodoo is a syncretic overlay of Catholicism and West African religions, combining saints with West African deities to create a pantheon that Rod Davis argues is "more than accidentally similar to Roman and Greek systems."[62] Davis (or his sources) implies that the pantheon of West Indian and American voodoo is ultimately descended from Egyptian cosmology. The Egyptian gods were transferred to sub–Saharan Africa and were then brought to the New World on slave ships. Europe, it is argued, as corrupted by the monotheism of Asia Minor while Africa held onto the idea of a pantheon that had been the way of things in Greece and Rome as well.[63] It is this similar pantheon of multiple deities with different spheres of influence and the similar votive nature of the Greek and voodoo religions (meaning sacrifice is made by mortals in order to receive a boon from the divine) that allows playwrights to use voodoo as a transculturative substitute for Greek religious belief and practice in modern adaptation.

The continued influence of both the performed rituals of African religions (especially West African) and the presence of religious leaders from Africa ensured a blending of old traditional and new (enforced) faiths that not only allowed for cultural preservation in the New World but also for the creation of a new social hierarchy and sense of community that is reflected in diasporan adaptation of Greek tragedy. Lawrence Levine explains:

> The slaves took their owner's religion and made it their own not only in terms of content, but also in terms of style. The ways in which slaves sang, moved, and danced in and out of church left no doubt at all about the extent to which they were able to amalgamate African cultures with the cultures they encountered in the United States. Indeed, the debate about whether slaves retained a sense of community is put to rest by the communal nature of their music. There was almost no solo music in slavery; slaves sang in call-and-response fashion, a distinctly African form of music. Because they'd fashioned significant elements of their traditional culture into an African American culture, slaves did not merely mimic European Americans but constituted a cultural influence of their own which had an impact on wide areas of American expressive culture.[64]

From Levine we might discern several key elements. As was discussed in chapter two, African culture undergirds much African American culture. Second, that the religious roots of this culture are performative. The singing, dancing, and movement (all aspects of performance) are African in origin, related to religion, communal in nature, and historically blended with European cultural influences (more enforcement than influences, but the end result is a blend). The use of Greek tragedy by African Americans, it might be argued based on Levine's position, is yet one more example of cultural blending, and not merely the mimicry of European American theatre.

In addition to performative elements and rituals, social structures were also preserved within religion. Those who held positions of religious significance in the Motherland, even if separated from members of their

own ethnic group, could still hold a position of social importance by blending new religion with old:

> Slaves were bought and sold irrespective of their background or trade.
> Among them, therefore, were those who held key positions in the reli-
> gions of their homeland, which explains how a large number of rituals
> could be preserved in the New World, rituals which had of old featured
> dancing, for example, at weddings or rituals.[65]

Epskamp and de Geus are specifically interested in the preservation of
dances, but the point they make can be taken even further for the purposes
of this study. The religious figure from Africa made into a slave in America retains his or her religious authority. Also note again the significance
of performance within the religious framework. The religious leader is a
preserver and teacher of culture, including performed culture.

The religious figure who connects Africa and the New World serves
as a central character in Afro-Greek adaptation. As the Greeks presented
on stage a world in which gods interact with mortals, a world in which there
are mysteries that one can only accept on faith, a world in which individuals have supernatural powers, a world in which the contemporary political, social, and cultural concerns are addressed through myth and ritual,
the use of African or African-derived religions becomes extremely prevalent in adapting these tragedies to the New World.

Another area of culture that allows for rewriting of cultural codes is
sexuality. Greek tragedies are full of explorations of sexuality, whether the
taboo sexuality of Oedipus's incestuous marriage to his mother or the
almost psychotic preservation of her virginity by the title character in Euripides' *Electra* or the rape of Silenus in *Cyclops*. Black sexuality is, as the title
of a Cornell West essay states, "The Taboo Subject." As Greek tragedy deals
with taboo subjects publicly, it lends itself to dealing with this one.

West argues that "Americans are obsessed with sex and fearful of black
sexuality."[66] In fact, West locates the fear of black sexuality in "visceral feelings about black bodies fueled by sexual myths of black women and men."[67]
As theatre is created by live bodies moving physically through space, the
theatre is one area where the public is confronted by the physical body.
Greek tragedy, according to Froma Zeitlin, among others, is the site of
misogynistic attempts to control women and female sexuality.[68] The larger
sexual concerns in Greek tragedy deal with the implications of taboo sexuality, specifically incest, as seen in *Oedipus*, the power and potential for
abuse that comes from the ability to rape (such as seen in *Cyclops* and *Hippolytus*, among others), and inter-racial sexuality as seen in *Medea*. These
three concerns connect to American history (and are transculturated into

Afro-Greek tragedy) through the national and historical concern over interracial sexuality, particularly as it leads to miscegenation and children of
mixed-race descent.

"Miscegenation" itself is a racist term, from the Latin words for mix
(*miscere*) and race (*genus*), it was invented in 1863 for political purposes by
Democrats involved in the presidential campaign against Abraham Lin-
coln. Greek tragedy's thematic concerns with generational curses (*Oresteia*),
taboo relationships (*Oedipus Rex*), the relationship between parents and
children, particularly when the children are taken as prizes or slaves (*Hecuba,
Trojan Women*), and the interaction of Greeks and barbarians (*Medea*) present opportunities to explore the anxiety and political, moral, and philosophical issues surrounding mixed-race relationships and their offspring.

The Code Noir (discussed at length in chapter four) led to the "one
drop" rule of racial identity in the United States: one drop of black blood
(i.e. any African ancestry, no matter how small the percentage) meant that
a person was regarded as non-white regardless of actual skin color. This rule
eventually resulted in legally designated identities based on the percentage
of "black blood": mulatto, quadroon, octoroon, etc.[69]

The laws concerning racial identity based on the races of one's parents represented an attempt not only to preserve the supposed purity of
the white race, but further to control the threat of miscegenation and also
deal with the complex legal, moral, and philosophical implications of the
existence of a group of persons of mixed-race descent in a system that establishes a binary (white/non-white) sense of identity and establishes one of
those groups (non-white) as slaves and possibly even not human.

Miscegenation anxieties were fueled by fears about black sexuality and
the creation of mixed-race offspring. Given these concerns, however, "The
white South combined the permissive sexual exploitation of black women
by white men with a fanatic 'protection' of white women from black men."[70]
Most Southern states passed laws dictating that children would inherit the
racial classification and legal status of their mothers. Thus, the child of a
white male/black female union would be a slave, whereas a child whose
mother was white would be free. Rita Dove uses this convention in *The
Darker Face of the Earth* to create an Oedipus-figure who should be free, but
is a slave.

In the face of fears over miscegenation, it often remained an open
secret, never discussed. There was, as Winthrop Jordan reports, "a wall of
silence around the circumstance," despite the rather common occurrence.[71]
Rita Dove also uses this fact in *Darker Face of the Earth* finding a commonality between the "open secret" of miscegenation in the American
South and the number of people in Thebes who must have realized who

Oedipus was at some point: "The institution of slavery could have fostered the same kind of intense scrutiny of a master from the populous, as well as having a secret that everyone knew about, but no one talked about," she observes.[72] Many masters owned slaves who were often children that they themselves had sired. The potential for tragedy and for the themes and issues that Greek tragedy addressed are manifold in the situation created by the laws surrounding miscegenation, and several playwrights have chosen to use it, particularly Rita Dove and the playwrights who adapt *Medea*.

The potential for ambiguity and blending of identities is yet another theme of Greek tragedy that lends itself to transculturation, particularly beginning in the 1960s. Hand in hand with concern over identity is the theme of power and its abuse that manifests in many tragedies, particularly in those of Euripides. Greek tragedy was a form of publicly questioning and castigating the leadership of the *polis* and of questioning what constituted the identity of citizen, or woman, or slave, or barbarian. Greek adaptation came into its own in that decade, when a large number of cultural shifts occurred in both the nation and the theatre. Young theatre artists turned to the Greeks for their archetypal depictions of generational struggles, inter-ethnic wars, and moral choice. African American playwright Robert Howard adapted several of Euripides' plays, including the *Bacchae*, into *The Death of Semele*. The play "questions the relationship between gods and men, or those in power and those who are powerless."[73] This sentiment could summarize many of the Greek adaptations of the sixties; the commitment to question authority could be dramatically manifested through Greek tragedy to connect the youth movement to the ideals of Western civilization while reinforcing the dominant ideas of the movement.

No production expressed this challenge to power within society and convention within the theatre more than the Performance Group's *Dionysus in 69*, an adaptation of the *Bacchae*. Directed by Richard Schechner and performed in New York City, the play used the actor's own identities and stories, combined with the Greek myth as expressed in Euripides' tragedy, to deconstruct theatrical practice and attack the government, mainstream culture, and society. Taking place in 1969, race played a large role in the play, and the mixed-race cast made use of recent African American popular uprisings in urban areas such as Watts, Detroit, Cleveland, Harlem, etc. in the dialogue. The show shifted each performance as all actors played all roles at one time or another, and certain sections were improvised.

At the end of the play, the actor playing Dionysus would issue commands and make predictions to the members of the cast. William Finley, for example, as Dionysus, would tell Richard Dia:

You, Richard Dia, shall change your name to Richard 37X. It is your fate to lead a great black army of black panthers. With a host so large its numbers cannot be counted, you shall burn many cities to the ground— Detroit, Cleveland, San Francisco, New Orleans, Chicago, Newark. Finally, your army will come to New York and plunder the Harlem Shrine of Apollo. There, your homecoming will be perilous and hard. Yet, in the end the great god Ares will turn you into a honky and bring you to live among the blest.[74]

The cities Finley lists were all cities that had seen racial unrest. Dia's name change to 37X is a reference to the practice among Nation of Islam members of changing their last name to X, the most well-known example being Malcolm X, standing for the unknown name they had lost when whites enslaved their forefathers. Lastly, a Greek word play is being made here. The "Harlem Shrine of Apollo" refers to the Apollo Theatre, located at 253 West 125th street in central Harlem, "the most important venue in black show business from the 1930s through the 1970s," according to Marian Aguiar.[75] The "perilous and hard" homecoming may refer to the famous Amateur Night at the Apollo, during which amateur black entertainers "had their talent assessed by the notoriously raucous Harlem audience," with a positive audience reception resulting in a successful career and a negative reception being particularly humiliating.[76] The Performance Group text demonstrates how Greek references can work on more than one level— the Greek god Apollo and Apollo theatre, for example, joined by a single reference that referred to both.

As Dionysus blends and confuses gender, the Performance Group also used the play about him to confuse and blend race. Richard Dia, who is white, is prophesied to become a leader of the Black Panthers until Ares (god of war) transforms him into a "Honky," a derogatory term for white people, to "live among the blest," another reference to privileged white people. By using the ambiguous nature of Dionysus to make race ambiguous, the Performance Group critiqued mainstream American ideas about race, economics and politics.

The second half of this chapter is a study of three later adapters of Greek tragedy into African American contexts, including three adaptations by Adrienne Kennedy: *Orestes*, *Electra*, and *Oedipus Rex*, Bob Telson and Lee Breuer's *The Gospel at Colonus*, and *The Darker Face of the Earth*. Each of the three approach Greek tragedy differently and handle the material in different ways. All plays will also be examined in terms of which paradigm they follow: "Black Orpheus," "Black Athena," or "Black Dionysus."

Adrienne Kennedy and Greek Tragedy

Adrienne Kennedy is arguably one of the best known and most significant female African American playwrights. She has won numerous awards for her plays, including Obies for *Funnyhouse of a Negro*, *June and Jean in Concert*, and *Sleep Deprivation Chamber* (this last play was co-written with her son Adam). She has written numerous plays dealing with issues of identity, gender, history, and ethnicity, including *The Ohio State Murders*, *A Movie Star Has to Star in Black and White*, *The Owl Answers*, *Motherhood 2000*, *She Talks to Beethoven*, *An Evening with Dead Essex*, *A Lesson in Dead Language*, and *The Lennon Play*. She has written a memoir, *People Who Lead to My Plays*, and has taught at numerous colleges and universities, including Yale, Harvard, New York University, and Berkeley. The Signature Theatre Company of New York devoted an entire season to her work. In short, she is a significant and accomplished playwright. She has also adapted or been involved in three productions of Greek tragedy as a writer.

Kennedy's first published writing, 'Because of the King of France,'' appeared under the name Adrienne Cornell in *Black Orpheus* while she and her husband were touring West Africa in 1960, a happy coincidence considering her later work with Greek tragedy.[77] Kennedy discovered Greek tragedy in her early twenties, realizing their potential when seeing Martha Graham's dance version of Greek myth after having read several of the plays in college. "Taken together," she told Alan Woods, "it was just a revelation."[78] It would not be until 1980, however, that Kennedy would have the opportunity to engage Greek material as a playwright.

In that year, Michael Kahn at the Julliard School of Music commissioned Kennedy to adapt two plays by Euripides: *Electra* and *Orestes*. Kahn then directed the two plays with music by Kirk Nurock and costumes by Mariann Verheyen. Kahn specifically chose Euripides's versions as "Euripides to me is much more jagged on the edge."[79] He specifically chose Kennedy as, "I always thought the power of Adrienne's plays was the underlying myth she tapped into...."[80] He therefore asked a mythocentric playwright to adapt Euripides's "jagged" dramas for production by the acting students at the Julliard School. Kennedy was not approached based on her gender or ethnicity, but rather due to her work as a writer, and her strength in engaging myth through interesting theatre.

The plays were performed November 5–9, 1980 as part of a performance project by the Julliard students, and were then presented in repertory again in April of 1981. Electra was played by Linda Koslowski and Orestes was played by a then-unknown Val Kilmer. Both performers are European American. The dominant word associated with the production was "primitive"—Randolyn Zinn, who choreographed the shows when original choreographer Martha Clark could not, and Michael Kahn "put it in a very primitive period," and Lois Overbeck describes Verheyen's costumes as "primitive and feathered."[81] All of the primitive aspects of the show were meant to suggest Greek pre-history, not any sense of Africa or African-primitive. Kennedy's versions of the play are devoid of any suggestion of ethnicity or of African culture.

The plays were subsequently published in *Adrienne Kennedy in One Act,* a volume that also contains *Funnyhouse of a Negro, The Owl Answers, A Lesson in Dead Language, A Rat's Mass, Sun,* and *A Movie Star Has to Star in Black and White. Electra* and *Orestes* are set apart from the other plays in a separate section called "Greek Adaptations." The split seems rather arbitrary, and no explanation is given why these two are separated out. In separating them out, however, the volume acknowledges that these two works are separate and different from the rest of the Adrienne Kennedy canon. The two Greek adaptations are not to be understood in the same vein as more political and Afrocentric works such as *Funnyhouse of a Negro.*

Kennedy does not so much transculturate the plays from the original Greek setting into a new one, or alter the dramaturgy so as to create new relevance or historicity as she does edit them. Both plays are greatly reduced in length from Euripides's originals. Kennedy's plays are not line-for-line translations of the originals, nor are they Afrocentric adaptations, they are freely adapted versions of Euripides's dramas that focus on telling the story in direct, simple, modernized language.

Euripides begins with the farmer that Electra has been forced to marry giving the backstory. Kennedy gives a truncated version of the lines to the chorus, allowing them to summarize the events to the point at which the play begins. Here, also, the farmer is called "Peasant." Other than these two alterations, the opening of the play follows Euripides very faithfully. Electra goes to fetch water and weeps for her dead father and lost brother. Orestes enters in disguise and claims to bring news of her brother. She explains her life to him, and her husband enters. The peasant's speech offers an opportunity to compare Kennedy's version with a traditional translation.

In the translation by Emily Townsend Vermeule as part of the *Complete Greek Tragedies* series, lines 341 to 344, spoken by the Farmer who, entering, sees Electra talking with Orestes and Pylades, are rendered thus:

> Hey there! Who are these strangers standing at our gates?
> What is the errand that could bring them to our rough
> courtyard? Are they demanding something from me? A nice
> woman should never stand in gossip with young men.

Kennedy renders the speech this way:

> Strangers what do you want at our door?
> Electra you should not let strangers
> come so close to our door.[82]

The language is much more direct and unaffected. No attempt is made to create formal verse or sound "classical"—the language is intended to convey simplicity. Again, Kennedy does not develop a line-for-line translation but tries to capture, in a modern, American manner, the spirit and intent of the lines and exchanges.

As in the original, an old man enters and reports that a sacrifice has been left at Agamemnon's tomb. When he sees Orestes, he recognizes him from a scar on his brow. The reunited brother and sister join the chorus, old man, and peasant in plotting against Clytemnestra and Aegisthus. The old man leaves to tell Clytemnestra that Electra has given birth to a son while Orestes kills Aegisthus.

After a choral interlude, a messenger arrives to report the death of Aegisthus at the hands of Orestes. The chorus chants and dances as the corpse is brought in, but Electra's lengthy speech against Aegisthus (lines 907 to 956) are cut in Kennedy's version. Instead, she jumps directly to the point when Orestes has second thoughts about killing his mother. Electra convinces him of the rightness of their planned action and he hides in the cottage to await his mother.

Clytemnestra enters and Electra accuses her of a variety of offenses, referring to herself as "fatherless." Clytemnestra defends herself with a lengthy speech, arguing that her actions were a justified revenge against her husband for the killing of Iphigenia. Electra's equally lengthy response is that if Clytemnestra's revenge was justified, killing a family member for their causing the death of another family member, then she and her brother would be justified in killing Clytemnestra.

In the Vermuele translation, Clytemnestra responds:

> My child, from birth you always have adored your father.
> This is part of life. Some children always love
> the male, some turn more closely to their mother than him.
> I know you and I forgive you. I am not so happy
> either, child, with what I have one or with myself.
> How poorly you look. Have you not washed? Your clothes are bad.
> I suppose you just got up from bed and giving birth.
> O god, how miserably my plans have all turned out.
> Perhaps I drove my hate too hard against my husband. (1102–1110)

Euripides's lines follow a thought process. Clytemnestra engages the complex family dynamic that existed in the house of Agamemnon, with conflicting loyalties and the literal sacrifices that have made what should be the strongest ties into the bitterest and bloodiest of enemies. She also notes the wretched condition of Electra and expresses concern and remorse.

Kennedy reduces this entire speech to the single line, "Electra, I regret that revenge now."[83] The line is simplified—perhaps even oversimplified. The subtlety, thought process, and nuances of Euripides's original are all lost. In one sense, Kennedy is re-mythologizing Euripides. If Euripides is often seen as the tragedian who is known for "depicting realistic behavior rather than the prescribed heroism of myth," and his extended exchanges insert realistic psychology where Aeschylus and Sophocles place heroic myth, then Kennedy in a sense, erases the psychological study, leaving a more simple, more primitive, indeed more mythic drama.[84]

Clytemnestra enters the cottage to see what she believes is her grandchild and make the proper sacrifices to the gods, but instead meets Orestes, who kills her offstage. The bodies of Clytemnestra and Aegisthus are brought out and displayed for the audience to see. In the Euripidean original, the Dioscuri—the twins Castor and Polydeuces (or Pollux)—appear as the *deus ex machina* and order that Electra must marry Pylades, as she never consummated her marriage to the farmer, and Orestes must go to face trial in Athens.

The *deus ex machina* is completely cut from Kennedy's rendering. That play ends with Electra and Orestes covering the bodies and expressing regret. Electra's last line before the entrance of the Dioscuri, "the one I loved and could not love," in reference to her mother (line 1231) is rendered, "We loved you ... although we hated you."[85] Whereas the Euripidean original has another 127 lines to go, Kennedy's play ends with the chorus responding to Electra's final line with, "This is the prophetic end of great sorrow."[86]

Considering that Kennedy was commissioned to adapt the plays based on her ability to "tap into the underlying myths," her removal of the last scene of the play is quite telling. The presence of the Dioscuri at the end acts as a corrective force—they describe the future, bleak as it is, for Orestes and Electra. They promise a continuation in the face of all the violence that the family has endured. By removing them, Kennedy evokes a more tragic sense of the play—nothing can be recovered from the murder of the mother and her lover. Euripides "exposes [the] psychology [of the characters] with a ruthless scalpel and pushes Sophocles' character to its logical extreme," in this play, but Kennedy then removes the one mythic concession that gives meaning to the suffering of all the characters.[87]

Orestes, similarly, is reduced in scope and lines with some minor changes and cuts, but remains a freely-adapted, straightforward version without any re-encoding of the text into a specific milieu. Electra's opening prologue is given to the chorus and reduced to the basic components of the backstory by Kennedy. Extended conversations in the original are reduced to quick and easily comprehensible exchanges in this version.

Kennedy, in fact, seems to take entire sections from the William Arrowsmith translation (again, part of the *Complete Greek Tragedies*) and edits them down to brief passages, still recognizable from their source. The chorus's plea on behalf of Orestes is translated by Arrowsmith as:

Goddesses of terror,
runners on the wind,
revelers of sorrow
whose rites are tears!
Women of darkness,
Eumenides whose wings
shiver the taut air,
demanding blood,
avengers of murder,
we implore you—
release this boy,
Agamemnon's son,
from madness and murder,
the blood that whirls him on!
Pity, pity we cry,
pity for the crime,
murder that came on,
drove from Apollo's throne,
the god's command to kill
breaking the hushed, the holy air,
with the word of blood—
blood drenching the shrine
of Delphi—
			Delphi,
holiest of holies
and navel of the world! (316–333)

Kennedy reduces this entire invocation, plea, and prayer to:

Eumenides, women of darkness,
avengers of murder
we implore you—
release this boy
from his madness.[88]

Kennedy simply inverted lines 321 and 322, and added lines 324 through the first half of 326 of Arrowsmith's translation, reducing the extended poetic plea down to a very simple, evocative one. In this case, Kennedy is not so much adapting Euripides' play as she is editing Arrowsmith's translation for a production by Julliard students, mostly by cutting.

Unlike in *Electra*, the *deus ex machina* of *Orestes* is kept; Apollo arrives to fix the situation. However, a great deal of other material is removed or changed. The nearly one hundred line exchange between Orestes and Menelaus, from 379 to 470 in the original, is reduced by Kennedy to a mere two page conversation. The encounter with Tyndareus, the father of Helen and Clytemnestra, is greatly reduced. The "Phrygian Slave" in the original becomes a "Trojan Slave" in Kennedy's text. This change is merely one of clarification for modern audiences. Troy was located in the country of Phrygia, and is its largest and best-known city, although not very many people who have not studied the classics might know this fact. Kennedy substituted the known name (Trojan) for the less familiar (Phrygia). While the change is not great, it should be noted that while all Trojans are Phrygians, not all Phrygians are Trojan. The change itself is indicative of Kennedy's larger agenda in writing this version: to simplify and de-classicize the piece for a contemporary New York audience in 1980.

Even the choice of pieces indicate a desire to create and remove distance at the same time. Rather than engage the *Oresteia*, the better known and more familiar version of these myths, Kahn (and Kennedy) chose to stage the less familiar Euripidean versions. The audience knows the story, but perhaps not this version of it. The audience is both familiar and unfamiliar with the story, the characters, the myth, and the language. By familiarizing the references, removing or reducing the extended speeches, generalizing specific references or situations, and keeping the language simple, but modern, Kahn and Kennedy present an unfamiliar familiarity, paradoxically distant and familiar at the same time.

This type of text would allow the production to focus on the acting, rather than developing a political or cultural message relevant to the play and the larger culture of New York in the 1980s—aesthetics without ideology. By not engaging in ideology, however, the productions privilege the European center to which the Greek plays are attached. These two plays by Adrienne Kennedy, after Euripides qualify as neither "Black Orpheus" or "Black Athena," primarily because they do not engage Africa or the African American experience at all. The two main actors (Koslowski and Kilmer) and the director are white. Kennedy, who so often deals with ethnic (read: black or multi-racial) identity in her work, does not do so here. This commission is an example of an artist of color attempting to sidestep the trap of Kobena Mercer's mentioned in chapter one, that an artist of color is never allowed to be just an artist but must always "visibly embody a prescribed difference." Kennedy accepted the commission and wrote these plays without regard to African American theatre or ethnic identity. These plays are almost outside the purview of this survey. Yet, because they were written by Adrienne Kennedy, they fall very firmly within the boundaries of the subject matter: Greek tragedy as adapted by, for, and/or about African Americans. This paradox demonstrates both the difficulty of Mercer's position and the complexity of determining what constitutes African American theatre. Kennedy is African American, the cast and director were Euro-American, the context was the audiences of the Julliard School of

Music. Can these two plays be called "African American" simply because Adrienne Kennedy wrote them? It is not an easy question to answer.

Kennedy was "happy" with the work at Julliard, and the plays received positive reviews at the time and in subsequent histories.[89] Samuel Hay, for example, calls *Electra* and *Orestes* "the bright spots" of "Inner Life versus Inner Life" drama in the late seventies and early eighties, although he does not explain why or offer further specific comment (60). Nevertheless, Kennedy's two Greek one-acts have faired well in critical histories of African American theatre, despite their lack of direct representation of African American life.

Kennedy accepted another commission to work with Greek material at the end of the twentieth century, this time from the Hartford Stage. Under the direction of Jonathan Wilson, the *Oedipus Rex* of Sophocles was reset in contemporary Africa during a production in January and February of 2001.

The Hartford Stage was certainly not the first to relocate Sophocles' play from Greece to Africa. Numerous African productions have done so, most notably Ola Rotimi's *The Gods Are Not to Blame*.[90] In the United States, several college, semi-professional, and professional companies have also set the play in Africa, most notably the African American Shakespeare Company of San Francisco, a group dedicated to presenting Western classics using African American performers, directors, and designers, who relocated the play to an African village during the colonial period.

What is unique about the Kennedy/Hartford Stage production is that the play was not set in the colonial period nor used to analyze the colonial relationship between African and the West, nor even to explore internal political struggles in Africa. This political dimension was ignored entirely and instead the play focused on the specter of AIDS.

The action is sparked in the original Sophoclean play by a plague that is decimating Thebes. A priest of Zeus pleads with Oedipus to do something to halt the disease:

> King, you yourself
> have seen our city reeling like a wreck
> already; it can scarcely lift its prow
> out of the depths, out of the bloody surf.
> A blight is on the fruitful plants of the earth,
> a blight is on the cattle in the fields,
> a blight is on our women that no children
> are born to them; a God that carries fire,
> a deadly pestilence, is on our town,
> strikes us and spares not, and the house of Cadmus

is emptied of its people while black Death
grows rich in groaning and lamentation. (23–30)

Oedipus responds to these pleas as a leader who shares their concern, and
sees the scope and size of the problem:

> I have known the story before you told it
> only too well. I know you all are sick,
> yet there is not one of you, sick though you are,
> that is as sick as I myself.
> Your several sorrows each have single scope
> and touch but one of you. My spirit groans
> for city and myself and you at once. (58–64)

The play begins with the supplication of the leader by the priest, representative of both the gods and the community, to help end the plague that
is destroying the people. The lines indicate that not only are people dying,

Oedipus Rex at the Hartford Stage. Note the difference between the
traditional African dress of the Greek characters and the more modern dress of the AIDS patient (right). Photograph © T. Charles Erickson.

but that as a result of the sickness and death the city is suffering serious socio-economic problems. The city is "reeling like a wreck" under the problems caused by the disease.

Hartford Stage Artistic Director writes in the program that, after considering doing the play, the artists involved realized that "the play reflects modern-day Africa amidst the AIDS plague."[91] He notes that the choice to use the Greek tragedy to engage AIDS and its effect in Africa also reflects the reality of AIDS in America, specifically in Hartford, Connecticut where the theatre is located. Wilson cites figures that show the dramatic increase in AIDS and HIV in Hartford, especially among teens, and especially in the young African American and Latino populations. Thus, the Hartford Stage uses the Greek play to link AIDS in Africa with AIDS in urban America.

The program furthers the connection by locating an excerpt from Thucydides on a plague that began in Ethiopia and eventually ravaged Greece next to an excerpt from *Time* about AIDS in Africa.[92] The linkage of Greek plague, African AIDS, and AIDS in America is not a straightforward one, and the production problematizes the link by using *Oedipus Rex* to casually link three rather different pandemics.

AIDS has devastated and ravaged African populations far worse than those of any other continent. Approximately thirty-six million in the world are HIV positive or have AIDS. Sub-Saharan Africa has one-tenth of the world's population but approximately 70% of the HIV and AIDS cases. In 1999, 2.6 million people in the world died of AIDS or AIDS-related causes. 85% of those deaths were in Africa. 90% of the AIDS orphans, or 12.1 million children, are African, 1.1 million of whom live in Uganda alone (an AIDS orphan is defined as a child 15 or under who has lost the mother or both parents to AIDS).[93]

In addition to the suffering, sickness, and death that HIV and AIDS bring, other negative consequences quickly emerged in Africa as a result of the pandemic. Political, economic, and social instability has resulted from the disease. The sheer number of orphans combined with the number of sick has increased health-care costs to a crippling level for most African economies, already in bad shape from colonialism, wars, etc. The poverty that is one of the causes of the spread of AIDS is worsened by the disease. The pandemic will have far-reaching consequences for Africa, many of which have not even yet been estimated.

Beginning in the 1990s, after a period of slow response, the African American community began to take note of AIDS, both within its own boundaries and within Africa. Although initially ignored, as demonstrated in Cheryl West's play *Before It Hits Home*, AIDS began to impact the African

American community in record numbers. Likewise, the African connection to AIDS was downplayed until a group of religious and political leaders such as the Reverend Eugene Rivers of Boston began to bring public attention to the growing pandemic in the Motherland.

Beginning in 1999, Rivers challenged American blacks to do something about AIDS in Africa. While much has been accomplished in the past three years, there is still concern in some quarters that "highlighting AIDS in Africa reinforces negative stereotypes."[94] Indeed, the fact that AIDS appeared to originate in Africa from a simian immunodeficiency virus was perceived by many African Americans as propaganda motivated by racism: all bad things come out of Africa, Africans have intercourse with monkeys, etc. Simon Watney has written extensively about the negative associations of "African AIDS," noting that the connection between AIDS and Africa in the Western media always centers around the "primitiveness" of the sexual and medical cultures, equating black Africans with drug-users and promiscuous homosexuals, and framing the entire pandemic as the latest in a series of perpetual crises (such as famine or the emergence of Ebola) that afflict the continent.[95]

The danger, of course, in setting Oedipus Rex in Africa, rooted in the AIDS pandemic is that the production might perpetuate some of these perceptions: the "primitiveness" of African culture and African medicine, distancing the crisis through the Greek metaphor. Furthermore, to argue, as Wilson does, that the production also therefore engages AIDS in America is also problematic, simply because there are some differences between AIDS in America and AIDS in Africa, many of which are economically and culturally based. Free HIV testing is available in Hartford, not so in many parts of Africa. Cultural attitudes towards sex are radically different in urban Hartford and Uganda, for example. For those with insurance or access to good community care facilities in the United States drug-therapies are available that are not available in most of Africa, even to the economically advantaged. The production, admittedly, might oversimplify some of the connections it seeks to make without any seemingly valuable insight gained. Watching the production does not teach the audience anything about AIDS, Africa, or AIDS in Africa.

The concept for the play that Kennedy and Wilson relied upon is that of a travelling theatre company in Africa which arrives to perform Oedipus for AIDS patients gathered at an AIDS clinic. The play then begins to subsume the reality around it as the clinic becomes the palace of Thebes and the AIDS patients become a chorus of sorts. This concept is problematic, however, inasmuch as the plague in Sophocles is but a plot device that is used to instigate the action of the play: the search for the murderer of Laius

Jocasta (Stephanie Berry) comforts Oedipus (Reg Flowers) in the Hartford Stage production of *Oedipus the King*. Photograph © T. Charles Erickson.

that Oedipus undertakes, only to have his quest turn into a search for his own origins, learning to his horror that the prophesy of his killing his father and marrying his mother has come true. The plague is not mentioned again after the first scene. Thus, the concept is rooted in something not central to the action.

Sophocles' play has been used as a parallel or overlay for many contemporary political, religious, sociological, and psychological situations. In this case, however, the play is linked to a larger situation that is seemingly irrelevant to the main action of *Oedipus*. Oedipus himself did not have AIDS, and, although the play certainly engages taboo sexuality, it does not do so in a manner that is readily and apparently linked to the AIDS crisis. As a result of Sophocles dropping the plague references after the opening scene and the linkage of the plague to AIDS, the production seemed to have difficulty sustaining the AIDS throughline.

In her review for the *Boston Globe*, Patti Hartigan observes:

> Yet the contemporary resonance is barely discernable, and after the first two minutes the folks who are supposed to be AIDS patients sit mute, awkward spectators who fail to blend in with the scenery."[96]

As noted above, the result is that the audience learns nothing about Africa or AIDS, and instead is given an uneasy marriage between a concept that is only really supported by the prologue of the play and not carried through the rest of the drama and a text that is ultimately not about disease or its effects on the population.

The concept does not even allow for the linking of the destabilization politically and economically of AIDS-afflicted nations as suggested in the prologue. The plague is brought about as a result of the city sheltering the murderer of the old king, and, although poor leadership might be very slightly to blame for the emergence of AIDS, much greater causes, such as poverty, gender roles, cultural attitudes towards sex, lack of sanitary health care, lack of HIV education, and a growing urbanization in sub–Saharan nations exist. Thus, the production suffers from a tenuous link between its text and its production concept that is not always supported. The text also problematizes the "Africanness" of the play, moving it into a "Black Orpheus" paradigm.

Kennedy, it should be noted, did not "adapt" the play. Although she was commissioned to write an adaptation, the Hartford Stage ended up using the Dudley Fitts and Robert Fitzgerald translation with Kennedy listed as "Text Consultant" in the program. It remains unclear how much of the text is her work, although the reviewers give her the credit for creating accessible, contemporary language.[97]

Hartigan notes that, "the language is subtly updated, but it remains scrupulously faithful to Sophocles."[98] One might ask how a play in contemporary English can be "faithful" to Sophocles' language, given that he wrote in ancient Greek. It seems what Hartigan means is that the language sounds how she believes ancient Greek tragedy should sound—no contemporary topical references or slang are inserted. Nevertheless, the text is translated and adapted, not Sophocles' language at all. The issue of "faithfulness" is questionable, as one can be faithful to literal language in translation, or one can be faithful to the "spirit," or one can be faithful to the culture, looking for equivalents in the target culture. In other words, for the ancient Athenians the tragedies were not ancient classics, but contemporary (in fact, brand new) explorations of contemporary political and cultural issues using myth. One might argue that a contemporary updating might actually be more "faithful" to the original experience of Greek tragedy.

It is important to note, however, that Hartigan sees the language as being Sophoclean, not African, or contemporary American. Many of the reviews of the production highlight the seeming "closeness" of the adaptation to the original. Bruce Weber in the *New York Times* argues:

> The production is purposefully race-based, yes, but it is not political. Even with casting and performances that reflect the variety of black experiences, and with costuming, a hauntingly percussive music score and intervals of dance that are all redolent of African culture, the show feels cross-cultural in a modern vein.[99]

Any review reveals much more about the reviewer and his or her assumptions than it does the production being reviewed, and Weber's reflections on *Oedipus* are no exception. Of course the show is political—to claim that it is not is intellectually dishonest. A play about AIDS in Africa, also intended to reflect the reality of AIDS in America, presented in a professional regional theatre in a major urban center in Northeastern America cannot not be political. In this case, however, the "Black Orpheus" paradigm seems to be in effect: the audience is shown the AIDS epidemic in Africa and then given a production of *Oedipus Rex* with an overlay of African visual and aural elements and an all-black cast intended to evoke Africa. Arguably, the perceived lack of political content is a form of political content—one should have sympathy for communities suffering from AIDS, but the status quo remains unchanged. Performances were arranged for Hartford public schoolchildren, but the vast majority of the Hartford Stage audience is culled from the upper-middle class, well-educated elite of central Connecticut, spreading as far north as Boston and as far south as New

Stephanie Berry as Jocasta, surrounded by a chorus of young girls and AIDS patients in the hartford Stage *Oedipus the King*. Photograph © T. Charles Erickson.

York City. The idea of framing Oedipus's story in AIDS-ravaged Africa does not give any additional insight into AIDS or Africa, although it creates a new way of seeing *Oedipus* for those familiar with it—a class-specific intention for the elite audience.

The show "feels cross-cultural in a modern vein," meaning that it doesn't strike him as African, but rather as a play accessible to European Americans. Given the uneasy marriage between concept and text, the "Black Orpheus" paradigm is most definitely operational here, the metaphor being that Oedipus seeking the murderer of Laius in a plague-ridden city is like the leaders of Africa looking for solutions to the AIDS crisis. Unfortunately, the production does not work as well as it could or should because of the inaccurate and inadequate concept.

Weber goes on to note of the director of the production:

Mr. Wilson's intent, I think, is not to distinguish the black experience but to affirm its inclusion within the corporal and spiritual plaintiveness of humankind—and within its literary tradition as well.[100]

Weber obviously privileges the West, stating as he does that *Oedipus* is part of the "literary tradition" of "humankind," in which now the "black experience" is able to be included. Such thinking represents Eurocentrism at its extreme. Weber perceives the production as having erased the difference between Africa and Greece, between non–Western and Western, between black and white. His review engages in the universalizing, humanistic enterprise of erasing all difference and acknowledging one world, centered around the culture and societies of humankind (read: the West, Euro-American, etc.).

Weber's comments reflect his view more than the reality of the production, but in all fairness, the Hartford Stage *Oedipus Rex* with Adrienne Kennedy does erase difference without locating African culture or the AIDS crisis anywhere other than a convenient dressing for a western classic. Kennedy's earlier Greek adaptations likewise ignored difference and African or African American culture. On the one hand, she deals with Greek tragedy as an artist, period. She does not allow ethnicity to be an issue, thus avoiding the issue of exceptionalism. On the other hand, while such erasure is unproblematic when doing *Orestes* or *Electra* at the Julliard School, no engagement of Africa is even attempted, so the plays are almost outside the African continuum, and only the ethnicity of the playwright locates them within it. *Oedipus Rex*, however, being set in Africa, engaging the issue of AIDS in Africa and in America, with an African mise-en-scene and an all African American cast does engage Africa, and also erases difference. In this case, *Oedipus Rex* follows the "Black Orpheus" paradigm by siting African culture in the same space as Greek culture, employing the Greek material as metaphor—AIDS in Africa is like the plague in *Oedipus* and expresses Africa in terms of the west.

Adrienne Kennedy is a fascinating and talented playwright who has profoundly influenced those who came after her and might be regarded as one of the preeminent African American playwrights of the twentieth century. Thus it is interesting that the two times she has engaged Greek tragedy it has been solely for the purpose of erasing difference and presenting a "Black Orpheus" paradigm that ignores the African at most and expresses the African in terms of the western at the least. In the case of the plays at Julliard, one wonders if the plays might even be considered African American theatre. If it were not for the ethnicity of the playwright, there would not even be a question.

Preaching from the Book of Oedipus:
The Gospel at Colonus

Lee Breuer and Bob Telson's Afro-Greek musical is, arguably, the "multiculturalest" and, paradoxically, the most mainstream of the plays considered in this volume: an adaptation of a Greek tragedy, written by two European Americans, set in a black Pentecostal Church, utilizing an all-African American cast and spiritual and Gospel-style music, presented on Broadway. After several years of workshopping at the Brooklyn Academy of Music (among other places), The Gospel at Colonus made its Broadway debut at the Lunt-Fontaine Theatre on 24 March 1988, running for 61 performances.

The work itself is an adaptation of Robert Fitzgerald's translation of Sophocles's Oedipus at Colonus, staged and presented in the form of an African American Pentecostal Church service. Telson composed the Gospel music for the show and Breuer adapted the text. Breuer was already known for his avant-garde work with Mabou Mines, focusing on American culture through the lenses of gender and race. His work has been called "interactive" and "intercultural," and his adaptations and more mainstream offerings tend to be "subversive rather than accommodat[ing]."[101]

Breuer writes in the acknowledgements to The Gospel at Colonus that, "Zora Neale Hurston made the connection between Greek tragedy and the sanctified church many years ago."[102] It is this connection that has been arguably the most controversial aspect of the play in critical reception, as will be explored below. Breuer's response to the argument that Greek religion and black Pentecostal religion are incompatible is that the doctrines do not matter, it is the purpose (what Aristotle would call the cause) of the experience that matters: catharsis. "As was the classic Greek performance, the Pentecostal service is a communal catharsis which forges religious, cultural, and political bonds. Should not the living experience teach us something of the historical one?"[103] The "living experience" of which Breuer speaks is modern production of Greek tragedy, and by using the Pentecostal church as a setting he hopes to evoke the spirit of the original experience of tragedy. While he is essentially correct that the experiences of ancient tragedy and modern worship are both active on many levels and similar in that they both forge a variety of communal bonds, his statement remains both simplistic and problematic.

Breuer, neither Greek nor African American Pentecostal, has a significantly different experience of these performances that one who is from either of these communities. He is responding intellectually as an outsider to his perception of the experience of these "performances." These same experiences which "forge communal bonds" can also prove divisive: witness Euripides, whose plays caused controversy and who continually upbraided the community for what the playwright saw as misguided action. Likewise, the sinner publicly castigated from the pulpit during a church service is as likely as not to leave the church as reform his or her ways in the cast of the Pentecostal community.

Furthermore, one might argue that the Festival of Dionysus was the theatre of the elite in Athens, the judges and participants consisting of the male citizens of the city, and while the audience consisted of members of society from all classes, races, and genders, only those who could afford to take the time to go would attend. Given that, however, the theatre was also the theatre of the entire city. The Pentecostal church, on the other hand, is not a large denomination in terms of the overall population of America, it is not even the majority church of African America. It is not the church of the elite: it has its roots in the slave experience and remains firmly ensconced in the lower income rural and urban communities of African America. In other words, the Pentecostal church does not hold the same place in contemporary American society that Greek tragedy held in Athenian society. One might argue that the Pentecostal church holds the same place in the African American community that Greek tragedy held in the Athenian community, but then this complicates both Breuer's role in combining the two and the audience to which he and Bob Telson brought their *Gospel*. We must be aware of these differences in order to understand both the criticisms of the play and how the play generates meanings for different audiences.

Mimi Gisolfi D'Aponte argues, correctly so, that *The Gospel at Colonus* is actually a blend of two modern genres: the Gospel musical and the postmodern reworking of a classical text, both of which developed in the 1960s and 1970s.[104] Gospel musicals began to develop in the mid–twentieth century as a genre of theatre created by and for African Americans.[105] Well known playwrights and musicians, such as Langston Hughes and Jobe Huntley, among others, began writing musicals to be performed by black actors for a target audience of African Americans. Musicals such as *Tambourines to Glory, Black Nativity, Trumpets of the Lord, Purlie, Your Arms too Short to Box with God,* and *Mama, I Want to Sing* were presented on Broadway, becoming crossover hits with both African American and Euro-American audiences attending, and, in many cases, are still revived in many American communities today. Despite being crossover hits, however, the target audience remained African American.

Joining a narrative to both traditional and original Gospel songs, the musicals tell a story through Gospel music and an acting style suggestive of the Pentecostal service. As Warren Burdine argues, the typical Gospel musical "has opted to give its audience the familiar ... to preach to the already converted," in other words, to present the known church service as entertainment, including reinforcing the same messages received each week at church.[106] Burdine reports that "this manner of thinking has been justified at the box office," as ticket sales for Gospel musicals is always high and many more African Americans attend this type of production than the standard Broadway fare of musical comedies.[107]

The African American community, however, was not the sole target audience of *Gospel at Colonus*, or even its main one. It is the blending of postmodern reworking of a classical text and Gospel musical combined with its production history that indicates Breuer and Telson were seeking to create a piece of theatre distanced from both of its sources (Greek theatre & African American religious experience) and yet paradoxically built on both. They created a theatre for the elite (as the original *City Dionysia* was) by presenting the play at the Next Wave Festival, whose audience is usually well-educated, economically well-off theatre aficionados—the economic and cultural elite of the New York area. Broadway, as well, tends to cater to those who can afford the time and the ticket price to see the show. To this elite audience, Breuer and Telson seek to distance Greek tragedy through Pentecostal ritual and gospel music.

But as critic Royston Coppenger argues:

> If the intention of *Gospel at Colonus* is to be described as a subversive one, that of undercutting the audience's intellectual preconceptions about the production of a certain type of play in order to free them for a direct emotional experience, we must also acknowledge the class-specificity of that intention."[108]

It is true, the target audience of this Gospel musical is the cultural, economic, and intellectual elite of New York. In one sense, *Gospel at Colonus* is a Gospel musical for European Americans. Yet, a large number of those who purchased tickets were also African American. This audience, however, did not see its "intellectual preconceptions" of Greek tragedy undercut by the production, but rather had its expectations challenged by the presentation of different subject matter for a Gospel musical than Christianity.

Gospel music is rooted in the Christian experience and Christian doctrine, which is one of the things that makes *Gospel at Colonus* a problematic blend of two incompatible belief systems. In *Black Culture and Black Consciousness*, Lawrence Levine notes the change in the figure of Jesus from spirituals, the early music of the black church, and Gospel, in which the congregation sings of "not the warrior Jesus of the spirituals, but a benevolent spirit who promised His children rest and peace and justice in the hereafter."[109] It is this promise of "rest and peace and justice" that Breuer attempts to link to Oedipus, who, like the "I" singing in a Gospel song, has known a life of hardship, misery, difficulty, and burden from which he knows he will be delivered. It is, however, an uneasy fit as the agency of deliverance is different.

Oedipus is fated to be delivered by death and his death will bring a blessing to the place where his body lies. This deliverance is a boon promised him by an oracle. The Pentecostal Christian is saved by Jesus alone. This doctrinal difference causes Greek theatre scholars such as Oliver Taplin to reject Breuer's linkage. Taplin, in his critique of the play in *Greek Fire*, argues that Sophocles's play is set "at the grove of the primeval terrifying Furies, not in the hallelujah-filled church," and that Oedipus does not go to Heaven but becomes a protective spirit.[110] Breuer finds the common point in spiritual deliverance from suffering, his critics object that the deliverance is of a very different nature in each of the worlds Breuer links.

Critics of *Gospel* argue that the philosophies and belief system behind Greek religion are incompatible with the philosophies and belief system of Pentecostal Christianity. Burdine, writing from the perspective of the theatricality of the black church, contends that the black church and Greek theatre are "too diametrically opposed" to allow *Gospel* to generate the meaning and experience for which its authors hope.[111] Robert Brustein, writing as a theatre critic, in his original review of the Broadway production entitled "Transcultural Blends," complains, "I'm not convinced that the story of the blinded, feeble Oedipus ... is entirely compatible with the rituals of Christian evangelism as practiced in the black church."[112] He claims Breuer and Telson are "no so much blending as banging" the two cultures together, ultimately doing a disservice to both. John Simon, writing in *New York*, even accuses Breuer and Telson of being "two white boys" who are "colonizing the gospel," appropriating African American culture and using it to frame European culture in order to enrich themselves.[113] These critics raise three separate issues: the inaccuracy of representing Sophocles's play in the Gospel musical form, the incompatibility of Greek tragedy and Afro-Christianity and the appropriateness of two Euro-American males using African American religion in order to recreate Greek theatre. We shall deal with each of these issues separately.

In response to the criticism that the production does a disservice to Sophocles, Penelope Fitzgerlad, wife of the translator Robert Fitzgerald, writes in the preface to the text of *Gospel* that, "*The Gospel at Colonus* uses the idea of reimagining in a striking and original way. The play is not meant to be Sophocles' *Oedipus*, but a whole new play derived from the original, different from it, and yet true to its original spirit."[114] While Fitzgerald is essentially correct, that Breuer and Telson's play is not Sophocles', but a new work, just as Sophocles' was not the myth but a new work, her response raises as many questions as it does answers. What does it mean to be "true" to the original? Why should one be "true"? Can one even be "true"? Are there other allegiances and representations that should be questioned here, such as the use of the Pentecostal church to represent ancient Greece?

Equally as problematic is Maryann McDonald's analysis of the play. She initially presents an almost "Black Athena" paradigm of the play, noting that, "It is possible that the African tradition from which Gospel music drew is even older than Greek tragedy."[115] If this is the case, McDonald presents an interesting possibility—that Breuer and Telson are blending one ancient form with the modern version of another ancient form in order to create a unique fusion of European and African cultures, blending as equals, equally ancient, equally modern. McDonald, however, does not pursue this line, preferring instead to universalize and erase the difference between African America and Euro-America: "For the most part, black traditional music has become an American product," which is how two Euro-Americans, she argues, are "allowed" to use gospel music in Greek tragedy.[116]

By calling black traditional music "an American product," McDonald focuses on the commodification of black culture while ignoring its origins. Cornell West can speak of "shared cultural space" when people of different ethnic backgrounds appreciate the same hip-hop music, or the work of an athlete, or a particular film, but this shared space does not in any way erase the origin of the form or suddenly transform it into national culture. For McDonald to say is this simply a way of avoiding the issue of "colonizing the gospel," and ignores the larger cultural issues that this piece of theatre engages, as shall be outlined below.

Alicia Kay Koger argues more forcibly and believably for a compatibility between the original and adaptation based on music, rhythm, and structure than on similarities between the church and the story of Oedipus's salvation. Koger claims that music plays "a role in the overall cathartic effect," and that this effect, present in the Greek original through the transformation of Oedipus, is achieved in *Gospel* through "layering."[117] She argues that just as most songs in the musical begin "solo voice accompanied by one musical instrument" and build by adding others until, by song's end, all are blended together into a thunderous whole, the play itself also has a layered structure of cultures: "Greek, Christian, and contemporary African American," which are then layered together, not representative of any single one of them, but rather a blend of all, complete in and of itself only when mixed together.[118] This musical metaphor of layered cultural structure offers a more suitable and interesting way of understanding how *Gospel* works as an Afro-Greek adaptation.

Mimi Gisolfi D'Aponte asserts that, "what takes place during *The Gospel at Colonus* is simultaneously, but in no hierarchical order, black church, participatory theatre, gospel concert, and Sophoclean drama. It is a combination which teaches, preaches, entertains and offers catharsis."[119] Although one can argue that the structures which support the institutions of the Pentecostal church and Greek tragedy are incompatible, those structures are rendered less important if one acknowledges *Gospel* as a postmodern *bricolage* of deliverance drama and pure theatricality. The objections of critics who desire a one-to-one correspondence of Greek tragedy and black Christianity are countered by the argument that the elements that do not match are not what Breuer and Telson are highlighting. No one connected with the project has ever insisted that the theology of Greek tragedy is compatible with the theology of Christianity as practiced in the sanctified church. The name change from *Oedipus at Colonus* to *The Gospel at Colonus* suggests that the project is not merely an adaptation along the lines of a "Black Oedipus," but rather a new entity to be considered on its own terms, rather than whether or not it is truly representative of Greek tragedy or a Pentecostal church service.

There is a third cultural presence in the play that also supplements and links the first two. As Marianne McDonald indicates, church services don't have intermissions.[120] They also usually don't have programs by Playbill, drinks for sale in the lobby, and different prices for different areas of seating. The conventions of modern theatre going, particularly those of the modern Broadway musical, are overlaid over the Pentecostal service and Greek tragedy. No audience member at the Lunt-Fontaine theatre, or any other theatre in which the piece has been presented, has believed that they were at an actual church service, although the familiar setting and conventions would cause some audience members to respond as if they were. Likewise, no audience member would believe they were watching historic Greek tragedy, with its mask and outdoor theatre. Instead, the meeting point of these two cultures was the theatre itself, which has a different set of conventions and "rules" than these other two cultural forms.

Koger's and D'Aponte's analyses work best if one accepts that the shared sense of catharsis is what links these two plays, the original and its adaptation. In fact catharsis is the most popular critical response in the face of the issues listed above. Catharsis is arguably the solution to the critical problem of the incompatibility of belief systems. Aesthetic and intellectual distancing is the solution to the critical problem of inaccuracy of representation and even, possibly, to the "problem" of the ethnicity of the creators.

As noted above, Breuer argues that "communal catharsis" is the common ground between black church and Greek tragedy. In an interview with Gerald Rabkin, Breuer stated that he believed "that if you go one step further with cathartic theatre you might find pity and terror turning into joy and ecstasy."[121] As noted above, Koger, D'Aponte and even Kramer acknowledge that it is the music of the production that makes it cathartic.[122] As the famous Gospel singer Mahalia Jackson claims, "Gospel songs are songs of hope. When you sing them you are delivered of your burden."[123] In other words, singing Gospel music is cathartic, at least for the singer. The effect, however, is also transferable to the congregation, in particular since the musical form is both individual and collectively expressed. The congregation joins the singer at certain parts of the song and are thus equally moved into catharsis.[124] If tragedy is defined as a play that achieves catharsis for the audience, then *Gospel* is much more of a real tragedy (in the Aristotelian sense) than any other play considered in this study.

Interestingly, Morgan Freeman himself, in an interview with Glenda Gill, argues that catharsis is the common point between Greek tragedy and the black church. "That hollering and shouting we do must have been to [Breuer] what the Greek chorus was really about," Freeman states. "The Greeks were so emotional. You've just taken two traditions that were compatible and stirred them together."[125] Freeman sees the two traditions as "compatible" based on their performance and on their effect—the celebration by black church or Greek chorus and the catharsis that either brings. Where European critics have seen only the incompatibility of theology and philosophy, Freeman sees the compatibility of effect and performance style.

Thomas M. Disch, in his review of the Broadway production for *The Nation*, wrote that he had seen the play three times, "and each time my heart has swelled, my throat has lumped, and I've cried a stead flow of wedding-march tears, feeling foolish and elevated and swept away."[126] If that is not catharsis, what is?

The second method by which *Gospel* becomes an effective transculturation of Greek theatre is through distancing. As noted above, the intent behind *Gospel* was to challenge two potential audiences. Those familiar with Greek tragedy would have their preconceptions undercut by a "direct emotional experience," whereas those familiar with the form of Gospel musical would be distanced by the different subject matter, the "Book of Oedipus" instead of the Bible. For the former group, the cultural elite of the Northeast, "what began as an intellectual appreciation ended as an emotional experience," in other words, catharsis.[127] Yet this very catharsis, this different experience of Greek tragedy, distances it, taking the familiar for this audience (the postmodern production of Greek tragedy) and radically transforming it. (Although, in fairness, as Coppenger argues, this approach is arguably class-specific and, what is more ethnic-specific.) However, the accusation of appropriation of African American culture is somewhat offset by those involved in the production, as will be argued below. For the latter, the conventions of church ritual are subsumed into the conventions of the Broadway musical and the subject matter of Christianity is exchanged for that of ancient Greece, also thereby presenting the familiar and unfamiliar simultaneously. It is the theatricality of the church that is used to rehistoricize the theatricality of Sophocles' text.[128]

The African American church has its roots in Africa and in the slave experience in the New World. The figure of the preacher, "an icon among Afro-Americans and since," comes from West African priests, who were "spiritual leader, counselor, and politician" in the slave communities according to Walter C. Daniel.[129] This communal role originated in Africa and continued in the New World, altering only slightly in the face of forced conversion to Christianity. The black preacher is a figure of religious, civic, and social power and importance who must be "a shrewd administrator and an engaging politician."[130] During the era of slavery, the preacher was not only a religious leader but a community leader and teacher. Even in the present day, many leaders in the African American community are also preachers or clergymen, such as the Reverend Jesse Jackson, Reverend Al Sharpton, and, of course, Dr. Martin Luther King.

In the early black church there was an emphasis on the Old Testament. Ulysses Duke Jenkins reports, "The plight of a people taken from their homeland became the text of their sermons and they could understand why Jeremiah asked, 'Is there no balm in Gilead?'"[131] The focus of the amalgam of West African religious social structure and New World Christianity was the ideas of captivity and deliverance, presented in a highly performative style. Michael Weaver explains the two "modes" of preaching in the black church as "teaching" ("the dispassionate imparting of information") and "preaching" (the "physically enlivened and vocally arousing" performance of experience).[132] Jon Michael Spenser, in his analysis of Gospel music, notes that the preaching of sermons is not simply the intoning of lines, but rather that there is musicality in black preaching. The preacher often delivers a "chanted sermon," accompanied by the organ, during which the congregation is expected to make responses via noises, phrases, clapping, etc., and which can rely upon such performance elements as melody, rhythm, repetition, call-and-response, polyphony, and improvisation.[133] The preacher thus serves as a lead performer of sorts in a service that can combine individual and communal singing, narration through "testifying" and readings from the Bible, and interactive dialogue through call-and-response centered around a performance of teaching and preaching by the central authority figure. It is this highly theatrical religious service that Breuer and Telson used to develop their own Greco-religious service/performance.

The play "begins" with an organist playing while the members of the chorus, a Gospel choir dressed in robes suggesting African, Greek, and "church Sunday" garb, enter and prepare for the service.[134] Eileen Southern, in her seminal history of African American music, indicates that two types of Gospel groups developed in the 1920s. The first is an "all male 'Gospel quartet'," called such even if it has five or three members instead of four. These singers will be dressed in business suits and most likely sing acapella or accompanied by a single instrument. The second group is a "Gospel chorus" or Gospel choir, a mostly female (but with some males) group in choir robes who clap in unison in order to accentuate the rhythmic patterns of their songs, often accompanied by an organ or a band.[135] Both of these groups are present in the play. The choir whose entrance by ones and twos opens the show is the "Gospel Chorus." The character of "Singer Oedipus" is played by a blind singer and a Gospel quartet (Clarence Fountain and the Five Blind Boys of Alabama were the "Gospel quartet" of the original production). There is also a Gospel quartet (actually a quintet) that takes the role of the Chorogos.

The band and other members of the congregation enter and sit in their designated places. All of the characters in the Sophoclean drama are presented by members of the congregation: a Deacon (who will "play" Creon), an Evangelist (who will "play" Antigone), and the Pastor (who will "play" Theseus). Finally, the Preacher enters and begins the "service" with a sermon that mixes Biblical reference, Greek tragic prologue, and Pentecostal preaching:

> Think no longer that you are in command here,
> But rather think how, when you were,
> You served your own destruction.
> Welcome, brothers and sisters.
> I take as my sermon this evening the Book of Oedipus.
> (*He begins to preach*)
> Oedipus! Damned in his birth, in his marriage damned!
> Damned in the blood he shed with his own hand.[136]

He then gives the background of the Oedipus story, telling in graphic detail the ending of *Oedipus Rex*. Thus, Breuer and Telson frame the story of Oedipus as a pseudo-Biblical narrative to be preached as an example to sinners in a Pentecostal congregation.

Marianne McDonald argues, correctly so, that this formulation of Oedipus as a sinner is even more problematic than the deliverance of Oedipus as a Christ-narrative. Oedipus is not an "everyman" figure, she argues, nor is he a sinner in the Christian sense.[137] In his analysis of the Greek

original, Ivan M. Linforth proves that there is no Christian sense of sin by
omission or even unintentional sin by commission: "no liability is incurred
by unintentional wrong-doing."[138] We might also note that there is no sense
of sin in the traditional Christian sense in Greek religion. There are moral
wrongs, but not in the sense of disobeying God. Oedipus is not punished
for his sins—he is fated to kill his father and marry his mother, fated to
blind himself and wander, fated to be transfigured at death and become a
protective spirit. No covenant with any deity is involved, no behavior, good
or evil, on his part will change this fate. Here is the theological point that
Breuer and Telson cannot overcome, except, as they do, by ignoring it.

"The Book of Oedipus" is actually the Fitzgerald translation of *Oedipus at Colonus*, which the Preacher, theatrically and metatheatrically, reads
from, comments on, and cites by actual line number, instead of chapter
and verse, as he would from the Bible:

> We direct you to lines 275 through 279,
> Wherein he cries out to his daughters:
> "I could say much to you, if you could understand me.
> But as it is, I have only this prayer for you:
> Live where you can. Be happy as you can—
> Happier, please God, than God has made your father."[139]

The quotation actually refers to lines 275 through 279 of the Fitzgerald
translation, spoken verbatim. Thus, the Fitzgerald translation of the Sophoclean play is raised to the level of the Bible, as quoted in a sermon. The
unfamiliarity of the text and of the use of lines rather than chapter and
verse, however, make the familiar style of preaching to an audience used
to traditional Gospel musicals or Pentecostal services unfamiliar. Likewise,
to an audience familiar with Oedipus but unfamiliar with Pentecostal
preaching, the experience is likewise distancing.

The choir then sings the Gospel invocation "Live Where You Can,"
in which the lines of the play are put to Gospel music, further distancing
the audience. The song is followed by the "Recapitulation from *Oedipus
the King*" in which the Evangelist appoints the blind singer as Singer Oedipus as she herself takes on the role of Antigone and they relate the experiences of Oedipus's life. In the form of a call-and-response dialogue they
arrive at the land where Oedipus knows he is fated to die, and the Gospel
quartet sings "Fair Colonus," taken from the lines of the choral ode appearing much later in the Sophoclean original:

> Fair Colonus, land of running horses
> Where leaves and berries throng
> And wine-dark ivy climbs the bough

The sweet sojourning nightingale
Murmurs all night long.[140]

We should note that Breuer and Telson not only have radically shifted the mise-en-scene, they also edit and adapt the text, even using lines from *Antigone* and *Oedipus Rex* to narrate the tale. This song is immediately followed by the Chorogos Quartet singing "Stop Do Not Go On," thus fulfilling the role provided by the "Stranger" in the original, who tells Oedipus and Antigone, "Do not go on;/First move from where you sit; the place is holy;/It is forbidden to talk upon that ground" (83).

A singer then mounts the pulpit and becomes Ismene, singing "How Shall I See You Through My Tears?," during which she informs Oedipus (and the congregation) about the battle at Thebes between Polynices and Eteocles, the lines of the song again taken directly from the Fitzgerald translation. Singer Oedipus refuses to return to Thebes and curses both his sons and those who would "them that would be kings of Thebes before sons of Oedipus."[141] He and Antigone go through "The Rite," in which Oedipus is blessed with "Holy Water," and then pours out a libation, linking both Baptism of the sanctified church and the pouring of libations to the dead and to the gods in Greek tragedy.

This action—the performing of anointing with water and pouring out of libations is another counter to the "incompatible theologies" argument. Both Greek religion and Pentecostal worship are first and foremost performed religions—active worship through performance. One cannot perform theology—one can perform ritual and action.

As the choir gasps at the revelation that Oedipus's daughters are also his sisters, the Preacher begins to tell the narrative again, quoting directly from Fitzgerald and, as the stage direction reads, "*He now speaks in his own voice*," reminding us of the metatheatricality involved in the scene (the Preacher is an actor playing a preacher playing Oedipus who is also reading out loud from the text of *Oedipus at Colonus*) and the theatricality of the black church (in which the preacher speaks for God, and Jesus, or might take on the persona of one of the prophets during his sermon). Again, it is the theatricality (and even the metatheatricality) that holds the piece together far more than theologies or belief systems.

In the song "A Voice Foretold," sung by singer Oedipus, it is revealed that Oedipus's body will bring blessings upon the land where he shall be buried. His sons in Thebes want his body, but Oedipus wants to die in the grove of the Eumenides outside Athens at Colonus. The choir responds with the rousing song "No Never," in which Oedipus is assured that, "We will never drive you away from peace in this land, no never!"[142]

An elderly deacon assumes the pulpit and, simultaneously, the role of Creon. "Creon" asks "Oedipus" to return to Thebes, and, when Oedipus refuses, the ushers of the congregation, acting as soldiers in the narrative, seize the singers who have been playing Oedipus's daughters and take them away. The Preacher then reiterates the lesson of the text at this point, simultaneously using the standard preaching elements of repetition and textual citation:

> God help him now. For don't you see
> That in taking his daughters he has effectively
> Taken his eyes and left him helpless
> As if "standing on the wind of death."
> Ode 1, strophe 2, line 6.
> As if "standing in the late wind of death."[143]

Again the play reminds the audience (or reader) that it is using the Fitzgerald translation of the original as a "Gospel text" from which the service is taken. Defamiliarizing the familiar.

The Pastor of the congregation, who assumes the role of Theseus in the performance within the service, then recites an ode from *Antigone*, "Numberless are the world's wonders," which the choir then repeats in song. This moment of reflection closes the first half of the performance. Unlike most church services, this one has an intermission.

The second half begins with the Deacon reminding the audience that he, as "Creon," has taken Antigone and Ismene and that Oedipus now waits for their return and his death. Singer Oedipus sings the lament "Lift Me Up," which foreshadows his end and is suggestive of the Rapture, an event in which those who believe in Jesus will be swept up to meet him in the clouds:

> I wish the wind would lift me up...
> I wish the Lord would hide me
> I wish the Lord would hide me
> In a cloud.[144]

A member of the congregation rises and becomes Polynices, testifying to his sins. He says, "I have been evil ... I didn't support my father ... In his hour of need," during which time the balladeer repeats his sins to the crowd.[145] Polynices then asks Oedipus for forgiveness, which Oedipus refuses. Pastor Theseus then stands with Antigone and Ismene, whom he has rescued from Creon. Cursing his son through song, Singer Oedipus brings about the collapse of Polynices, symbolizing his death at Thebes.

After Evangelist Antigone recites an ode to love from *Antigone* (the third choral ode, "Love, unconquerable"), Preacher Oedipus preaches "with tuned response" the speech from Sophocles' original, which is actually the third choral ode:

> Though he has watched a decent age pass by,
> A man will sometimes still desire the world.
> I swear I see no wisdom in that man.[146]

The entire choral ode is transplanted by Breuer into the final message of the sermon of Preacher Oedipus: this life is a misery to be endured and death waits for all. Royston Coppenger sees the similarity between Greek tragedy and Gospel preaching in these scenes. Both the preacher sermonizing on Moses in the Wilderness and the re-enactment of the story of Oedipus in the theatre of Dionysus are performances that use stories from the past to "teach a lesson for the present day."[147] Whether the death of Polynices or the faith of Daniel in the lion's den, the stories performed are fundamentally pedagogical—they are designed to present models of behavior, positive and negative, for the purpose of teaching the audience how to live their lives. When the teaching is over, the performance ends, and the same hold true in reverse.

Theseus then tells Oedipus, "your hour has come," and Oedipus promises salvation for Athens.[148] Oedipus and Theseus begin a call-and-response dialogue of "The Teachings," that is, the things Oedipus told Theseus before he died. When it is announced that Oedipus has passed away, the Choragos Quartet sings "Eternal Sleep," in which they ask God(s) that Oedipus be allowed to "sleep well."[149]

Oedipus does not go to heaven, however, as Taplin objected to earlier. However, the play does not state that he goes to heaven. This Pentecostal church (which, it should be noted, is not the Pentecostal church but a theatricalized one that uses Greek tragedy for sermons) subscribes to a theology of that incorporates Hades:

> Down, down, down he goes
> He goes among the ghosts
> Down, down, down below...[150]

Oedipus is delivered out of this life of misery and into death. The Hades that awaits him is, arguably the same as the Christian Heaven, inasmuch as it represents a deliverance from this life of misery into eternity. Pastor Theseus reminds Antigone and Ismene, who mourn their father, and the congregation (and therefore the audience), of the lesson of the Book of Oedipus: "Rejoice, sisters. He has left this world."[151]

Following the "Doxology," during which the chorus sings "Life Him Up," a paean to those who have been "set free" of this world and "lifted up," the Preacher gives a final brief sermon on the manner of Oedipus's death, informing all that it was painless and wonderful. He closes the service with:

> Now let the weeping cease,
> Let no one mourn again.
> The love of God will bring you peace.
> There is no end.[152]

The choir then sings the closing hymn, "Let the Weeping Cease," again taken directly from the Fitzgerald translation. Breuer, however, has altered one line in order to fit the concept better. In Fitzgerald's original translation, Theseus intones, "Now let the weeping cease;/Let no one mourn again./These things are in the hands of God."[153] The Greek ending is not that mourning should cease because of the love of God and the peace it brings (which also provided a nice closing rhyme), but rather because mourning will not change fate. Breuer needed to alter this line in order to better fit Pentecostal Christianity, perhaps evidence that the critics who say the two forms are ultimately incompatible have a point.

Breuer and Telson use the structure, terminology, and social roles of a black Pentecostal church to frame and narrate the story of *Oedipus at Colonus*. But in doing so, they not only acknowledge their original source, the Fitzgerald translation of Sophocles's play, the incorporate it into their adaptation metatheatrically. Rather than a straightforward adaptation, they alter the text slightly but present it within a whole new cultural frame. The Fitzgerald translation of the play becomes a theatrical Bible, quoted line and verse by the Preacher in order to teach the congregation about the nature of suffering and redemption and the mysterious ways of God. The forms that the plays draw upon are completely incompatible in terms of their theology, but the play isn't intended as a theology lesson, or even an attempt to blend the two belief systems. Instead it is the theatricality of the black church, of Greek tragedy, and of Broadway theatre-going that unites the disparate elements that make up the play. In doing so, Breuer and Telson have rehistoricized Greek tragedy to include a new religious focus, religion so often being the element missing from many modern adaptations of Greek tragedy. In doing so, they do not do a disservice to religion so much as revitalize the theatre, although the theatre of an elite, admittedly.

Given that the Greek theatre was a theatre of the elite, Telson and Breuer have recreated that aspect as well. However, they also drew upon an African American audience, primarily because of the strength of the material and the abilities of the performers.

Morgan Freeman played Preacher Oedipus. Reverend Earl F. Miller, a black Pentecostal minister, played Pastor Theseus. In his introduction to the text, he notes that he sees no difference between the play and his actual services: "What I do every Sunday is drama, but I am performing for the Lord."[154] The musicians were not actors playing Gospel singers, they were actual Gospel singers.

That the performers were performing from experience and from their own culture adds an element of authenticity to the production. Yet one might also ask how The Gospel at Colonus, written and produced by two white men, to be performed by an all-black company for audiences of all ethnicities is different than, for example, the South African show Ipi Tombi? or other African shows created and developed by whites to showcase indigenous African culture? In other words, on some level is The Gospel at Colonus exploitive? If it is or if it is not, can it be considered African American theatre?

It is interesting that most critics choose to focus on the incompatibility of the belief systems of Afro-Christianity and ancient Greece, rather than the ethnicity of the creators. Eileen Southern calls the play "a glorious summary of the black Gospel sound" despite being "conceived and produced by whites."[155] Other than John Simon's critique, hers is one of the few writings that even makes an issue of it in passing.

Simon's critique itself, white calling attention to the ethnicity of Gospel's creators verges on the racist:

> To chop up this text, coarsen its language, drop in bits from the other Theban plays ... and give it all al faux-naïf, gospel-service verneer is vulgarization of the crassest kind.[156]

In other words, Simon's real objection is not that "white boys" have "colonized the gospel," but rather that in doing so they vulgarized classical Western culture by changing the language and giving it an African American setting.

Mimi Kramer, in her review of the play for The New Yorker, observes that Breuer and Telson have not written a play about ancient Athens; "it's about American values, specifically black culture and black music."[157] Amy S. Green finds that that is the strength of the piece and why it is ultimately not exploitive: "The genius of Breuer's transformation was to be found in how the production reflected life in black America."[158] In other words, the play is not meant so much to give insight into Greek tragedy (although it does) as to reflect the spirit and vitality of the Pentecostal church. The larger question which no critic to date has answered is, did the Pentecostal church need two Euro-American theatre artists to reflect it to elite audiences?

There are no simple answers to the questions raised by *The Gospel at Colonus*. It is arguably the most written about play in this study. Some people love it and believe it epitomizes both the best that modern production of Greek tragedy can be as well as the spirit and vitality of the black church in America. Others find it to be exploitive and another example of the mainstream Euro-American cultural world appropriating black culture as a commodity or novelty to momentarily fix a dying theatre.

Slavery and Fate: *The Darker Face of the Earth*

> I will stand to the opinion that the institution of slavery degrades the white man more than the Negro and exerts a most deleterious effect upon our children.
>
> Ella Thomas
> Georgia Abolitionist, 1858

In Rita Dove's *The Darker Face of the Earth* we find a blend of elements from Kennedy and Breuer: an African American playwright adapting a Greek tragedy for a mixed-race cast that engages the history of Africans in America and uses Africanisms in its action and language.

Dove is first and foremost a poet, having won the Pulitzer Prize for poetry for her poetry collection *Thomas and Beulah*, one of seven she has published. She served as the Poet Laureate of the United States from 1993 to 1995 under President Clinton. Also a short-story writer, Dove's writing has been highly awarded, including a National Humanities Medal and a Fulbright Fellowship. She is also a professor of English at the University of Virginia. Dove has written several one-acts, but *Darker Face* is her first full-length play.

Her influences as a playwright include Adrienne Kennedy, Lorraine Hansberry, Ed Bullins, LeRoi Jones, and Derek Walcott, several of whom have also engaged Greek cultural material. She also cites such European and Euro-American influences as Tennessee Williams, Elmer Rice, and Shakespeare.[159] In short, Dove , a novice playwright albeit a very celebrated poet, turned to both the African diaspora and Euro-American culture to shape a play that uses a Greek tragedy to explore slavery and fate.

The Darker Face of the Earth was first written in 1979, according to Dove, but when it was sent to publishers and theatres they declined to publish or present the work, and she set it aside.[160] She rewrote the play in verse in 1989 and it was subsequently published by Storyline Press in 1994, having never had a theatrical production or workshop. In July and October of 1996 the play was workshopped at the Oregon Shakespeare Festival in Ashland, where it began to undergo revision as the needs of the stage began to shape and change the text. Subsequently the play underwent a number of staged readings that continued to shape and develop the text. The Round House staged a reading, as did the Roundabout Theatre in New York, the Crossroads Theatre, and a reading at the 12th Street YMCA, directed by Derek Walcott, himself a playwright with a great deal of experience in adapting Greek tragedy as will be analyzed in chapter five. Ricardo Kahn then directed the play at the Crossroads Theatre Company in New Jersey in October 1997. A month later that production transferred to the Kennedy Center where it ran for a month.

In August of 1999, London's National Theatre produced the play in the Cottesloe Theatre, directed by James Kerr. According to Dove, she was hardly involved in this production and was very unhappy with it.[161] In that same year, however, Oberlin College presented one of a dozen or so college productions of the show. Directed by Oberlin faculty member Caroline Jackson-Smith, Dove thought the production, had it been professional, could have transferred to Broadway. The play continues to enjoy both professional and academic performances, including a joint production in March of 2000 by the Guthrie Theatre and the Penumbra Theatre Company of St. Paul.

The play has undergone some revision, although the basic plot remains the same. Gone from the definitive third edition are the characters of Ned, a conspirator, and Rose, a slave midwife. The lines and characters were also altered to give more power to Amalia. The last name of the plantation owners was also changed from Jennings to LaFarge, for reasons discussed below.

Set in the antebellum South, somewhere in South Carolina, the play has a prologue set in 1820 and then two acts set twenty years later. In the Prologue, slaves named Phebe, Psyche, Alexander, and Scylla whisper about a "hard birthin'" occurring in the plantation house. Also waiting is Hector, a slave who seems to be very interested in the birth in the house. He waits apart from the other slaves. The scene immediately shifts to the bedroom of the mistress of the plantation, Amalia Jennings LaFarge. She gives birth to a son. Scylla, who is a "conjure woman," has a pain and realizes that the baby has been born and fate has been set into motion: "It's out in the world," she gasps to the other slaves, hinting at something greater than a baby having been born.[162] Hector says, "Eshu Elewa ogo gbogbo!," a chant often repeated during the play, but never translated.[163]

The child is clearly of mixed race parentage, meaning it is not Amalia's husband Louis's son. Based on his behavior on the porch, we are led to believe the child is Hector's. When Louis expresses outrage, she counters that both of them exploit the slaves for sexual pleasure. She tells him that she knows that he goes after "little slave girls" at night, and "God knows what you do to them/in the name of ownership."[164] This context is significantly different than the original story. The Laius-figure is not killed by his son before the beginning of the play, the child has not been prophesied about, and both the Laius and Jocasta figures are presented as being sexually promiscuous with their salves. In other words, Amalia is not Jocasta. Louis is not Laius. Hector is not Laius. In one sense, the Oedipus figure has two fathers in this play: a biological (and cultural) father in Hector and a father figure in Louis, the white plantation owner. Dove's Oedipus has two fathers to kill. Dove does not construct an exact parallel, but rather borrows the dramaturgy and places in the narrative different characters in a new social and cultural context.

In the original version, Amalia suggests selling the child instead of killing it. In the new version she wants to keep the child, and the doctor who has been summoned for the birth is the one who suggests selling it. As Amalia weeps when the baby is taken from her, Louis slips his spurs, a Christmas present from his wife, in the basket holding the child without the knowledge of his wife or the doctor. He hopes that the spurs will cut the child, causing it to bleed to death. The doctor leaves, taking the baby in a basket to bring to another plantation to be raised as a slave. The LaFarge plantation slaves are told the child died. The prologue ends.

The names of the slaves are meant to evoke Greek myth (Pysche, Scylla, Hector), Roman myth (Diana), and Greek history (Alexander). Yet they are also historically accurate. Dove reports that during her research for the play she found all of the names listed in plantation records. "There were plantations where all the slaves were Greek or Roman," she states, indicating the names given to the slaves.[165] As argued in chapter two, the use of classical names by plantation owners was, in part, an attempt to frame American slavery on the model of classical slavery, promoting the enslavement of Africans on the grounds that the Greeks and Romans, who were model civilizations, had slaves.

The prologue shapes a backstory based upon but significantly different from the Sophoclean original. Rather than a prophesied fate of killing his father and marrying his mother bringing about the abandonment of a legitimate child by his parents, who also cripple him, the birth of an illegitimate child of mixed race descent brings about his sale into slavery and the use of spurs to scar him for life. The fear of breaking the taboos of incest and patricide drive both his parents and Oedipus to action. The fear of the taboo of miscegenation and the social stigma it brings drive LaFarge to action, just as his own assumptions about his mixed-race origins will drive Dove's Oedipal figure to another course of action that will bring about the tragedy.

Historically speaking, the selling of the child into slavery is illegal. As children inherit the legal and racial status of the mother, the child, even though of mixed-race parentage, was legally free-born and could have and should have been raised as a free citizen. Thus, the actions of the Doctor and LaFarge, already morally wrong in the eyes of a contemporary audience, are also illegal and against custom. One might argue that it is this action that is the *hamartia*, or tragic mistake, that brings about the tragic change of fortune for the hero.

The original thirteen scenes are now reorganized into two acts. The first act begins twenty years after the prologue. Amalia now runs the plantation and is seen by the slaves as a cruel woman verging on evil. Psyche has a daughter, Diana, now, but otherwise the population of the plantation remains unchanged. Hector now lives out in the swamp and catches snakes. Scylla describes him as "Hector, son of Africa—/ stolen from his father's hut/sold on the auction block!"[166] Hector, despite his slave name, is African. In fact, he is the first generation of African Americans—Africans brought to America. He is both the link to Africa, and, as father of Amalia's child, one of two father figures that the Oedipus figure must kill.

Amalia has made arrangements to purchase Augustus Newcastle, a slave known for his rebellious behavior and "the most talked about nigger along the Southern seaboard."[167] He has committed "twenty-two acts of aggression and rebellion."[168] More problematic for the plantation: he can read and write. His previous master taught him, although doing so was illegal according to American law at the time. Augustus is an Oedipus figure, but he is not Oedipus. He is a riddle-solver, known for his intelligence and rebelliousness and arrogance, but he does not arrive in the community as one who conquered the Sphinx. He does not marry the queen and become ruler of the city. He is a leader, yes, a leader in the slave rebellions, but he is not the same as Oedipus. Dove, however, creates the same qualities as Oedipus in a culturally appropriate manner.

Jones, the overseer, introduces Augustus to the other slaves in scene three of act one. Set on a Sunday, when the slaves do not work, they are free to converse in the fields. Augustus is left in chains while the others question him, in particular about his name. Scipio asks, "What kind of name is that?" when Augustus is first introduced. Augustus responds, "The name of a king," suggesting that he is, in another sense, like Oedipus the ruler of the city as he sees himself as a king.[169] When introduced to Phebe and Diana, he remarks, "The sun and the moon all in one morning," explaining to the slaves that Phebe refers to Phoebus Apollo, the sun, and Diana is the goddess of the moon.[170] Thus Dove demonstrates the cleverness of Augustus, much as Oedipus was known for his cleverness. He is also a learned man, capable of classical reference, generating another level of meaning and another link between African America and ancient Greece.[171]

In the fourth scene of act one Scylla prophesies danger for Phebe, who then meets Augustus, kept in chains, while leaving Scylla's cabin. Augustus reveals his own origins and shows contempt for Scylla's abilities and religious beliefs. He is ignorant of his African link—he is not interested in African culture. In some ways Augustus is a symbol of those who stand for revolution and the quest for freedom without the cultural link to the Motherland. Though he despises the whites, he himself is more Eurocentric than the other slaves who maintain their ties to Africa. He can recite Greek poetry, but remains unconnected on a personal level to Africa. Augustus's *hamartia* is the rejection of things African while fighting for his freedom against Euro-Americans. He rejects slavery but remains firmly ensconced in colonial culture and, like the original Oedipus, remains unaware of his own origins.

Hector sees Augustus leave the plantation to meet with the slave conspirators who are planning an uprising that that of Nat Turner. Of particular importance is the password exchange that the conspirators use to identify themselves:

> May fate be with you.
> And with us all.[172]

This exchange introduces the idea that a slave revolution is fated and that the conspirators perceive fate as being on their side: they are fated to revolt and fated to win. Dove introduces the larger theme of fate in this exchange, how different characters perceive fate, and mostly how the slave system in the American South actually served as a form of fate: one's destiny was determined at birth by ethnicity and social place, not by anything one did. This theme of Dove's will be explored in greater depth below.

In the subsequent scene, the slaves pick in the cotton fields as Jones the overseer watches. Augustus has an extended monologue in which he tells the other slaves about the Haitian slave revolution, which excites them.

The threads of fate, the ties that bind, and the chains of slavery are visualized in a scene from *The Darker Face of the Earth* at the Oregon Shakespeare Festival. Photograph © T. Charles Erickson.

In the previous scene, Augustus had been commanded by the conspirators to "sow discontent" among the slaves and inspire them to join the revolution when it comes.[173]

Amalia overhears the speech and invites Augustus to the house after nightfall, in opposition to the original version in which he comes to the house in response to a summons from her when she is curious about him. Instead, Dove has brought about a confrontation between rebellious slave speaking of slave revolutions and the plantation owner who has been known to take lovers from the slaves.

At the house that night she questions him about his learning. He states that in addition to Milton and the Bible he read "Tales of the Greeks."[174] She hands him the book she was reading and when he declines to perform for her she snidely remarks that he would "do better with the Greek original," a line that can only be read ironically in this context. He responds, however, that "the Greeks were a bit too predictable."[175] The two characters flirt and jockey for power in this exchange, but Dove is also commenting on her own actions here. A self-aware, metatheatrical exchange acknowledges the shifts that have occurred in the Greek narrative that she is adapting and that the audience might be more comfortable with the original tragedy, as they knew what was going to happen, whereas an adaptation often creates meaning by veering from faithfulness to the original, the meaning lying in the unpredictable differences between original and adaptation.

Amalia shares the plantation history with Augustus. Louis' parents, it is learned, were among the French plantation owners displaced by the Haitian revolution. The plantation belonged to Amalia's father and when he died, she and Louis took it over, although Amalia is the one who runs the plantation. Louis avoids her and stays to his own chambers. Both are wary of slave revolts for their own reasons. Amalia, it would seem has two reasons to seduce Augustus. The first being to continue to attain revenge on her husband for unfaithfulness, punishing him for being "the Big White Hunter with his scrawny whip."[176] She also seeks to control Augustus and keep him in his place. Amalia uses her sexuality to control the men in her life who may seek power over her. She is a strong, independent woman.

She tells Augustus the story of the Amistad, the revolt on the Spanish slave ship, which had occurred in 1839, with the trial of the slaves ending over a year later. Intended seemingly as a warning to Augustus about slave revolutions, she inaccurately reports the result of the incident: "They managed/to land on our coast and deliver/Cinque and his followers to execution."[177] While it may be that Dove is in error here, it seems more likely that the mistake (if indeed it is a mistake) is the character's. Even Augustus does not believe her, noting, "A bit of a storybook ending, isn't it?.... It's just so perfect a lesson."[178] One possible explanation is that the play takes place in 1840, after the capture of the Amistad in July of 1839, but before the end of the trial in March of 1841, in which case Amalia is making assumptions about the outcome of the trial.

In response to this lesson, Augustus counters with the story of Isaac, a black preacher who would not stop preaching even after repressive measures were put into place after Nat Turner's uprising in 1831. Isaac was flogged repeatedly and his family was sold off. Isaac himself was then sold, but dropped dead off the auction block. "They couldn't break his spirit," Augustus tells Amalia, "so they broke his heart."[179] As Amalia warned him about the dangers of revolution, he warns that some will not stop until they die. He also, however, evokes the tragedy and human suffering of slavery. He forces Amalia to see the slave not as an enemy who must be put down, but a human being who can feel loss and pain. Amalia, familiar with human loss herself, changes the topic of conversation, asking if Augustus had ever been happy.

He tells her that he has not been happy, and the reason is the circumstances of his birth. His response reveals that Augustus, like Oedipus, is unfamiliar with his true origins:

> One soft spring night
> when the pear blossoms
> cast their pale faces
> on the darker face of the earth
> Massa stood up from the porch swing
> and said to himself, "I think
> I'll make me another bright-eyed pickaninny."
> Then he stretched and headed for
> my mother's cabin.[180]

Augustus, the child of parents of different races, believes that his father was the white one, sexually using and abusing his black mother to make another slave. The likelihood was that the white parent of a child of mixed race descent was the father at the time. Besides, had his mother been white, then Augustus, by law, would have grown up a freeman. Augustus sees in his origins all that is wrong with the place of Africans in America. He hates the man he believes is his birth father and has been seeking him whenever and wherever possible in order to revenge himself and his mother on him.

This passage is also from whence the title comes. The title refers to the visual image of pear blossoms falling to the earth. The personification of the blossoms evokes the idea that at this point in history it is always the white that instigates a cross-race relationship ("cast their pale faces/on the darker face of the earth"). The title also links the African American characters with the land and the soil, in a manner that the Euro-American characters are not.

The scene ends suggesting that Amalia and Augustus are about to kiss, and perhaps even more. The suggestion of the sexual tension between them leading to a full sexual relationship is made as a slave sorrow-song swells, and the curtain falls on the end of the act.

The second act begins with a dream sequence in which Augustus tellingly sings, "Sometimes I Feel Like a Motherless Child." We sense his loss and his desire to connect to his mother, whom he believes was a slave, and his desire to kill his father, whom he assumes was a white slave owner. After the dream is over, Phebe and Augustus talk and we learn that Psyche died of a fever after Louis punished her severely.

Augustus then meets with Scylla and tells her that her voodoo keeps the slaves in place. They will not revolt, he argues, if they are afraid of curses and if they are promised that suffering in this life leads to happiness in the afterlife. He again displays an ignorance of things African. He has no appreciation for cultural survival. He would gladly sacrifice all African cultural elements in the New World for freedom from slavery. In this scene Dove furthers the concept that Augustus has no idea who he really is or from where he came.

In the following scene, Hector hunts snakes in the swamp where the conspirators meet. Henry, a fellow conspirator, and Augustus meet and plan further. Hector overhears and tells Augustus to stop. Hector grows afraid that Augustus is "planning a great evil" that might hurt Amalia, whom he still loves on some level. Augustus, fearing discovery, chokes him to death and hides the body, unaware that he has now killed his own father. Like Oedipus, the murder was performed with no knowledge of his relationship to the victim.

Jones informs Amalia that Hector has disappeared and that a cold spell is threatening the cotton crop. After Jones leaves, Augustus enters. They talk about their relationship. He calls himself "a nigger," and she argues he is not, to which he reminds her that she best not forget that he is a slave and their relationship will never be anything else.[181] She states:

> Don't you think I see the suffering?
> Don't you think I know I'm the cause?
> (With sarcasm and self-loathing)
> But a master cannot allow himself
> the privilege of sorrow. A master
> must rule or die.[182]

Dove demonstrates how limited Amalia is by the system as well. She loves Augustus and ironically regards him as an equal in a way that she never has her white husband. She desires to transcend the system, but cannot. The system will not let her, and Augustus constantly reminds her that he can and will never be anything more than a slave to her. This larger theme of the system oppressing whites and limiting their choices as much as blacks will be discussed in more detail below.

She asks him if he has ever killed anyone. He avoids the question, and she then asks about his scars. He avoids that question as well, and they embrace passionately as the scene ends.

The following scene is Hector's funeral. African rituals are carried out as Augustus keeps his distance. Phebe then confesses her love for Augustus, but is afraid he hates too much for him to love anyone. Conversely, the conspirators Benjamin and Henry fear that his romantic relationship with Amalia will compromise their plans for a slave revolution like Haiti's. They arrive with orders to bring Augustus to the revolt's headquarters. Amalia orders Phebe to bring Augustus to her, implying that she knows something is going on.

In a flashback the audience is shown the conspirators order Augustus to kill Amalia and Louis in order to prove that he hasn't betrayed the cause. Augustus enters the house and goes to Louis's study. Louis pulls out a gun, which Augustus throws to one side. Louis cries out that he was a fool not to have killed the slave child in the basket, which stops Augustus. He asks Louis to describe the basket, and when Louis does, he further asks if Louis put spurs in the basket, which Louis confirms.

Augustus reveals that he was the child, has now returned from revenge on Louis, believing him to be his father, and demands to know who his mother is. Louis, Tiresias-like, tells Augustus to ask Amalia about the child, "She knows your mother better than anyone!"[183] The revolt begins outside the house as Augustus kills Louis with the knife.

Here Dove makes a significant departure from the original. Whereas earlier he inadvertently killed Hector, his real father, Augustus now kills Louis, who he believes was really his father. The original Oedipus, however, did not want to kill his father and did everything in his power to avoid killing his father and marrying his mother. As Jean-Pierre Verant argues, Oedipus, ironically, did not have an Oedipus complex—he did not want to kill his father.[184] Augustus clearly does want to kill his father, whom he perceives as the embodiment of all that is wrong with the slave system.

Augustus goes to Amalia's bed chamber and accuses her of attempting to destroy Louis "with his own son."[185] He assumes Amalia knew that he was Louis's son and was using him to destroy her husband. He accuses

Rita Dove's *The Darker Face of the Earth* at the Oregon Shakespeare Festival. Amalia (Elizabeth Norment) and Augustus (Ezra Knight) confront their inequality and fate in this antebellum *Oedipus Rex*. Photograph © T. Charles Erickson.

her of being the one who put the spurs in the basket with him as an infant. He demands to know who among the slaves his real mother is. She says that she will tell him who his mother is and when she does, "You will wish you had never been born."[186]

At this point Phebe enters to see if Augustus has killed their masters yet. Amalia reminds her that Hector went into the swamp when he thought his baby died. At this moment, the reversal and recognition occur as Phebe and Augustus both realize that he is Amalia's and Hector's child. Amalia stabs herself and dies as Augustus goes mad with grief and realization. The slaves enter the room chanting "Freedom." They carry Augustus triumphantly out as Scylla sets fire to the bed room.

This ending is significantly different than the Greek original. In the Greek original, Oedipus begins the play by seeking for the murderer of Laius, learns of the deaths of his adoptive father, learns that he was adopted, and then learns his true identity. Instead, in Dove's play, Augustus searches for freedom and for his (assumed) white father, so that he might have revenge for his and his (assumed) mother's sake. Rather than blinding and exiling himself at the end, however, the mad Augustus is carried out in triumph by the slaves in celebration of the successful revolution. In the face of the change that he brought about, he has learned his true origins and gone mad. His mother was white, his father African. He who hated his European father and mourned his black mother and despised all things African learns his true origins.

If Adrienne Kennedy's *Oedipus* erases difference, and *The Gospel at Colonus* re-religisizes Greek tragedy via African American music and spirituality, then Dove re-historicizes Sophocles's play by framing slavery as a tragedy for both whites and blacks forced to live under it. The system of slavery serves as a form of fate.

Dove explores in detail a number of different conceptions of fate as expressed by the different characters in the play. In her essay "Oedipus in America" in the program for the Kennedy Center production, Dove notes, "There was little chance of altering the course of one's life if one were a slave."[187] She equates fate with the forces of "history."[188] In other words, as in *Oedipus Rex*, fate in antebellum America meant being born into a system in which one's role was predetermined by one's race. No action or activity could alter that fate. The system dictated the fate of African Americans: if one was born black, or one's mother or anyone on one's mother's side was black, then one was a slave for life. What ultimately happened to one was determined by the system, society, and the individual white people who owned the slaves. As Dove wrote in the program, "The white power structure must have seemed all-encompassing for the Africans whose roots

... had been decimated."[189] Elsewhere, interestingly, she compares the white power structure to "the implacable will of Zeus."[190]

Like Oedipus, African Americans had been cut off from their true origins and instead were forced to construct histories and identities based on the new culture and society in which they found themselves, to the point of taking one's master's name as one's own. The white power structure in the pre Civil war South was fate itself. There was no individual reason for this fate: Oedipus did nothing to bring his fate upon himself, nor did any of the people born of color bring the fate of slavery upon themselves. Whites had set up a society in which blacks were slaves, those who were born black, like Oedipus, were given an undeserved fate that nevertheless had to be lived out.

Interestingly, Dove takes this idea and expands it through the characters of Amalia and Louis. Jocasta and Laius are as much the victims of fate as their son. Just as Oedipus was born to kill his father and marry his mother, Jocasta was born to marry her son and Laius was born to be killed by his son. In much the same way, Dove demonstrates how the whites were just as system-bound as the blacks, albeit in a better position. William Liston observes in his review of the Oregon production that there is a strong theme of "the bondage of white masters to the system."[191] The whites needed the slaves economically. Without the system of slavery the South's economy would have fallen apart. The white power structure could only be held in place by the slave system. White masters who wanted to free their slaves, such as Augustus's first master, could not do so because the economic, social, and political systems that the whites had put into place were dependant on slavery for their survival.

Amalia was forcibly sent to finishing school, although she was not suited to the life of a "Southern Belle." Her father taught her to run a plantation, but still expected her to behave like a daughter—darn his socks, cook his food, mend his clothes, etc. Louis is not suited to be a "massa," retiring to his chambers to read and study the stars after he learns of his wife's infidelity. Both, however, were required to play the roles that they had been born to, despite being unsuited for them and made unhappy by them.

The legal system, which dictated that people of color were property and dictated every aspect of their lives also therefore controlled the lives of those who owned and used them. The Code Noir, for example, issued by the king of France for the territory of Louisiana in 1724 contains as many rules for whites as it does for blacks. "We forbid our white subjects of either sex," section six begins, "to contract marriage with blacks under pain of punishment and arbitrary fine.... We also forbid our white subjects ... to live in concubinage with slaves."[192] Likewise, masters can be punished and fined for the behavior of their slaves, or for mistreating their slaves. Slaves "who are not fed, clothed and kept up by their masters" can be taken from them by the local authorities, for example. While no one would argue that the whites under the system were anywhere near as unfortunate or as dehumanized or even suffered at all in comparison with the slaves, the point is made that whites were just as bound to the system as blacks. That they had a much better deal goes without saying.

In Dove's play Amalia is forced to give up a child she loves and wants to keep because he is half-black. Her relationships with Hector and Augustus are illicit and punishable, even though they are open secrets. Louis is equally trapped by his role. Whites were not as limited as blacks, as whites had created the system. Individual white people, however, could become caught in the system, i.e. in their fated places in a social order not of their choosing.

What Dove has done is use the idea of fate as explored in Sophocles' *Oedipus Rex* in order to explore the American psyche and the ways in which the institution of slavery worked as a form of fate on all who lived under it, black and white. Interestingly, just as Jean-Pierre Vernant argues that Greek tragedy is an ambiguous form, and *Oedipus Rex* in particular explores ambiguity, Dove has created an adaptation that also consciously explores its own ambiguity.[193] As the playwright said in an interview, "There aren't any answers embedded in it. If anything, there are questions embedded in it!"[194] Dove has taken the story of the riddle-solver, the question answerer, and used it to pose questions about and to America in the face of its tragic history.

In an interview with Dove from the Kennedy Center Homepage while *Darker Face* was in performance there, the interviewer observed that Dove had "taken every artistic element that somehow repels mainstream America—classical Greek tragedy, poetry, the incest taboo, and the uncomfortable reminder of slavery and its implications" and put them into a single work which somehow transcended their alleged repellant nature.[195] Without taking issue with the idea that Greek tragedy is "repellant," one might argue that Dove's play is therefore much like original Greek tragedy itself. Both confront society with ugly truths in distanced form. As with Kennedy and Breuer, Dove rehistoricizes a Greek play through adaptation, making it relevant to a modern American audience through elements that both distance and familiarize.

4

Black Medea

Now I'm indeed Medea. My genius
Has grown with all these evils I have done.

Medea
Seneca's *Medea*, 909–910[1]

The Modern Medea

From 1866 through 1867, a "much acclaimed" production of *Medea*, an adaptation of Euripides by French dramatist Ernest Legouvé, starring Italian actress Adelaide Ristori in the title role, toured the post–Civil War United States, beginning and ending in New York City.[2] And, as Steven Weisenburger reports, the young nation not even a century old had already experienced Euripides' most famous tragedy in other translations and adaptations, such as Giovanni Mayr's opera version, Richard Porson's translation, and, in 1848, Harriet Fanning Read's adaptation.[3] Ristori's performance was inspirational to visual artists, and was the subject of numerous drawings and engravings, and even the subject of a series of photographs. It was in this atmosphere of representing the dramatic character through a visual medium that Kentucky painter Thomas Satterwhite Noble was commissioned to paint what is arguably his most famous work: *Margaret Garner, or The Modern Medea*.[4]

Margaret Garner was a twenty-two year old African American slave, mother of four and pregnant with a fifth child, when, in January of 1856, her husband Robert Garner, Margaret and their children fled from Boone County, Kentucky across the frozen Ohio River to Cincinnati. Archibald Gains, her owner, tracked the party to a cabin owned by a freedman where the Garner family and the other slaves with whom they had escaped were

132

planning to follow the Underground Railroad to Canada and freedom. Gains had secured a warrant and the assistance of the U.S. Marshals under the Fugitive Slave Act and surrounded the house. Determined not to allow her children to be slaves, Margaret used a butcher knife to nearly decapitate her two to three-year old daughter Mary and tried to kill the other three children when the slave catchers broke in to capture them. She was hitting her one-year old daughter Priscilla with a shovel when the men entered the room.[5]

The story immediately captured the public's attention on the eve of the Civil War. To abolitionists, the Margaret Garner case demonstrated the horror of slavery: that a mother would rather kill her children than allow them to live as slaves.

Created over ten years after the event it depicts, the painting *Margaret Garner* depicts the moment that the slave catchers break in on Garner. Two bodies lie at her feet, while two live children cling to her skirts as if in fear, although whether fear of her or fear of the slaver catchers is uncertain. She points at the bodies defiantly while the slave catchers react in horror and Gains stares at her with unbridled hate. According to art historian Leslie Furth, "An exchange of theatrical gazes and rhetorical gestures charge the space with tension."[6] In other words, the painting is a highly theatrical, even melodramatic, formulation of the moment of discovery. It is not historically accurate: Garner killed only one child, a girl, but Noble painted two dead boys on the floor at Garner's feet.

Noble himself was raised in a slave-owning family and later served in the Confederate Army. The painting was commissioned by a New York City leather broker named Harlow Roys, and was shown in an 1867 exhibition at the National Academy of Design.[7] The painting was photographed by Mathew Brady and then reproduced as a wood engraving in *Harper's Weekly* 18 May 1867 issue, accompanying the story of Margaret Garner. A smaller version was also painted by Noble and was exhibited in Cincinnati in 1868.[8] It was *Harper's* that named the depiction of the mother over the bodies of her children "The Modern Medea."[9]

It was also in the article that accompanied the engraving in which Garner is more substantially compared to Medea: "Margaret Garner, with a far nobler jealousy than that which actuated the mythical Medea, finding her children were about to be given up to the slavery she had endured, seized a knife and took the lives of two of them."[10] Thus, Noble's painting became more real than the actual history in which only one child was killed. *Harper's* states that two were killed, thus keeping Garner more in line with the Medea myth, as opposed to the historical reality. The anonymous *Harper's* author was writing more than ten years after the event, and actually was

The Modern Medea—A photograph by Mathew Brady of the lithograph based on the painting *Margaret Garner* by Thomas Satterwhite Noble and reproduced in *Harper's Weekly* in the 18 May 1876 issue. (Courtesy of Denison University Library).

writing a brief article to accompany the Brady photograph. The article also introduces the motive of jealousy, rather than resistance to slavery as the cause of the infanticide.

The very name "The Modern Medea" is highly problematic in its historic context, as Weisenburger argues, as it is:

> ...a title with deeply troubling influences. In Euripides' drama, a Medea already suspected of practicing the "black arts" of witchcraft kills her two children to spite their father, Jason. Jason had cut Medea to the heart by rejecting her for a racially "purer" wife; she countered by cutting off his royal lineage. Noble's title therefore implies that Margaret Garner destroyed Archibald Gains' property—and the child of their illicit union —out of *jealous rage*. "The Modern Medea" thus plays on the themes of miscegenation, sexual bondage, and the black woman as alluring and dangerous other.[11]

Gains was most likely the father of one or more of Garner's children. Mary, the daughter that was killed, was described as "practically white" by sources at the time.[12] Weisenberger interprets this action as Margaret having "destroyed her master's *property* with the same stroke that destroyed his *progeny*," in other words, by killing her child by Gains she struck a blow against the patriarchal system of slavery.[13] By referring to Medea in the title of the lithograph, the editors of *Harper's Weekly* cast Garner in the role of the mad barbarian who would slaughter her own children to be revenged on an unfaithful lover.

Nor was Medea the first Greek figure to whom Margaret Garner compared. In the 8 February 1856 edition of the *New York Tribune*, editor Horace Greeley (of "Go west, young man" fame) compared Margaret Garner to Greek hero Mithridates, who killed his own sister and his wife rather than let them become concubines.[14] The comparison did not stick, though. Mithridates was male, a hero warrior, and not very well known to the general public, all of which stood in the way of readily identifying Garner with him. Medea, however, seemed to strike a chord with the public and seemed to be a more apt comparison. Garner was not a hero defending the honor of loved ones—she was a crazed mother who killed her own children out of vengeance.

Beyond these concerns, however, the painting and lithograph both display, as art historian Leslie Furth observes in her analysis of the painting, a very real ambiguity towards the subject of Garner. The painting certainly shows the horror and despair of the slave's condition, but also shows a "wariness ... about emancipation."[15] She notes that, "...while some aspects of Noble's interpretation heighten the viewer's sympathy for Garner, others, conversely, intensify the sense of horror generated by her act of infanticide."[16]

This analysis parallels Euripides' version of the story in which the audience is inclined towards sympathy for Medea initially, especially as we see her treatment by both Creon and her husband. It is only when we see her plan and then carry out the murder of her own children (including hearing their offstage screams as they are killed) that the audience is repelled by Medea. While we sympathize with Medea, we do not empathize with her. Nor, in the case of Noble's painting, can we empathize with Garner. The painting, Furth argues, "incarnates the myth of the savage African American."[17]

The deranged expression on Garner's face and the forceful pointing to the bodies of her children indicate a woman on the verge of madness, if not one who is already clearly insane. Noble's painting not only reinforces the myth of black savagery, it reinforces what Sander L. Gilman calls the "arcane stereotypical myth" of blackness and madness being synonymous.[18]

According to the 1840 U.S. census, there were 17,000 insane people in the United States, of whom 3,000 were black, a largely disproportionate number, considering the size of the African American population.[19] This fact was used as an argument that blacks were "emotionally unfit" for freedom, and eventually white doctors began to "explain" black insanity in the medical literature of the day.

In 1851, Dr. Samuel Cartwright developed a typology, subsequently published in the *New Orleans Medical and Surgical Journal* that only blacks displayed. "Drapetomania," according to Cartwright, causes slaves to run away.[20] As Gilman concludes, "manifestations of the black's rejection of the institution of slavery were fitted into the medical model of insanity."[21] Thus, if a slave tried to escape, the cause was not the cruel, barbarous life of slavery but rather that the slave was insane. The danger of Noble's painting, then, is that even two years after the end of the Civil War, it still reinforced the idea of escaped slave as insane and savage: Margaret Garner was mad, just as in the mid-nineteenth century sensibilities of the United States Medea was regarded as insane and dangerous.

Interestingly, Weisenburger demonstrates that the murder of a child by her mother in a cultural landscape that included all of the *Medea* variations listed in the opening paragraph of this chapter connected the Margaret Garner story to the myth of Medea, and gave the black and white, Northern and Southern populations of the United States a way of interpreting and understanding the event in terms of Greek tragedy:

> By 1856, therefore, it would have been possible to understand Margaret Garner in terms of three different Medea: a Southern version in which abolitionists goad her to child murder (Mayr), a bourgeois Northern view of her as murdering from an altruistic mother love (Legouvé), and an abolitionist view of her as a wrong woman of color wreaking vengeance on her white husband for his sexual and racial betrayal of her.[22]

In other words, the Medea that one sees Garner as is dependent upon both one's political views vis-à-vis slavery, and which translation, adaptation, or performance of *Medea* one has encountered. The Margaret Garner/"Modern Medea" episode may be the first American use of Greek tragedy to frame the African American experience in the "Black Orpheus" mode, i.e. explaining an historic event in terms of a Greek tragic metaphor. The first "Black Athena" use would not occur until a century later.

The entire episode eventually served as the inspiration for Toni Morrison's Pulitzer Prize-winning novel *Beloved*. Garner is fictionalized as Sethe, who lives in an African American community outside of Cincinatti after the Civil War. Sethe lives with her daughter Denver and her mother-in-law Baby Suggs. Paul D., one of the former slaves from the Sweet Home Plantation where Sethe had been a slave, joins them and becomes Sethe's lover.

The family is joined by a mysterious young woman, Beloved, who, it is eventually revealed, is the spirit of a daughter that Sethe murdered Margaret Garner-like when she and her children attempted to escape slavery. The Archibald Gains figure, a harsh master known as the School Teacher, pursued Sethe's family to Ohio from Kentucky and witnessed her butcher their child. Eventually, the characters must come to terms with what has passed, and the results of their choices. Beloved vanishes, but her death and the reasons for it remain scars in the lives of her family.

In her analysis of Beloved, Drucilla Cornell argues that Morrison's novel presents a very different construction of the Medea story: "It is not her revenge on the Man, but her desire to protect her children from the Vengeance of the Father that leads her to kill her children."[23] In other words, the motive for the killing of children in Beloved is not revenge by the Medea figure (Sethe) on the Jason figure (the School Teacher), but motherly love: "She cannot protect them from slavery. And so she protects them from the white patriarchal order in the only way she can. She takes their lives before they are turned over to him."[24] Morrison rescues the Medea figure from being Medea—she kills out of motherly love. Sethe is not the violent mother who kills her own children to spite their father, she is the mother who loves her children so much she will not let them live in slavery under his tyranny. One might argue that the School Teacher is only part of the Jason figure. In Morrison's Beloved Jason might also be perceived as the institution of slavery.

We must be wary, however. Beloved is not Medea in an new form, although it both invokes and reworks the myth of the child-murdering mother. Beloved is also not an historical narrative—it is a work of fiction. It is not the story of Margaret Garner, though it is based on the events in her life. Beloved is a psychological exploration of the character of Sethe and, perhaps even a mythologizing of this period of American history. Morrison contextualizes African American motherhood in the slave era to remythologize and rehistoricize the tragedy of a mother driven to kill her own children.

Medea is the most popular figure in the Afro-Greek world. Adaptations of Euripides play have exploded in the twentieth century, not just in African American adaptation, but also in a variety of environments and cultural contexts. The advances of feminism and postcolonialism in the theatre and the academy in the latter half of the twentieth century have also rescued Medea from being portrayed as the tragic, violent, insane child-killer, shifting her to an empowered feminist figure.

This chapter begins with a survey of Medea as written by Euripides, as seen by the Greeks, and as understood by scholars today. Next, productions that have cast women of color in the role of Medea are considered.

Four adaptations of the play are then analyzed, two of which are by European-American men and two of which are by African American men. Lastly, the Medea Project: Theatre for Incarcerated Woman, created by Rhodessa Jones and launched with an adaptation of Medea by and for women in prison (the only other use of the character by women of color than Morrison's novel) will be examined.

(Non) Greek Medea

Medea, as related by the Greeks, was not a Greek herself, although Blondell, after Edith Hall, notes that in the original myths she might have been Greek and Euripides may have been the one to make her a barbarian.[25] Euripides may have also been the one who invented the murder of the children by their mother, as in other versions they are killed by the people of Corinth, or even live.[26] Even if Euripides is the one who created these aspects of the legend, it would not matter. His is the version that has come down to us as the definitive one. The story is related or referred to in the writing of Apollodorus, Hesiod, Hyginus, Ovid, Diodorus Siculus, Plutarch, Pindar, Cicero, Apolonius Rhodius, Pausanias, Valerius Flaccus, and Silius Italicus. But it is the tragedy of Euripides that serves as the source of the story for many writers from ancient Greece to the present day.

Medea is not Greek. She is barbaroi (a non–Greek speaker), apolis (without city), agrioi (savage), xenon (stranger), and a woman. In Greek society she is completely disenfranchised.[27] Medea comes from Colchis, on the shore of the Black Sea in modern day Georgia. Herodotus claims that people from Colchis were "black skinned and wooly-haired."[28] This quotation has convinced some Afrocentric classicists that Medea was African, or that Colchians were of African descent.

Bell calls Medea "one of the truly complex women in mythology."[29] She is intelligent, passionate, cunning, and assertive. She comes from very noble stock: her grandfather is Helios, the sun. Her father is Aeetes, king of Colchis and the brother of Perses, Circe, and Pasiphae, three powerful magic-using women in their own right. Her mother, depending on the source, was either Idyia, the daughter of Oceanus, or Hecate, goddess of witches. Regardless of which mother is correct, Medea is the child of supernatural beings and comes from a family with a long history of powerful women who use witchcraft and magic.

According to Apollodorus, Medea is central to the story of Jason, although her story continues after the two of them part ways. Jason, a disenfranchised prince seeking to reclaim his throne from Pelias is sent by Pelias to get the Golden Fleece, the skin of the ram on whose back Phrixus and Helle fled Boeotia. Helle fell off and drowned in the Hellespont (named after her). Phrixus reached Colchis and married one of Aetes's daughters. The ram was sacrificed and its golden fleece was hung in a sacred grove and guarded by a dragon.

Jason ordered a ship built by Argos and gathered fifty-five companions, including Heracles, Castor and Pollux, and Orpheus. They traveled from Greece to Colchis, "the first expedition of Western Greeks against the Eastern barbarians."[30] Aeetes, Medea's father, demanded that Jason must yoke the bulls with bronze feet and which breathe fire (a gift to Aeetes from his relative Hephaestus) and then sow dragon's teeth if he is to take the golden fleece back to Greece. Medea offered to help Jason if he promises to marry her. He promised, and she gave him a magic ointment that protects him from the bulls' fire. Jason plows the field, plants the teeth, and, similar to Cadmus's experience at the founding of Thebes, discovers that fully armed warriors spring up from the teeth. Like Cadmus, Jason throws a stone amongst them, causing them to fight each other to the death, and allowing Jason to complete the task.

According to myth, Aeetes plans to burn the Argo and kill the crew, thus keeping the fleece. Medea, however, drugs the serpent that guards the fleece and steals it, giving it to Jason who then escapes and flees with the crew of the Argo.

The greatest source of information about Medea, and the text that most people are most familiar with, is the play by Euripides. Even Apollodorus used the *Medea* of Euripides for his shaping of the narrative. The play opens with a prologue from the Nurse, lamenting what has come to pass. In Rex Warner's translation for *The Complete Greek Tragedies*, the opening passage is rendered:

> How I wish the Argo never had reached the land
> Of Colchis, skimming through the blue Symplegades,
> Nor ever had fallen in the glades of Pelion
> The smitten fir-tree to furnish oars for the hands
> Of heroes who in Pelias' name attempted
> The Golden Fleece! For then my mistress Medea
> Would not have sailed for the towers of the land of Iolcus,
> Her heart on fire with passionate love for Jason;
> Nor would she have persuaded the daughters of Pelias
> To kill their father, and now be living here
> In Corinth with her husband and children. (1–11)

In addition to giving the setting and backstory, the Nurse's lament also frames the tragedy on a very personal level—she wishes the Greeks had never come to Colchis because then Medea would not be facing the problem she is now: her husband leaving her for another woman while they live in exile. The adaptations of the play will often change key elements of the Nurse's opening speech to frame the tragedy on other levels, as will be seen below.

When the nurse finishes the tutor enters with Medea and Jason's two sons. The tutor shares that Creon has exiled Medea and her two children and Jason accepts this. Jason has agreed to divorce Medea and marry the daughter of Creon, king of Corinth. The children are taken inside the house as a chorus of Corinthian women join the Nurse and encourage Medea to accept her fate.

Medea then makes her famous speech to the chorus, which we might assume was also aimed at the women in the audience. "Women of Corinth, I have come outside to you," she begins, stating that she does not wish to be misunderstood by remaining silent within the house. Instead she unleashes a complaint about the place of women in Greek society:

> We women are the most unfortunate creatures.
> Firstly, with an excess of wealth it is required
> For us to buy a husband and take for our bodies
> A master; for not to take one is even worse.
> And now the question in serious whether we take
> A good one or bad one; for there is no easy escape
> For a woman, nor can she say no to her marriage. (231–237)

She continues, lamenting that husbands are free to take mistresses, if unhappy, but wives may not have lovers. Men fight wars, but women must bear children. Yet she has it worse than the women of Corinth (and Athens): "You have a country. Your family home is here.... But I am deserted, a refugee, thought nothing of/By my husband—something he won in a foreign land" (253, 255-6).

Medea frames the life of a woman, even the daughter and wife of a citizen, in terms of slavery. She outlines the oppressive state of marriage and the unequal status of women within society. Euripides presents a very sympathetic portrait of her at the beginning of the play.

Creon, enters and orders Medea into exile with her sons. He openly admits his fear of her powers. Again, in adaptation the origin of this fear is often transculturated into other things—fear of voodoo, fear of slave revolutions, fear of Africans, etc. She asks Creon for a single day to prepare for exile, which he grants. After he exits, however, she announces to the chorus her intent to use the time to gain revenge on those who wrong her.

Jason arrives to justify himself to Medea, arguing that she got more from him than he ever received in return from her. He blames her for her own misfortunes and exits. After a brief choral interlude Aegeus, king of Athens enters. He has no children, and Medea offers to use her magic to make him fertile again if he will offer her sanctuary. He readily agrees and exits. Medea then decides to kill Jason's bride and her own children at that point—"And when I have ruined the whole of Jason's house,/I shall leave the land and flee from the murder of my/Dear children, and I shall have done a dreadful deed" (794–6).

The chorus, which was accepting of revenge on Creon and Jason, reject the idea of killing her own children. Medea herself will wrestle with the idea several times during the course of the play before accepting and committing to it. Medea summons Jason, who returns and she send for the children to say goodbye. He announces that he has changed his mind and intends to keep the children in Corinth. He will oversee them as they grow up and Medea must go into exile alone. Medea sends the children to Jason's new bride with a robe that she has poisoned, and he departs.

A short while after the children return and are taken into the house by the tutor, a messenger arrives and informs Medea of the death of Creon's daughter when she put on the robe, and Creon, who attempted to help, was also consumed by flame. Medea enters the house and the children's screams are heard as she kills them.

Jason arrives with his men and attempts to break into the house. Medea appears on the roof *ex machina* in a dragon-drawn chariot. She has the bodies of the children which she refuses to give to Jason, instead burying them on the roadside on the way to Athens so that he will have no grave at which to pour libations. The chariot bears her off as Jason curses her.

Medea, as rendered by Euripides, is a powerful and compelling figure. Several scholars agree that the playwright presents her in the manner of a typical male tragic hero, not like the women of tragedy.[31] As Nancy Sorkin Rabinowtiz indicates, Medea is not like any other woman in Greek tragedy: she is not a virgin sacrifice, she is not a willing victim, she pays no price for her revenge, she does not commit suicide, she is not executed, she is not silenced—she is a woman who does what she wants and gets away with it.[32]

Euripides presents Medea the foreigner within the Greek cultural context. Page DuBois notes that Medea "is not whole other culture, but the other within the city."[33] Rabinowtiz agrees, arguing that Euripides does not treat her "as the representative of a full-blown culture of her own"— the setting and point of view of the play are both Greek.[34] For the purposes of adaptation, we must also remember that at play's beginning, Medea and Jason have been living in Corinth for quite some time—years, in fact.

It is this foreignness within the culture, the outsider who has been among the citizens for a while that also makes Medea a strong candidate for transculturation into African American contexts. She left her home and family, far away, and was taken to a land across the sea where she was expected to live by their laws, abide by their customs, and was feared for her different appearance, abilities, and manners.

Scholars identify two main sources of her revenge. The reason why she revenges herself on Jason is first and foremost because he has broken his oath. She kills his bride, father-in-law, and children, not out of spite, but in revenge for his having perjured himself. He made her promises in Colchis that were broken in Corinth, and that her revenge is therefore divinely sanctioned (and also why she gets away with it)—the gods will not abide an oath-breaker.[35]

The other source of her revenge is her sexuality, which Rabinowitz also links to Jason's oath-breaking: "She links male sexuality with linguistic duplicity."[36] Female sexuality becomes the agency by which she achieves revenge. The sexuality of Medea is a strong focus in some of the adaptations, such as Steve Carter's Pecong. Anxiety over miscegenation (the children, after all, are of mixed race descent) forms a further concern in plays by Magnuson and Ferlita, and in a different way in Jones's play.

Emily A. McDermott, who sees both the play and the character of Medea as "an embodiment of disorder, observes that, Jason had the "legal right of the fifth-century Athenian husband to marry and have children by a citizen woman, while keeping a foreign non-citizen woman as a concubine."[37] In other words, Medea did not have to be exiled because of Jason's new bride. It was fear and concern over her powers that forced Creon to exile her and Jason to agree.

Likewise, in the American South, while it may not have been entirely legal for the husband to have an African American concubine, it was certainly common practice to make black women available sexually to white men whenever the white man desired. Lisa Anderson outlines the history of black women as a "sexual outlet" for white men in her book Mammies No More.[38] What is unique in Medea and in its adaptations set in the American South, is that Medea consented to be Jason's wife and, until Cornith, both believed their children to be the result of a legitimate union. It is only in the context of Corinth (or in a Euro-American environment in the adaptations) that their different ethnicities become an issue.

Medea has proven extremely popular in performance, both in translation and adaptation. In the twentieth century Dame Judith Anderson,

Zoe Caldwell, and Diana Rigg, among many others, have played the role in major productions of translations. Pierre Corneille wrote one of the first early modern adaptations in 1635, followed by Gustav Charpentier's 1693 opera which used Corneille's text. Jean Georges Noverre choreographed *Médée et Jason* in 1763, and nearly two centuries later Samuel Barber scored *Cave of the Heart* for Martha Graham's Medea adaptation. Maxwell Anderson's *The Wingless Victory*, Brendan Kennelly's *Medea*, Marina Carr's *In the Bog of Cats*, Tony Harrison's *Medea: A Sex War Opera*, Heiner Müller's *Medeamaterial*, and Güngör Almen's *Kurban*, among hundreds of others, are modern versions of the Greek tragedy. Ninagawa Yukio created a Japanese version in 1983, while in Taipei the Contemporary Legend Theatre created a Beijing Opera version entitled *Lolanna*.

Pier Paolo Pasolini directed a film version, shot in Turkey, starring Maria Callas. Though the opera star played Medea, Pasolini, whose *Notes for an African Oresteia* was examined in chapter one, sees the film as being about the conflict between western and non-western cultures:

> Medea could easily be the story of a third world people and its disastrous encounter with materialist Western civilization, while Jason's inability to understand such a pre-industrial culture marks him as part of the modern world we all inhabit.[39]

His positing of the "modern world" as the one "we" inhabit indicates his position and the assumed position of his audience. He assumes he is speaking to other westerners and not to the third world people he purports to represent. Pasolini also roots the "disastrous encounter" in materialism, ignoring the other causes of colonialism, including racism.

Yet Pasolini is not alone in locating the primary conflict in *Medea* between western colonial power and third world colony. Willy Kyrklund set *Medea fra Mbongo*, performed and published in his native Danish and in French, in Africa. Guy Butler, the South African playwright set the play in early colonial South Africa, with Medea as a Tembu princess, Jason as an English settler and Creon as an Afrikaaner. *Demea*, as it was called, could not be performed when it was written in the late fifties, only seeing production in 1990 after apartheid began to be dismantled.[40] Another *Medea* in South Africa, created and performed by Mark Fleishman and Jenny Reznek in 1994, explored the sexual and racial oppression of their culture as modeled in the play: "Greek and Colchian relations are presented as a metaphor for South Africa's own history of colonizing encounters."[41]

More recently, numerous multi-ethnic transculturations have been performed in the Unites States and Europe, using Euripides' play to critique western racism and sexism. A recent article in *American Theatre* highlighted a large number of productions and adaptations being performed at the beginning of the twenty-first century.[42] Seattle's Northwestern Asian American Theatre, for example, mounted three different adaptations that transculturated the play to three different environments in a single season: *The Hungry Woman*, setting the play in contemporary America, *wAve*, which located with play within Korean culture, and *American Medea* by Silas Jones, which locates the play in colonial America and is analyzed later in this chapter.

In her introduction to *Medea in Performance, 1500–2000*, Fiona Macintosh outlines five modes that the character of Medea is presented as in production: witch, infanticide, abandoned wife, proto-feminist, and outsider.[43] Of these, adaptations that posit a black Medea often focus on the character as an outsider first, then as proto-feminist and abandoned wife second. All, however, look for an African equivalent of her supernatural powers, so while the witch aspect of the character may not be the main focus, it certainly is engaged and explained. Ferlita and Carter offer a Medea with voodoo powers, Silas Jones locates her abilities in Egyptian religion, while Magnuson relies on African magic. Only the Medea Project's version ignores the supernatural aspects of the character.

Marianne McDonald sees Medea as a "revolutionary symbol"—as Antigone is "an inspiring symbol of civil disobedience" in the twentieth century, so, too, is Medea a "freedom fighter."[44] Medea is viewed as an "exploited other" who fights back. McDonald argues that the Euripidean original begins the tradition of Medea as postcolonial appropriation of imperial culture for resistance to that culture: "The play of the oppressor (since *Medea* is from the colonizers' literary tradition) is co-opted as a weapon directed at the oppressor's heart."[45] McDonald correctly sees Euripides' play as the model for all adaptations to follow and arguably a model for the "Black Dionysus" paradigm of Afrocentric adaptation.[46]

What follows is a brief summary of productions of *Medea* that, while not always adaptations per se, rely upon the ethnicity of the actress playing Medea to develop the "Medea as outsider" model of the character. Many of these productions fall squarely in the "Black Orpheus" paradigm, but some move towards "Black Athena" and "Black Dionysus" paradigms.

Black Medeas

One of the first productions to feature a Medea of color was not in the United States. Hans Henny Jahnn, the German artist, adapted *Medea* in 1926, performed in Berlin with a black actress as Medea in a play that presented Jason as a "predatory pedophile" and Medea as a woman from Africa. The play's focus, as summarized by Corti, is on "interracial strife and the sexual abuse of children," demonstrating a critique of European colonialism through the story of "the African protagonist who is ostracized because of her race and gender [who then] vents her rage on offspring whose racial and sexual identity is ambiguous."[47]

Jahnn's production featured black actress Agnes Straub in the role of Medea. The script indicates that Medea is "Negrin"—black.[48] The chorus consists of "Sklaven des Hauses"—the slaves of the house. Jason is white and their children are the product of an interracial marriage. The play has enjoyed a number of revivals, always with actresses of color in the lead role—Käte Wittenberg in 1927 in Hamburg, Traute Fölss in 1964 in Wiesbaden, Rosalinde Renn in 1980 in Bern, Doris Schade in 1981 in Munich, Eva Mattes in 1983, also in Munich, and Lore Brunner in 1988 in Cologne, directed by noted German playwright Manfred Karge. An adaptation was performed in 1989 which now titled the play Medea, Barbarin focusing on the outsider status of Medea and contrasting the attitudes of the characters with the waves of anti-foreigner sentiment then sweeping the cities of Germany in the face of the Berlin Wall falling.[49]

One of the earliest, if not the earliest intended theatre productions of Medea in the United States was written by Countee Cullen and set to star Rose McClendon was abandoned at her sudden and tragic death from pneumonia.

McClendon, born in 1884, was a co-founder of the Negro People's Theatre and co-ran the Negro Theatre, one of five Federal Theatre Project units in New York City in the thirties. Dick Campbell, a close friend of Rose McClendon's reports that in the early thirties McClendon would read aloud from a translation of Euripides's Medea to friends and guests at her house by means of entertainment.[50]

Countee Cullen, born 30 May 1903, received his BA from New York University and his MA from Harvard and taught French and creative writing at Fredrick Douglas Junior High School in New York. He was also a poet and playwright. In 1934 he began to write a new version of Euripides' Medea with seven choruses set to music by noted American composer Virgil Thompson. The play was published in 1935 and was set to star McClendon in a production in 1936 when she died. As a result, the play was not performed until 1957 at Howard University, where Cullen's text was further adapted by Owen Dodsen, setting the play in Africa.[51]

Cullen had not set the play in Africa, keeping it in Greece, set "outside Jason's house in Corinth." Cullen made no attempt to "Africanize"

the play, the characters, the setting, or the message in any way—the prose
language is straightforward American dialect of the 1930s with no indication of ethnicity. Medea refers to Colchis as "my native land," but no connection to any specific ethnic group is made.[52]

The Nurse's lament, likewise, makes no indication of a specific ethnicity:

> Those Greeks! They should never have come to our country. The Argo
> should never have sailed and the pines from which her oars were cut
> should still be standing in the forest of Pelion. They should never have
> heard of the Golden Fleece, the cause of all our troubles.[53]

Cullen removes many of the site-specific Greek references, but the play
remains mainstream, with no indication of any attempt to link the play to
African America. The original production with McClendon was intended
to be an integrated show, with McClendon as Medea and both black and
white actors performing in the show. As a result of McClendon's death,
however, the play was never produced and the meaning that such a production would have generated in depression-era New York was lost.

Nevertheless, critics responded (and still respond) to the text with
Cullen's own ethnicity and the fact that Rose McClendon was to play the
role in mind. The Nation carried a review of Cullen's book entitled "Euripides in Harlem." Philip Blair Rice praises the translation, tinged with a typical pejorative attitude, common to white critics of the day confronted with
black artists. Rice states that most Greek translations are "stilted, archaic"
and "repel" readers and audiences. "Where Oxford dons have so often
failed," he exults, "an American Negro has succeeded."[54] He praises Cullen's
"living and utterable English." Rice prophesies (and hopes for) more African
American translations of Greek tragedy: "If there is to be a popular revival
of Greek drama, it appears that this is more likely to originate in Harlem
than in the universities."[55]

Rice's contrast of "Harlem" with "the universities" not withstanding,
Cullen's play, un–African in content and form, appealed to Americans.
Despite the lack of African American cultural presence in the play, critics
saw the ethnicity of the playwright first and read the play as a "black translation." Even more than half a century later, in 1998, Lillian Corti sees the
play in terms of its place in African American culture. She connects Cullen's
line "Would that your mother's milk had been poison in your mouth and
killed you at her breast" with Cassie's poisoning of her child in Harriet
Beecher Stowe's Uncle Tom's Cabin.[56]

In this volume, I, far from guiltless myself, have included Cullen's version in a study of African American Greek tragedy. Cullen may be victim

of Mercer's contention that artists of color are never allowed to be ordinary, but his play is perceived and received as being an Afrocentric translation of *Medea*, linked to black American culture in spite of the lack of a black cultural presence or African American references in the play. Arguably, his play is one of the first to bring audiences to see Medea as a woman of color. The potential production with McClendon opened the door in America for other actresses of color to play the role.

Beah Richards, who passed away in September of 2000, was well known for playing Medea. Born during the era of Jim Crow and raised under segregation in Mississippi, she became an actress, writer, and teacher. She was nominated for an Academy Award for her work in *Guess Who's Coming to Dinner* and played Baby Suggs in the film adaptation of Toni Morrison's *Beloved*. She played Medea in a production directed by Frank Silvestra at the Theatre of Being in Los Angeles.

Richards sees a strong link between *Medea* and *Beloved*, not simply because of the archetype, but because both concern a mother scorned and the effect of love and what it makes a human being do: "When I played Medea I was so mad at that man [Jason]! I thought he was terrible and from that you could learn to hate all men, and yes, you could kill the boys."[57] But ultimately it is not the child killing that shapes Medea, according to Richards. Both Medea and Sethe in *Beloved* are women who are "trying to reconstruct her life ... reconstruct her soul, reconstruct her self, regenerate, to throw off all of the excess stuff."[58] For Richards, Medea is a character who gave up her self to be with Jason, and, in the face of his rejection, and the loss of family, her own culture, and everything she had both before and after him is forced to build a new self. She completes the process he begins. She cut all ties to her former life to join Jason. She cuts all ties to life with him when he leaves her, including their children. Sethe and Medea are both women who must recreate themselves anew in the face of what has happened to them.

Another well-known African American actress who played the role was Phylicia Rashad, better known as "Clair Huxtable" on *The Cosby Show*. The Alliance Theatre Company presented Euripides' play in May and June of 1998 under the direction of Kenny Leon, the Artistic Director. As in many other productions with a black Medea, Jason was white. Leon states that, "It was important to me that Medea be black and Jason be white" in order to "look differently visually and culturally."[59] Yet though reviewers perceived the ethnic differences, the production was primarily understood as "a battle of the sexes," as one reviewer put it.[60]

Of greater importance than her ethnicity was Rashad's television persona, which shaped audience reception of the play. Leon relied upon this

viewer recognition to generate meaning in the play: "If everybody's mom—
which is how Phylicia is known from television—can kill her kids, what does
that say about our society?"[61] Leon's point is that Rashad is known as a loving mother (although so is Medea—Blondell notes that Euripides portrays
her as an "intensely loving mother."[62]), but his perception if her is rooted
in class-specificity. This production is, in many ways, the opposite of the
Medea Project. Whereas the script for that show is rooted in the urban
lower class, showing the life-threatening and life-changing frustrations that
plague the lives of the disempowered, Rashad's alter-ego is completely disconnected from that reality.

The horror of the Rashad Medea is not that "everybody's mom" kills
her children—but that a well known, upper middle class housewife kills
her children. Clair Huxtable is, after all, the wife of a doctor (played by
Bill Cosby!). She is the mother of five, who keeps a nice house and has
ensured that all her children dress well, are polite, and get the best education money can buy. The Huxtables represent the bourgeois aspirations
of many. That a lower class, disempowered Medea kills her children as
revenge is acceptable and understandable in American culture. That an
upper middle class doctor's wife would do the same is what is terrifying.
The Alliance Theatre Medea relied not on Rashad's ethnicity but on the
television persona which she projects to generate meaning and frame the
horror of Medea's actions.

The idea of a "Black Medea" had become so cliché by the early 1990s
that George C. Wolfe was able to parody it in his satire The Colored Museum.
In the "exhibit" entitled "The Last Mama-on-the-Couch Play," itself a parody of plays such as A Raisin in the Sun, Walter-Lee-Beau-Willie Jones lives
with his Mama, his wife who is named "The Lady in Plaid" (an indication
that she is meant as a parody of the characters in Ntozake Shange's For Colored Girls Who Have Considered Suicide/When the Rainbow is Enuf in which
all of the characters are named after the colors of the rainbow: Lady in
Red, Lady in Blue, etc.), and his sister. Every day he must go out and work
for the Man and be oppressed by the Man and come home and be robbed
of his manhood by his domineering Mama. His sister's name is Medea
Jones. Medea "moves very ceremoniously" and speaks and gestures "as if
she just escaped from a Greek tragedy."[63]

Medea enters after her brother's tirade and speaks in verse in coun-
terpoint to his dialect:

> Mother, wife of brother, I trust
> the approaching darkness finds you
> safe in Hestia's busom.[64]

Her classical posing and verse speaking confuse and annoy her brother who asks her, "Girl, what has gotten into you?" To which Medea replies:

> Julliard, good brother, for I am no
> longer bound by rhythms of race
> or region. Oh, no. My speech, like my
> pain and suffering have become
> classical and therefore universal.[65]

Wolfe satirizes several theatre conventions in this scene and this speech. First, as noted above, the speech is a parody of black Medeas, Medea being the tragic figure most identified with women of color. Second, the scene is a parody of "Black Orpheus" productions that dismiss difference by universalizing—black suffering is the suffering of all. Medea Jones is a self-aware stereotype of sorts who mocks that which she praises. One might even read a possible parody of Adrienne Kennedy in there as well, the reference to classical productions at Julliard could reference her adaptations performed there.[66]

Wolfe's pastiche reminds the audience of the dangers of Greek adaptation into African American environments. It also serves as a reminder of how strongly Medea is identified with the African American experience. Euripides' play is easily the most adapted of all the Greek canon into black environments. What follows is an analysis of five different contemporary adaptations of Medea by American artists from the late sixties through the mid–nineties.

Revolutionary Parallels: Magnuson's African Medea

James Magnuson is the director of the James A. Michner Center for Writers at the University of Texas, Austin, where he has been a professor of creative writing since 1985. He is the author of over a dozen produced plays, seven novels (including Windfall, Without Barbarians, Open Season, and Ghost Dancing), and has written for television. He was a playwright-in-residence at Princeton University for four years. Yet in the late 1960s, having just graduated from the University of Wisconsin, young playwright Jim Magnuson arrived in New York City, had several street-theatre productions of his play No Snakes in this Grass (a one-act about the Garden of Eden with a white Adam and a black Eve) in Harlem, and taught playwriting at the James Weldon Johnson Theatre Arts Center.[67]

Mikal Whitaker, the director of the East River Players who had been involved in a production of Medea while a student at Howard University, suggested Magnuson write an adaptation of Euripides's play. After some consideration Magnuson decided to set the play in Angola, which was still a Portuguese colony undergoing a war of liberation at the time. In 1968 the East River Players presented African Medea with direction by Mikal Whitaker and with Detra Lambert as Medea. The response to the production "was terrific," according to Magnuson, which brought about a second production the following year at Hudson's Guild that was not as strong or as well-received.[68]

In his adaptation, Magnuson changes only some of the names of the characters. Medea is still Medea, and Jason's name remains the same. Creon becomes Barretto. Magnuson adds the character of the beggar, and turns the messenger into a soldier who catches slaves with Jason. The beggar serves as a voice of revolution, as will be described below.

The play is set in "A large African city on the west coast" in "the early part of the nineteenth century."[69] The colonizers are Portuguese and the chorus is a group of "poorly dressed African women."[70] The significance of this specific setting will be discussed below, but making it a Portuguese colony (as opposed to English or French) sets up a specific context of black nationalist movements in both Africa and America in the late 1960s and provides for a specific revolutionary parallel.

The west coast of Africa, it should be noted, is a distance from Medea's original home, which is in the interior, just as Corinth, the setting for Euripides's play is a distance from Colchis. The chorus reports that Medea "comes from far away, from a savage tribe beyond the Congo.... How different from us."[71] Medea is therefore outsider. Yet, she is also "African nobility," born the daughter of a chief of the Bono.[72]

Jason, being Portuguese is also an outsider, but like his Greek antecedent, comes from the ruling class and is therefore a powerful outsider. Jason is further empowered (and made into the villain of the piece) by his position and occupation. He is "a slave trader [and a] dealer in ivory." Despite his relationship with Medea, he is marrying "a golden-haired Portuguese girl, child of the governor," named Cecelia.[73] Celelia, though she is never seen on stage seems from her description to be the opposite of Medea in many ways: European, blonde-haired, etc. It is not enough that she is the child of the governor, she must embody the Aryan ideal, supposed white European superiority in breeding and beauty. Jason leaves Medea for an individual whose physical traits are often offered up as the embodiment of the white ideal.

The play opens with the beggar begging from the chorus, thus creating a difference between this adaptation and the Greek original. The beggar is blind and has only one arm, the other was cut off by the white imperialists for stealing. The beggar serves as a second chorus of sorts, and the voice of the displaced and resentful. No "nervous condition" for him, he speaks openly of rising up against the European colonizers. He cries out in front of Medea and Jason's house: "Your many kindnesses to us—slavery, death, disease—are soon to be repaid, the time is near."[74] Thus, the play begins with a prophesy of revolution, unlike the Greek original, which begins with the Nurse's lament.

The lament in this adaptation follows the beggar's foretelling the fate of the colonizers, as the nurse enters, gives him a coin, and shoos him away. She is an old slave woman who followed Medea out of the interior to serve as nurse to her children. She begins the opening lament, rendered as:

> I wish the long slave ships had never passed down the Congo...
> I wish that these powerful white traders and adventurers had never traveled to the heart of Africa. We would all be happier now.[75]

In several of the adaptations considered in this survey, most notably Father Ferlita's below, the Argo of the original Nurse's monologue becomes the slave ships which came to Africa, not only to take away the Fleece, but in this case, the human cargo of slaves. The Nurse's lament is no longer the personal one of Euripides, the tragedy of Medea, but rather the extended tragedy that resulted for Africans as a result of contact with the Europeans, the tragedy of Africa.

The tutor, who in this version is a more active presence in the play and represents the voice of indigenous African identity, enters with the children. He tells them (and the audience) several African folktales to teach them common sense. He then informs them that they are "African children," and that "they will not be pale Portuguese gentlemen with bows on their shoes," but will grow up to be Africans.[76] These lines might be read in the parallel context of both Africa and America. In Africa, the colonial education system, teaching African students in a European language, from a Eurocentric point of view, the topics of European history, religion, and culture results in a loss of African identity by the students. It is this loss the tutor wishes to avoid. Likewise, in America the school system, only recently desegregated, is entirely centered on Euro-American culture and history, ignoring the contributions of African Americans, depriving African Americans of their culture and identity. The same impulse that began the decolonization of education movement in Africa also began the "Black is Beautiful" movement in America, moving the focus on African achievement, rather than European.

The tutor then informs the nurse that Baretto (Creon) will drive Medea and her children from the city. Medea is then heard screaming and cursing inside the house. The tutor takes the children away as the chorus moves closer. They express sympathy for and solidarity with Medea. "When a black woman grieves," they state, "it hurts us also."[77] Much as in the Greek original, in which Medea's plea to the Athenian women in the audience must have struck a chord of sympathy, Magnuson's choral statement of identification with a suffering woman of color is intended to strike a chord with a contemporary audience. Both Euripides and Magnuson encourage at least part of their audiences to identify with and support the protagonist who shares their situation. Such support is magnified when the nurse brings Medea out of the house: "Don't think that you are alone," the chorus tells her, "We are black women, too."[78]

Medea responds with scorn: "You have had all pride and honor pounded out of you by whips, praying to the crosses your masters have nailed you to."[79] Medea rejects both the slave mentality that physical, spiritual, and emotional oppression creates and the religion that the Europeans have brought. She rejects their support as they do not rebel against oppression as she does.

She swears the chorus to silence as Baretto approaches. As in Euripides's play, he banishes Medea and her children. He is worried because "the fire of revolt" hangs in the air; the city that used to be "a delight, a small proud European city—the finest in Africa" has become a brutal, violent, dangerous, squalid, and miserable place: "slave-trading is more brutal than ever" and the city is falling apart."[80] Governor Baretto dislikes Medea in particular because, as a "black princess" she is a figure that people can rally around and bring strength to a revolt. She protests her innocence, but he will not be swayed. Instead, as a gesture of his merciful nature, as in Euripides, he allows her a day to get her affairs in order: "We Portuguese are not cruel and barbaric with the blacks like the English," he states as he leaves.[81]

His last statement is an inversion designed to critique the English-speaking American audiences. Again, following the parallel revolutionary discourse present in the play, the remark is intended ironically. The audience, living in New York in 1968, knows that all Europeans (and those of European descent) have been cruel and barbaric to people of color, and that others have been worse is a fallacious argument used to justify one's own acts of cruelty. There is a second inversion here, as well. "Barbaric," meaning "uncivilized and savage," equates the English with the Africans, instead of with the Europeans. The Portuguese governor assumes his superiority to not only the Africans, but also to the English. When engaging in an act of cruelty and incivility to a woman he assumes the height of superiority to all. "Barbaric," of course, also comes from the Greek root word meaning "speakers of nonsense," used to designate non–Greeks, who were therefore inferior to speakers of Greek. Magnuson, in a single sentence, engages in a series of meanings that demonstrates the irony of Baretto's attitude, and, in doing so, indicts White America's attitude of benevolent racism and superiority.

In defiance of Baretto, Medea plans her revenge. The beggar who opened the play reenters and tells Medea that Adago, chief of the Mbamba and his warriors have arrived. They are the only indigenous Africans to be allowed to stay at the governor's house for the wedding, so great is both their prestige and the governor's trust in them. The beggar exits as Jason enters. He demands his sons, as he wants them to be educated in Europe, and he wants her to leave as Baretto has demanded. When Medea lists the many ways she has served him, he replies: "You forget what I've done for you ... Because of me you have discovered European culture and refinement, and been appreciated in return."[82] In other words, Jason argues the white man's burden: that it is the role of Europe to civilize and educate the heathen, savage, African, itself a racist, culturalist position.

Magnuson's Jason takes the same position as his Euripidean forebear, who makes very much the same argument:

> You have certainly got from me more than you gave.
> Firstly, instead of living among barbarians,
> You inhabit a Greek land and understand our ways,
> How to live by law instead of the sweet will of force.
> And all the Greeks considered you a clever woman. (535–539)

Medea is fortunate, he argues, having been civilized and educated by the Greeks, which is a far better gift than her having given up her family, her culture, and her identity for him. Greek superiority sees Greek culture as its own reward. To be appreciated by Greeks means one is worthy of merit. Magnuson's Jason takes the same superior, racist view—leaving her culture behind, giving up her identity and living among Europeans is its own reward and Medea should be duly grateful.

The irony, of course, is that in both cases, Greek and Portuguese, it is not in fact "law" but "the sweet will of force" that has allowed them to impose their "superior" culture on those they have conquered or otherwise engaged. While claiming moral superiority in their dealings, they actually rely upon violence and force to impose this "superior" culture. As Fanon argues, colonialism is violence and force on every level—and only violence can enforce colonial power. Fanon also argues, however, that such violence can, will, and should be met with resistive violence in return.[83] One must fight back with violence, which is what will happen to Jason, the Portuguese, and, by extension, mainstream America unless something changes.

Jason repeats his demand to see his sons. Medea refuses him and he departs, threatening to return to take his sons and send them to Europe. Adago then enters. As the Aegeus figure, Adago's request is the same as his Greek counterpart: he is heirless and wants a child. He has come to the city for the wedding, but has come to Medea to make this request especially, as he knows she has power. Medea, as in the original, agrees to help him sire children if he will agree to shelter her with his people.

Adago, who is staying with the governor and who desires to remain on the good side of the imperialists instead offers to send her to a ship that will take her "far from here. Across the sea. A land of hope where you could be safe and free."[84] The irony, of course, is that Adago is promising to send Medea to America. It is not stated categorically in the script, but the possibility exists that the ship to which he would send her is a slave ship, thus allowing him to take advantage of her powers and then ensure that he will not be beholden to her. This possibility is mere supposition, however.

One might also interpret his offer to send her to America, which he identifies as "a land of hope where you could be safe and free," as ironic, considering the cultural context of America in 1968. Dr. Martin Luther King had been assassinated in April. Fred Ahmed Evans and his group of community activist black nationalists were involved in a shootout with the Cleveland police in the summer, for which Evans would receive a death penalty sentence for the murder of all seven dead, both police and activists, even though it was never conclusively proven he was even present at the time of the shootout.[85] This incident was but one in many in the explosive political and racial climate in the United States in which violence both by and against the police would be blamed on politically active African Americans who would be imprisoned, and in some cases executed, for it.

The Civil Rights movement of the fifties and sixties had been met with violence from both white citizens and white law enforcement. Resentment, fear, and anger was the response of many African Americans in the late sixties to what was perceived (accurately) as a racist society intent on not only continuing oppression, but actively working to undermine and destroy those who would empower African Americans. Racial uprisings occurred in many major American cities in the summer of 1968. As Magnuson states, "There was more and more feeling that non-violence might not work and there was a certain revolutionary rhetoric in the air."[86] When Magnuson, in 1968, has Adago tell Medea that America was a land where a woman of color "could be safe and free," the audience would have recognized the irony of the remark.

Medea agrees to go to America and she and Adago exchange promises to do as they have said. He exits and the chorus comes forward as Medea plans to send gifts to Cecelia and the first act closes.

The second act, taking place in the evening, a few hours after the first act, opens with a discussion between Medea and the nurse. Medea plans to send her husband's new bride a gold dress and a golden coronet. She prays to Nyame, the sun god (let us remember that in the original, Medea is the grandchild of Helios, the sun god—Magnuson gives an African equivalent). Jason and the tutor enter together, while simultaneously the nurse and children enter from the other side of the stage.

Jason proposes that the boys be sent to Lisbon or Paris to study. The tutor objects, prompting an exchange that is the first indication of the extended revenge Medea has planned:

> TUTOR: Medea, he must not have the children.
> MEDEA: No one will have the children.[87]

The Tutor's concern, as a representative of the older generation, is that the boys not go to Europe and lose their African identity. Medea's line, however, is a foreshadowing of her revenge.

As in the original, Medea gives her children the gifts to give to their father's new wife. Jason takes the children bearing the gifts and the nurse to the wedding. After they exit, the chorus begs Medea to stop. She refuses and enters the house.

The beggar enters and reports that, "There is fighting throughout the city; black against white, black against black, white against white."[88] For a revolutionary play, this line is particularly striking for its suggestion of disunity among the revolutionaries. The line is not entirely inaccurate, however, as in Angola the various rebel factions fought each other just as often as they fought the imperialist forces, as will be discussed below. In a specific American context, however, the line was also meant to reflect the larger problems that the revolutionary fervor could create. Magnuson himself explains:

> When riots broke out, it always seemed to be the have-nots that ended up losing. Rage, however justified, so seldom seemed to find its target back in '68. Violence keeps turning in on itself.[89]

The statement of "blacks against blacks" in this context, therefore, is meant to suggest that the riots that occurred in the sixties, while aimed at white oppression would occur in black neighborhoods, in which many, if not most of the injured and killed would be African American, and the property that

was destroyed was black-owned. Violence was kept within the black areas
by the police, while the targets of the riot were mostly unaffected by them.
Magnuson, both in his letter and in the play, laments the fact that too
often the violence created in response to colonialism is not directed at the
colonizers but other colonized, even in New York in 1968. This unfortunate consequence has been analyzed by Fanon, who recognizes the need to
redirect such violence towards the oppressors.[90]

Magnuson believes tragedy is "a form that distrusts excess" and "an
inherently conservative form," which is debatable, especially as Greek
tragedy could be both extremely conservative in content and/or context
(witness *The Oresteia*) or extremely progressive and disturbing (witness *Medea*
itself).[91] Given the revolutionary context of 1968, tragedy, even in adaptation, is problematic. Andrew Gurr argues that tragedy, having a "static
world-view," is in opposition to progress and therefore incompatible with
Marxism and the idea of revolution.[92] Biodun Jeyifo, however, believes that
revolutionary tragedy is possible in Africa, because of the experience of
colonialism.[93] By extension, revolutionary African American tragedy may
be possible in the face of the experience of slavery and continued oppression, not merely because of class , but because of race. It is possible to have
radical tragedy, but what is depicted will not always be a positive image of
progression. *African Medea* in one sense depicts a successful revolution, but
in another sense shows the tremendous sacrifice required for revolution:
the children must die. Magnuson reports that a "very political friend" criticized the play for not giving hope, and Magnuson's response: "how can
the tragedy of Medea give us hope?"[94]

The beggar wears a Portuguese hat that he has stolen from a man he
killed in the uprising. He swears he will kill one Euro for every finger on
the hand he lost to them. The tutor enters and questions the beggar. He
learns that the fighting is in the center of the city. The governor's house,
where the wedding is taking place, is on the hill overlooking the city, so
the governor and the members of the wedding don't know of the fighting
yet. The revolution is not merely suggestive of the freedom struggles in
Angola and the other colonies of Portugal. The revolutionary rhetoric and
uprisings are meant to parallel what is occurring in the cities of the United
States in the summer of 1968.

The nurse and children enter, returning from delivering the gifts.
Medea asks what happened and, in a departure from the original (as is the
nurse's accompanying the children), informs Medea that the bride looked
at the gifts and set them aside without putting them on. Medea cries out,
"I've been tricked by the gods."[95] Medea's response is a moment of doubt,
when her powers and prayer seem not to have worked. The line seems to

exist more to create a moment of dramatic tension than to reflect either the Euripidean original or the concerns of the revolutionaries in Africa or America.

The nurse takes the children inside while Medea contemplates her next move. Her resolve that "no one will have" the children is further strengthened by the fact that Jason accepts the children and wants them to be Europeanized—taken to Europe and educated how to behave like the whites. She sees in the children literally the blood of Jason:

> So, my children, you have a city, you have a home, and I have none. You can leave your mother behind. Why? Why? Because Jason's blood runs in your veins. Because of that Portuguese blood, you draw justice. I cannot bear it. I want no whiteness, no tenderness near my heart. I will cut it off like fat from lean meat.[96]

We might note two things going on here—first is a new motive to kill the children, not present in the original. Magnuson's Medea decides to kill her children, at least in part, because they are part white, because they are part Portuguese. She has been so driven to hate the Europeans that she can kill her children since they are part white. This response is in accordance with the "nervous condition" that Fanon argues is present in colonized people and is a "direct product of the colonial situation."[97] Fanon presents a number of case studies in which colonial subjects developed mental disorders, including violent homicidal mania, due to the psychological stresses of having one's identity questioned and destroyed by colonialism. Second is an inversion of the idea of tainted blood due to miscegenation. As will be discussed in the section on Ferlita's work below, most colonial laws state that one drop of black blood is enough to make a person non-white, regardless of actual skin color. Here the idea is reversed—it is their white blood that contaminates the children of Medea and Jason, and makes them less than African in her eyes. As they are half white, she believes killing them is acceptable, much as the European laws dictate that someone who is of mixed race descent (even if only a small percentage of their ancestry is of color) is therefore not white and can be enslaved.

A black soldier, one of Jason's men "who kept the slaves in line," runs in. He throws down his gun and tears off his uniform, which might be read as a visual rejection of his place in the colonialist enterprise now that the revolution has begun. He no longer wears the uniform that is the symbol of the authority vested in him by the Portuguese imperialists. He tells Medea the story of the wedding: that Cecelia put on the gold dress and burst into flames at the wedding. When Baretto attempted to save his daughter, he, too, caught fire and died. The soldier warns Medea to escape and then flees from the uprising. Medea instructs the nurse to bring the children to her.

As the boys enter, drums begin to play. Medea says, "That is the sound of the future. Our people, black people, have a future. The black man will live freely in Africa one day and possess a future all his own."[98] This statement is obviously a reference to the revolutions and independence movements in Africa and America, a celebration of the Black Power movement, a prophesy that the revolutions on both continents will succeed. This statement, contrary to Magnuson's friend's critique, is also the suggestion of hope that in spite of the tragedy of Medea, people of African descent will succeed in freeing themselves of oppression, both within and without the continent.

Medea considers the physical bodies of the children she is planning to slay: "Your eyes are like mine," she tells them, "The lips, the fine lips, they are ... Jason. The nose, mine, the forehead ... Jason. The skin ... do they call you mulatto, the other children?"[99] The children possess various physical characteristics they have inherited from both parents. Medea is able to recognize that the children possess characteristics and quality from both Jason and herself—they are truly the product of the union of two people, with one large exception: their skin color. It is obvious to Medea that her children will never be accepted fully by the Europeans because they are biracial, and therefore will always be seen by the Europeans as black or colored and therefore inferior at best and tainted at worst.

The nurse urges Medea to flee with the children. Instead, as in the original, Medea takes them in the house and kills them. That her last word on the subject was concern that her children might be called "mulatto" gives yet another motive for the murder of the children: to spare them from growing up in a world that will reject them for being biracial. She justifies her revenge by seeing it as a mercy killing for the children as well. This idea, as we have seen and will continue to see, is a fairly common one in adaptations of Medea in which the children are biracial or will grow up slaves: the killing is an act of mother's love.

Jason enters and interrogates the chorus about Medea's whereabouts. The nurse enters and tells a stunned Jason that Medea killed the children, then herself. It is unclear why she does so, other than to possibly buy time for Medea to escape, or protect her from Jason's wrath.

Medea then enters with bloodstained hands. Unlike the original, Magnuson literalizes the metaphor that she has the children's blood on her hands. Jason may be the motive for their death (why they died), but Magnuson visually reminds the audience that Medea is the means for their death (how they died). Jason threatens to kill Medea and demands his sons.

She throws open the house doors, much like in the original Greek production, in which the skene would open to reveal in tableau a previously described scene. Revealed are the bodies of the two boys, pinned to the Golden Fleece. Magnuson thus outdoes Euripides and reminds the audience of what Medea did for Jason, allowing him to plunder the Golden Fleece from Colchis, and what bonded the two of them together: the experience of the Fleece and the children they had. The death of the children is linked, therefore, to the stealing of the Fleece, in a manner that it is not in Euripides.

Medea tells Jason that he "betrayed" her love, and now his land "is stained with [his] children's blood."[100] When Jason demands the bodies of his sons for Christian burial, Medea refuses. Instead, she tells him:

> You go down to the ships, Jason, weep your tears by the sides of the rotting hulks that hold the corpses of the slaves you took, find two small bodies and bury those.[101]

Medea links the bodies of slave children, who are young people of African descent whom Jason has taken, chained, imprisoned, and sold into slavery, and the bodies of his children, who are also of African descent. She attempt to show that there is no difference between his own children and those whom he enslaves. Given the laws of Europe at the time, technically the children are African, and black, not European or white at all. As children inherit the racial classification and legal status from their mothers by most laws of this period, the children of Jason and Medea are African. They are legally non-white and can therefore be enslaved and, unless they become *assimilados*, have no legal rights. Medea, by her words, indicates to Jason that there is no difference between his children and the children he enslaves.

Medea then re-enters the house as Jason collapses on the steps of the house. In an interesting shift, her departure is not supernatural. Magnuson gives the audience (or reader) no dragon-pulled chariot or pillar of flame. The stage direction reads, "MEDEA *comes out of the side door bearing the two boys.*"[102] Presumably she takes them to be buried somewhere and departs from the province of the Europeans. As in the original, it is ultimately Medea that maintains control over herself, her children, their bodies, and the situation. Medea successfully resists colonialism, albeit at the expense of her children's lives.

The chorus then ends the drama, observing that, "The Golden Fleece is black with blood," and that "all we can do now" is to "huddle together against the rising storm and wait, wait for the morning sun."[103] After the riots and the violence, after a woman has been driven to kill her own children, we are uncertain if this revolution has been successful. The chorus, always representing the community, states that all most can and will do is watch and wait and see if any real change has occurred as a result of the tragedy.

By setting the play in a west coast Portuguese colony, Magnuson specifically links two nationalist struggles: the African American nationalist and civil rights movement in America and African nationalist movements in Portuguese colonies, specifically in Guinea-Bissau and Angola.

In the late sixties, the idea of Black Power and the need for revolution was particularly strong in urban America. Race riots had occurred in Harlem in 1964, Watts in 1965, Cleveland and Nashville in 1966, and Newark and Detroit in 1967. At the root of these riots was the fact that poor, urban African Americans suffered from a high rate of unemployment, inadequate housing, a corrupt and racist police force, and limited opportunities in everything from education to employment to social services. Many young African Americans, disenfranchised, disempowered and oppressed by the system turned to revolutionary beliefs and the idea that the revolution was coming.

The assassination of Dr. King and the perceived failure of his principles of non-violence and interracialism led to the emergence of more leftist, more revolutionary groups. For example, the Black Panther Party was founded in 1966 to protect the residents of the African American ghetto of Oakland, California from police brutality. By 1968 major branches existed in numerous American cities such as Chicago, Atlanta, and New York. Politically, the organization was a Marxist revolutionary group committed to taking control of their own lives and fighting the white establishment that continued to oppress people of color. A solidarity was felt with the struggles in Africa of nations and peoples to free themselves of colonialism.[104] Stokely Carmichael, chairman of the Student Nonviolent Coordinating Committee and active proponent of Black Power, openly advocated revolution against the United States in 1968 and was "paying homage to Frantz Fanon as the prophet of decolonization through violence."[105] Carmichael and others saw African Americans as a colonized people, just like those of Africa. In the late 1960s, there was, as Fredrickson notes, "a willingness to identify with Africa," including the adoption of African hairstyles, clothes, holidays, foods, and cultural practices. Out of the "revolution" was bred a "validation of black ethnic solidarity and action.[106]

By the late 1960s, Britain and France (two of the three principal colony-holders in Africa) had seen numerous colonies win independence, either through agreement or armed struggle: Ghana, Egypt, Guinea, Benin, the Congo, Nigeria, the Gambia, Kenya, Mali, Senegal, Zaire, Tanzania, and Gabon, among many others, all achieved independence in the early sixties. Portugal, then under a dictatorship, did not grant a single colony independence or self-rule during this period and actively worked to oppress independence movements.

Accordingly, nationalists in these colonies began counter-violent movements and insurgencies: Angola in 1961, Guinea-Bissau and Cape Verde in 1963, and Mozambique in 1964.[107] The Portuguese had first made contact with the west coast of Africa in the late fifteenth century. Initially peaceful trade had been the primary form of interaction between Africans and the Portuguese, but beginning in the sixteenth century and continuing through the early nineteenth the Portuguese saw their colonies in Africa as a primary source of slaves and raw materials such as sugar, coffee, and cocoa. Angola, for example, has been called "the Mother of Brazil," as an estimated four million indigenous Africans from that area were taken by the Portuguese in slave ships to their colony in South America, making it second only to Nigeria in loss of people to the slave trade.[108]

In Portuguese colonies, indigenous Africans who learned to speak Portuguese, converted to and actively practiced Catholicism, and pledged allegiance to Portugal were granted the legal status of *assimilado*: Africans (usually of mixed race descent) who were assimilated to Western ways and therefore granted equal rights under Portuguese law.[109] All other indigenous people were second-class citizens at best, and more often victims of internal forms of exploitation that "amounted to slavery in all but name."[110]

In Magnuson's *African Medea*, Jason wants his sons to become *assimilado*—by being educated in Portugal and assimilated entirely into the European culture, they will legally become full citizens under the law, with all the rights and freedoms that such status entails. Otherwise, Jason knows, as likely as not they will end up pressed into service as soldiers, laborers, and slaves.

In Angola, the armed struggle began in 1961 with two different groups rising up: the National Front for the Liberation of Angola (FNLA) rising up in the north and Popular Movement for the Liberation of Angola (MPLA) in the capital city of Luanda. In 1966 the Union for the Total Independence of Angola (UNITA) split from the FNLA. These three rivals would often fight with each other during the revolutionary struggle, and after independence fought a twenty year civil war, which explains the soldier's story about "blacks fighting blacks" in addition to fighting the Europeans. Even in the struggle for independence from the Europeans, anti-colonial conflict could quickly become inter-ethnic struggle or disunified fighting between different factions.

Similarly, Guinea-Bissau, between Senegal and Guinea, was a source of slaves for Portugal. Slaves were shipped to Portugal, Cape Verde, and Brazil. In the nineteenth century, after the abolition of slavery, the Portuguese imposed forced labor and extended limited civil rights only to the *assimilados* in the twentieth century, who were only 0.3 percent of the population.[111] In 1963, the African Party for the Independence of Guinea-Bissau and Cape Verde (PAIGC), which had been founded in 1956 as an independence movement, began armed resistance to the Portuguese imperialists. "By the end of the decade," reports Ramsay, the movement "had gained a mass following and was in control of two thirds of the countryside."[112]

The world of Magnuson's play, a nation on the West African coast under Portuguese control, was, in 1968, a world of revolution and anti-colonialist struggle. The world in which Magnuson's play was first written and performed, New York City, was, in 1968, a world in which racial tensions, racial uprisings, racial rioting, and violence against blacks, in particular by law enforcement, was at an all-time high. In both the Africa of the play and America of the production, conflict between white oppressor and angry, violent, vengeful black victim dominates. The revolutionary rhetoric present in the play reflects a world on the cusp of change, violent, revolutionary change if need be. By setting the story of Medea in Africa during the eighteenth century, Magnuson paralleled the struggle of Medea to resist oppression by Jason and Creon and present day resistance to colonialism and racism in both Africa and America. The play is a warning—one Fanon had sounded but a few years before: unless something changes, the violence of oppression will be met with the violence of revolutionary resistance. In Africa the revolution was already happening. In America, it was coming.

Thirty-three years after the East River Players' Production, in September and October of 2001, the San Diego Black Ensemble Theatre mounted the play again. In the twenty-first century the play was seen "through the lens of feminism—Medea as a sorceress and a strong black woman."[113] In the new context, however, the "revolutionary" aspect of the play "had totally disappeared."[114] Although the L.A. Riots of 1992 and other race-related incidents have occurred in contemporary America, this play is now in a new era of historicity. MTV tells us that, "The Revolution will be televised." Films and plays are made about the Black Panthers which highlight the positive aspects of these organizations and cite them as sources of black pride, unthinkable in mainstream America in 1968.

In short, *African Medea* is already in an era of new historicity. Outside the revolutionary context of the sixties, the play is no longer a warning of revolution, but a celebration of a powerful black woman, more in keeping with the cultural world of America in the early twenty-first century.

Medea as Voodoo Priestess: Ernest Ferlita's *Black Medea* and Steve Carter's *Pecong*

We have already seen the use of Voodoo to create a cultural context into which Greek tragedy may be transculturated in Dove's *Darker Face of the Earth*. Medea, known as a sorceress or witch in many contexts throughout history is a natural candidate for adaptation involving the use of voodoo as practiced in the United States and the Caribbean. Two plays in particular use the practice of voodoo to transculturate *Medea* into the African Americas. Father Ernest Ferlita sets Euripides's play in New Orleans at the beginning of the nineteenth century in *Black Medea*, whereas Steve Carter creates a fictitious and fantastic Caribbean island for the setting of his *Pecong*.

Ernest Ferlita, S.J., completed a degree in playwriting at the Yale School of Drama in 1969 and subsequently began teaching in that same year at Loyola University in New Orleans. A Jesuit, Father Ferlita has written many award-winning plays that have been presented off-Broadway and around the nation, including three adaptations from Greek tragedies: *The Krewe of Dionysus* from *Bacchae*, *The Twice-Born* from *Hippolytus* (which will be discussed below), and *Black Medea*. All three adaptations of Euripides are set in New Orleans at various points in that city's colorful history. Father Ferlita finds Euripides "especially fascinating," as his plays "and his psychological insights resonate with modern reality."[115]

Black Medea was written in 1976. Father Ferlita claims the impetus behind the play was the suggestion of a local reviewer that Loyola's theatre department do a production of *Medea* while Ferlita was looking for a role for an African American actress. Unsatisfied with any translation he found, Father Ferlita, who had a few years before transposed *The Bacchae* to present-day New Orleans during Mardi Gras, set about adapting *Medea* to historical New Orleans. New Orleans was "right," states Father Ferlita, "because of Voodoo."[116] The period following the Haitian revolution created a situation that the playwright found conducive for French and African characters to interact in a city not their own, much like the end of Jason and Medea's relationship occurs in Corinth, where both are strangers, but

Jason, as a man and a Greek has more recourse both to the law and to the local society than Medea.

Since its original production in New Orleans at the Marquette Theatre at Loyola University in April and May of 1976, the play has been presented several times nationally, winning several awards.[117] In 1977, the play was presented at the Dock Street Theatre in Charleston as part of the first Spoleto Festival USA over four days in May and June—the only American play to be featured at the festival. The following year the drama received its first Off Off Broadway production. The New Federal Theatre presented the play over two weeks in December, 1978 to good reviews. The NFT was founded in 1970 by Woodie King, Jr. in the Lower East Side with a mission "to integrate minorities and women into the mainstream of American Theatre by training artists and presenting plays by minorities and women to multicultural audiences."[118] It is a credit to the writing of Father Ferlita (who is a Euro-American male), and an argument against the idea that it is ethnicity of the playwright that determines whether or not a play is "black," that his play was chosen to fulfil the mandate of the NFT.

Washington Theatre Arts Productions revived the play at Loyola University in September 1984. Three years later, in 1987, the play received its second Off Off Broadway production by the Actor's Outlet Theatre in New York City where it ran for four weeks in April and May. Another production followed in the form of a revival by Actor's Outlet at the Fifteenth Annual Black Theatre Festival in October of 1987.

The festival production of *Black Medea*, then subtitled "A Tangle of Serpents," and directed by Glenda Dickerson, who had directed the original Actor's Outlet production was very well received, winning four awards in the festival: Dramatic Production of the Year, Best Actress, Best Choreographer, and Best Music Creator. Again, as with the NFT, that Father Ferlita's drama was included in the Fifteenth Annual Black Theatre Festival is an indication that ethnicity of the playwright is less of a factor in the identification of a drama as "African American" than subject matter and perhaps ethnicity of performers and the venue and context of the production. As part of its continuing success, the production was revived again by the Actor's Outlet in March of 1990, marking its third production Off Off Broadway. The play, however, has yet to be published.[119]

In 1808 the United States prohibited the importation of slaves from Africa. In 1812, Louisiana was admitted as a state to the United States, the same year that a new conflict broke out between the United States and Great Britain, cumulating in the Battle of New Orleans in 1815, two weeks after the war ended. New Orleans itself is, as Robert Farris Thomas argues, a "culturally strategic city," blending Kongo, Malian, Nigerian, Dahomeyan,

Cameroonian, French, Spanish, English, and Native American cultures.[120]
Geographically a port city and a link between the United States and the
Caribbean, sharing a Francophone history with islands such as Haiti, New
Orleans was a very international city for the time and represented not just
a blend of peoples, but a blend of cultures. This is the world in which *Black
Medea* occurs.

Set in New Orleans in 1810, the play is essentially a voodoo ritual that
uses flashbacks to show the conversations between the Medea figure and
the Creon, Jason, and Aegeus figures. The "suggested set" is a bare stage
with "two triangular columns that revolve like periaktoi," with black, red,
and mirrored faces.[121] The chorus was reduced to three women who serve
not only as chorus but also as assistants in the rituals of Tante Emilié, the
Nurse figure. The play begins with the chorus dancing and praying in invocation to Damballah. After the invocation Ferlita renders the prologue
thus:

> If only the ships had never come,
> great white whales with empty bellies
> prowling the coast of Africa
> to swallow up my people. If only
> the royal house of Dahomey
> had not been scattered, its remnants sold
> in the market place of Port-au-Prince
> in Haiti. For she who is my mistress,
> Madeleine, daughter of a prince,
> never would have coupled with Jerome
> Comte D'Argonne, and fled with him
> in secret to the city of New Orleans.[122]

In addition to giving the necessary background information, Ferlita transforms the original Nurse's lament for the arrival of Jason and the Greeks
into a lament for the slave ships, with which this Jason (Jerome, Comte
D'Argonne) was uninvolved. Jason did not go to Africa and Medea fell in
love with him and helped him. Instead, Europeans went to Africa and
enslaved the royal house of Dahomey. Jerome and Madeleine met in Haiti
and fled there after a revolution. In other words, there is no Golden Fleece
in *Black Medea*. Instead there are two noble people who were ousted from
their homes and positions of power; one by European slavers and one by
revolting Haitian slaves. The audience learns from Tante Emilié that
Jerome's family came from France to Haiti and that Madeleine and Jerome
fled together from the uprising and now have two sons: Placide and Moise.

The chorus and Tante Emilié summon Madeleine, telling her "Now
is the hour, the time," and "Damballah goes before you.... He will show

you the gate."[123] Madeleine enters and begins her first speech with a prayer: "Damballah, I am ready," and cries out that she has been wronged.[124]

Interestingly, both plays posit the Medea figure as being in the service of the voodoo *loa* (or god) Damballah. Madeleine in this play is consecrated as his priestess, and Mediyah in Carter's play is eventually revealed as his daughter. Damballah Wedo, also known in Louisiana as "Li Grand Zombi" is the central figure of Louisiana voodoo. In Haiti, where he is identified with Moses and Saint Patrick, he is significant, but not as important as in the American tradition.[125]

Damballah comes originally from West Africa where he figures most strongly in the Dahomean pantheon. A snake cult, the worship of Damballah involves serpents and possessive trances. "Often represented by the snake," states Anthony B. Pinn, "Li Grand Zombie is intimately associated with the activities of voodoo practitioners—'Queens'—such as Marie Laveau," and, for that matter, as Madeleine.[126] Damballah is a principle of cosmic order who "sustains the world and prevents its disintegration."[127] In bringing themselves into direct conflict with Madeleine, his priestess, the "Voodoo Queen," Jerome and Croydon bring themselves in conflict with order and with the spirit being that literally sustains the world. In short, it is not a fight that they can win.

The fact that Madeleine is a priestess of Damballah and a princess of Dahomey, a Haitian slave, and now a freewoman in New Orleans makes her the embodiment in many ways of the worship of Damballah that traveled from Dahomey to Haiti to New Orleans. The word "voodoo" comes from the Dahomean word *voda*, meaning "spirit" or "deity."[128] As Mulira notes, "The most renowned and earliest voodoo leaders in New Orleans came either directly from Africa or by way of the West Indies."[129] Madeleine comes to New Orleans from Africa by way of Haiti. In her, Ferlita has literally embodied the history of voodoo and Damballah-worship in New Orleans.

In a flashback, Madeleine relates her conversation with Colonel Croydon, the Creon of this adaptation. "Four days ago," she tells the chorus and the audience, "a man came to see me, and Croydon enters.[130] Ever the southern gentleman, Croydon states that he does not know how to properly address Madeleine. This remark begins their battle for her identity:

MADELEINE: I am Madeleine, Comtesse D'Argonne.
CROYDON: No! That title was never yours.
MADELEINE: The Comte D'Argonne is my husband.
CROYDON: He is not your husband.
He never *was* your husband.[131]

As with his Euripidean counterpart, Croydon wants Jerome to marry his daughter, in this case named Corrine. He therefore rejects Jerome's earlier marriage, as Madeleine is African and therefore has no rights. When Madeleine states that she and Jerome exchanged vows "before God" in Haiti, Croydon snaps, "God has not informed us."[132] He argues that Madeleine is Jerome's mistress, nothing more. She asserts her royal lineage and her status as a freedwoman:

> But I am no man's slave. My father
> was a prince of the house of Dahomey.
> It was people like you that enslaved him, shipped him
> to the island of Saint Domingue—or Haiti,
> as they call it now.[133]

Madeleine's father, the prince, was freed by Jerome's father and Madeleine with him. Madeleine and Jerome fell in love and married after she was consecrated to Damballah. "I am as free as you are, sir," she concludes. Croydon counters, "In New Orleans, you are free and you are not free."[134]

This paradox refers to the complicated laws regarding the status of people of color in Louisiana, especially before it became a state in 1812, two years after the action of the play. Madeleine is an example of the *gens libre de couleur*, the free people of color in the Francophone New World to whom Louisiana's Creole culture may be traced. Between 1719 and 1731, the French who settled in Louisiana brought approximately 6000 Africans to serve as slaves, making people of color almost sixty percent of the population in the area around New Orleans. Their lives were dictated by the Code Noir, issued by King Louis in 1685 to cover all French colonies, and its subsequent and specific reissue as the Code Noir de Louisiana of 1724, which was also retained under the brief period of Spanish rule (1768–1800, after which it returned to French control). Subsequent legal codes which had jurisdiction over the lives of both people of color and those of European descent in Louisiana include the Code Napoleon, the 1794 declaration of emancipation as issued by the French Republic, and eventually, after the Louisiana Purchase in 1803, the laws of the fledgling United States of America.

All aspects of slave life were dictated by the Code Noir, which, of course, meant that the activities and practices of slave-owners were also dictated by the code. Under the Code Noir, all slaves were required to be baptized into the Catholic faith. They could not carry weapons, and those that struck their master or other free person were required to be put to death. Section six of the code applies to relationships between blacks and whites. White subjects of either sex were forbidden to marry slaves, or even engage in any kind of romantic relationship or sexual encounter: "We also forbid our said white subjects, even freed blacks or those born free, to live in concubinage with slaves."[135] Although such liaisons were forbidden, the code contained provisions for the identity of and disposal of the children of such a union. Should a child be born to a slave and a free person, both the slave and the child would be taken from their master and sold to someone else and the master had to pay a heavy fine. The child's legal status was that of the mother—should the mother be a slave, the child was a slave, should the mother be free, the child would be free. Other laws were subsequently enacted to further prevent miscegenation. Thus, Madeleine and her children are technically free, but the Code Noir does not acknowledge them as the legitimate children of Jerome.

Croydon orders Madeleine back to Haiti before sunset the following day. Unlike Creon, Croydon does not rule the city. He is only a colonel in the militia. But, his wealth "makes [his] opinions important" and makes him a friend of the mayor and those who do rule the city.[136] In an interesting departure from the original, in antebellum New Orleans Ferlita equates wealth with power. Croydon does not need to be the ruler of the city—he need only have enough money that those who do rule will obey his wishes.

Croydon states that the Louisiana Purchase and the Haitian revolution have increased crime and unrest in the city. Most objectionably, voodoo has come to the city. Croydon sees voodoo as "the way to revolution:" "It was voodoo that stirred up the slaves to revolt in Haiti; it was voodoo that massacred the French."[137] Croydon is not entirely wrong, although his fear is motivated by racial prejudice and a desire to hold onto power and wealth at the expense of others.

Historically, voodoo was used as a counterhegemonic and oppositional force to slavery. Voodoo brought with it organization, leaders, and a ideology of revolt. As Jessie Gaston Mulira observes, the African priests whose religion would become voodoo were the first leaders of slave revolts in the Caribbean and the United States. They could conduct meetings under the guise of ceremony, they already had a leadership role in the African community, and thus were respected and obeyed, and they could assure supernatural support and inspiration for the revolts.[138] The leaders of revolution in Haiti—Toussaint L'Ouverture and Henri Christophe, for example, relied upon voodoo to support their successful political and military campaigns. Likewise, in New Orleans, beginning at the start of the nineteenth century, "Voodoo Queens" wielded tremendous power over individuals and the city. In 1782, when the area was under Spanish rule, Governor Gálvez of Louisiana prohibited the importation of slaves from Martinique because "he believed them to be steeped in voodooism and that they 'would make the lives of citizens unsafe.'"[139] In 1792 a ban was placed on importing slaves from Santo Domingo for the same reason, neither prohibition being lifted until the Louisiana Purchase in 1803. Mulira even goes so far as to argue that voodoo and African religions "also survived because of the organizational role they played in slave revolts throughout the New World but particularly in Haiti and Brazil."[140] In other words, revolt against the Europeans and voodoo practice were both mutually reinforcing and mutually empowering. Voodoo would organize and support an insurrection and the insurrection would then allow voodoo to flourish. Both voodoo and insurrection are forms of resistance to slavery and colonialism. Croydon in many ways is right to fear voodoo, not because it is different or heathen, but because voodoo has been a tool in all successful overthrows and resistances of white European hegemony in its mutually-reinforcing and empowering role.

Lastly, voodoo, as a performed religion, is a system of belief rooted in the human body. Voodoo possession, as Joseph Roach observes, "pointedly focuses attention on the autonomy and ownership of living bodies, an attention most unwelcome to slaveholders in antebellum times."[141] Croydon distrusts voodoo because it is a form of control of black bodies, the same black bodies over which he desires to have complete control.

Madeleine makes clear that she holds no grudge against Croydon, only Jerome. She recognizes Croydon has "acted reasonably" under Louisiana law. It is, of course, the clause "under Louisiana law" that renders the line satirical. Under the insane laws of the Code Noir and the laws for people of color, Croydon's unreasonable behavior appears reasonable. Madeleine is therefore not the revolutionary that Croydon fears her to be, nor even that Magnuson's Medea is. Madeleine does not seek to overturn an unjust system, merely hold the one who seemed to transcend the system responsible when he suddenly begins to adhere to it for personal gain.

Croydon demands that she leave and she acquiesces, asking that her sons be allowed to stay. He insists the children go back to Haiti with her. She then asks for more time and he grants her three days. He departs and the flashback ends.

The next choral interlude begins, again in the form of a prayer to Damballah. Madeleine, Tante Emiliè and the chorus invoke Damballah again. Madeleine states her grievance again, this time acknowledging the reality of both the law and the slave market:

> The law strips me in the marketplace
> makes a mockery of my marriage
> laughs at my claim to freedom...

Yes, if I wanted justice
I knew I would have to get it myself.[142]

Given her position as a *gens libre de couleur*, Madeleine is nevertheless little better off than her enslaved countrymen. When in direct conflict with Europeans, she will never receive justice as they control the laws in order to ensure she receives no recourse. In the absence of recourse to human law or justice, she must appeal to supernatural law and supernatural justice. She will become the agent by which Damballah repairs the breech of order caused by the whites.

Then begins the second flashback. We are shown the events of three days before, when Jerome comes to accuse her. He blames her for making voodoo threats against Croydon, arguing that that is the sole reason she and their sons are banished. She tells him that she learned of his new wedding through the newspaper—he is to marry Croydon's daughter Corinne.

Jerome blames love for his predicament, arguing that he "had only his title," as Madeleine's father had taken all of Jerome's family's property after the revolution, leaving him without money or property. He had wanted to send their sons to school in France, as "In France, it's blood that counts, not skin, and theirs is like the best of wines..."[143] By saying so, he acknowledges that his aristocratic heritage will help his sons in France, but in democratic America, where blood is not an indicator of class, bur rather racial purity, black-skinned sons are a liability to him. He admits to Madeleine that he needs to marry Corinne as he wants (and legally needs) legitimate (read: white) sons to carry on his name and title. Under the Code Noir, of course, the sons are not legitimate, so Jerome's romantic notion that their "blood" is all that matters is likely inaccurate at best and completely wrong at worst.

Interestingly, at this point in the play there is a flashback within the flashback. The audience is shown how, in Haiti many years before, Tante Emiliè sacrificed doves and a goat to Damballah when Madeleine, then just a young girl, was initiated into the cult of Damballah as a young priestess. During the ceremony, she fled out of the hut where the sacrifice took place and ran into the forest where she met Jerome, who was riding his horse around his family's estate the night before he was to leave for France for school. They made love on the spot and pledged themselves to each other. Jerome acknowledges he returned to Haiti for the land and for her. She tells him, "I am Africa. I am the New World."[144] As the embodiment of the practice of voodoo, as noted above, Madeleine is the visual and physical embodiment of the link between Africa and the New World. She speaks for herself, but she also speaks with the voice of Damballah, who links New World and Motherland. Jerome therefore knows from the beginning that his wife is a powerful woman and connected both to the higher reality of Damballah and to the more earthbound African and American nations.

Jerome then flees, afraid of the spirit and afraid of Madeleine's power. Both flashbacks end simultaneously with his retreat and another choral interlude begins.

In each choral interlude at this point, Ferlita repeats the phrase:

> What you tell to Damballah you tell to us.
> What you tell to us, you tell to Damballah.[145]

The entire play is structured as a voodoo ritual taking place in the moment. The flashbacks are designed to indicate the past events that have led to the ceremony being performed now, a summoning of Damballah for the purposes of taking revenge on those who wronged Madeleine. The worshippers of Damballah acknowledge a oneness with the god and acknowledge themselves, like Madeleine, a conduit to the loa. In voodoo, community is a strong focus and believers can be "ridden" by the loa—the gods manifest themselves by possessing their followers in order to pass along blessings or information and accept worship and sacrifice.

Following this interlude comes the third flashback, set two days before. Pierre Laguerre, a pirate and privateer and Ferlita's Aegeus figure, came to visit Madeleine. When the revolution came to Haiti, it was Laguerre who saved Madeleine and Jerome, taking them on his ship and bringing them to New Orleans. He brings news to Madeleine of Haiti, how it is now split into two lands: Henri Christophe rules in the north, where voodoo is outlawed, but Madeleine would be welcome in the south of Haiti. He tells her he will take her to Haiti right away if that is her wish, but she informs him she wants justice first. He tells her he will think about helping her, as he does not want additional trouble. This exchange differs from the original in which Aegeus gladly accepts Medea in exchange for the ability to father children. In Ferlita's adaptation, Laguerre is a friend of Madeleine's who does not require anything further of her and who is uncertain if he can help her, knowing she is planning a terrible revenge on those who will follow her. Laguerre also differs from his Greek progenitor as Aegeus was king of Athens, and while Laguerre is the captain of his own ship he does not have the weight of a nation behind him (other than the south of Haiti) to offer sanctuary to Madeleine.

After the flashback, a choral interlude with drumming and chanting in praise of Damballah is followed by a monologue in which Madeleine

Black Medea by Ernest Ferlita, performed at Loyola University, New Orleans, 1976. (From left to right) Alana Villavaso, Francesca Roberts (as Tante Emiliè), Carol Sutton (as Madeleine), and Adella Gautier. (Photograph courtesy of Father Ernest Ferlita).

tells what she has done that morning. She sent her sons to the bride with "a bracelet made of gold beaten into slender coils, with a clasp like the head of a sleeping serpent," which has fangs that bite into the wearer and that Madeleine has "filled with a swift poison."[146] Again, Ferilta's version differs from original, in which Medea sends a robe or dress and a crown for

Jason's new bride. The serpent bracelet Madeleine sends invokes Damballah, but ironically also makes the action less supernatural, as the device that destroys the new bride and her father is mechanical, not magical. Thus, Ferlita allows for more direct and human agency in his Medea's revenge, even as it is done in the name of Damballah and, ostensibly, with his blessing.

The first part of the play ends with Madeleine intoning, "What is done to me will be done to them," indicating the scope of her revenge to follow, and further indicating that she will reduce her enemies to the level at which they have reduced her.[147] The second part of the play begins with the re-enactment of the morning's action. Madeleine had summoned Jerome back and he plays with the children. She deceives him by begging him to ask Croydon to let the children stay in New Orleans. She tells him she will send a gift to Corinne—the serpent bracelet. Tante Emiliè brings it in and, after a moment's hesitation, Jerome takes it and leaves.

Switching back to the present moment, the voodoo ritual then begins in earnest. Tante Emilié invokes Damballah, as well as Baron Samedi, Erzuli, Ogun, and the other *loa*. She sends the first woman of the chorus into a trance, and she serves as the messenger, relating what has happened offstage, at a distance, as seen by the *loa*. The first woman is possessed, ostensibly by Damballah, and the ritual begins to reach its climax. Jerome and the children arrive at Croydon's house, she reports, and gives Corinne the gift. The other members of the chorus chant to Damballah, asking him to bring about vengeance for Madeleine.

Corinne, it is reported, goes to a room full of mirrors and puts on the bracelet. The first woman then describes the death that follows. The arm with the bracelet swells and turns brown as the poison takes effect. Croydon tears the bracelet off and throws it against the mirrored wall, shattering it, but he is too late. His daughter dies convulsing. Jerome sends the children home, fearing for their safety.

It is at this point, and not earlier, as in Euripides, that Madeleine decides to kill her children:

> They must die. Jerome has already
> killed them in spirit. I will make
> the murder visible to every eye.
> I gave them life; I will take it away.[148]

After debating with herself, as her Greek predecessor did, Madeleine commits to killing the children. Tante Emiliè argues against the murder, advising her to take her children to another city. Again, the children are killed for a different reason than in Euripides. She argues that her husband has "already killed them in spirit," which means that in her world view they are already dead anyway. Her responsibility is to manifest the reality that he has already created. She will "make the murder visible to every eye," speaking not of her killing the children, but of his killing them. She will realize in the physical bodies what he has already done to them on all other levels. As their mother, it is her responsibility to protect them from harm, and if their father has already irrevocably harmed them, then she takes away the life she gave.

Jerome enters and interrogates Tante Emiliè. He tells her that Croydon was nicked by the fang when he pulled the serpent bracelet off of Corinne, and the little venom that entered the scratch was enough to kill him. The entire family is now in danger. The first woman of the chorus, still in her trance, screams, reporting that Madeleine has slit the children's throats with a knife. The description of their killing echoes the earlier description of the sacrifice of the goat at Madeleine's consecration to Damballah. Thus, the children also become sacrifices to Damballah. Their deaths also end the ritual around which the drama has been structured. This vision is how Jerome (and the audience) learns of the death of the sons.

The final confrontation between the two is very brief and not face-to-face as it is in Euripides. Instead of Medea on the roof as Jason screams at her, Jerome remains in front of the house alone, dropping to his knees and crying out "Why?" Madeleine's face appears on a scrim behind him "in the heart of a fire," and tells him:

> I am the earth, the shape of the hills
> and the bend in the road. I open the night.
> I am Africa, I am the New World.
> I am the ocean that burst its bonds
> to thunder on every shore. I am fire
> and lightning, the great passion of your youth!
> I am the way to God for you![149]

The play then ends with Jerome screaming the word "NO!" as a blackout occurs.

The play's conclusion is also the conclusion of the ritual. The "I" of Madeleine's final speech is not her, but Damballah. As Damballah is the principle of cosmic order, his will has worked out to reduce Jason to the status that he reduced Madeleine. Damballah unites Africa and the New World and the European-Americans made the mistake of underestimating his power.

An interesting question that the play begs is why a Catholic priest would write a play that posits the dominance of Damballah in the New World. I am not prepared to psychoanalyze Father Ferlita, nor do I think it necessary or appropriate. But we must bear the play's origins in mind when considering where on the continuum of Afro-Greek tragedy it falls. Ferlita has written an historic tragedy set in New Orleans. There is nothing in it that is patently anti-western religion or even openly anticolonial. While the primacy of Damballah is presented and the rejection of colonialism in Haiti is present in the play, the work remains firmly ensconced in the United States and in American culture. The play is rooted in a voodoo ritual, using it as a dramaturgical device, as an organizing principle, rather than because the author implies the legitimacy of African-centered religions in the New World.

Ultimately, Ferlita's play posits that slavery is bad, colonialism is bad, and Jerome and Croydon reap what they have sown. Such statements, while essentially correct, do no necessarily make the play "Black Dionysus," but rather leave it firmly in the model of "Black Orpheus." While the practices of imperialism and slavery are critiqued as part of the narrative, the play itself neither uses the Greek material to critique western culture, nor alter the audience's perception of the place of people of African descent in America. It is an interesting and worthwhile play. But less than ten years after Magnuson's play, the revolution is over. Just as the Haitian revolution is over in Ferlita's play, the revolutionary fervor of the sixties had settled into the complacent seventies. The play concerns the fallout of failed revolutions, but is not a revolution in and of itself. To say this is not a criticism of the play, simply to point out the shift from *African Medea* to *Black Medea* that slides even further away from revolution in *Pecong*.

Steve Carter's *Pecong*, an adaptation of Euripides's *Medea*, was written for the Victory Garden Theatre in Chicago. The production, under the direction of Dennis Zacek, opened on 9 January 1990, and the play was subsequently published three years later. It also enjoyed major productions in 1991 at St. Paul's Penumbra Theatre in London, in April of 1992 by the American Theatre Festival at the Symphony Hall in Newark, New Jersey, and in October of 1993 at San Francisco's American Conservatory Theatre, all to fairly positive reviews.[150]

Carter was already well known in African American theatre circles for such plays as *Eden*, *Primary Colors*, *Shoot Me While I'm Happy*, and *The Inaugural Tea*. In *Pecong*, Carter has created an African American adaptation of a Greek tragedy that sets the play in the Caribbean and incorporates elements of both the "Black Orpheus" and the "Black Athena" paradigms. He adapts the Greek material to a setting within the African diaspora, but characters also voice the opinion that classical culture is African in origin.

The play is set on an "island of the mind" called Trankey Island (or Ile Tranquille) and on nearby Miedo Wood Island. Carter has transformed Euripides's character names into Caribbean equivalents" Medea becomes Mediyah, a young island girl on her way to being an Obeah Queen, a powerful practitioner of magic. Assisting and teaching her is Granny Root, who serves the function of the nurse in the original, although her name suggests the roots and herbs used in her magic, thus making her a more powerful figure than her Euripidean forebear. Granny Root also dies in the first scene, but her spirit lingers over the play, and Mediyah is in contact with her. In a departure from the original, it is the spirit of Granny Root that seems to drive the action as much as anything, which has the effect of placing focus on the supernatural elements, which, in the words of one reviewer, "are often avoided in conventional productions of the classical Greek drama."[151] In other words, the reviewer does not accept the supernatural when presented in "conventional" production, but the Caribbean setting with Obeah Queens creates an environment in which the presence of magic, curses, spirits, gods, and the supernatural are acceptable. This idea will be explored in depth below.

Jason becomes Jason Allcock, whose very name "all cock," suggests the phallocentric nature of the character whose power and weakness both stem from his sexuality: he is literally "all cock," thinking of nothing but his own gratification. Unlike the Euripidean original, Carter's play begins with the meeting of Mediyah and Jason, called "Jason the Ram" from Tougou Island, another allusion to his sexuality and phallic power.[152] Their relationship is openly sexual in nature: from their first conversation it is apparent that their mutual attraction is rooted in physical appearance and sexuality. Jason collapses naked at her feet while trying to get Calabash wood and cat gut to make a quatro for the Pecong contest. Mediyah cries out, "Oh, God! But you is a pretty piece of flesh."[153] They exchange initial flirtations, and then the stage directions read, "*He pulls her down to him,*" and they kiss.[154] The kiss overwhelms him, as he is already exhausted, but she "*throws herself savagely on Jason who, though asleep, reacts in kind.*"[155] Later, Mediyah tells Granny Root, "Each time I does look at that man, I does want to jump he."[156] However, this sexuality and sexual obsession on Mediyah's part is also her undoing, as Granny Root observes at the close of Act One: "A woman, too much in love, ain't have no power."[157]

The play engages this problematic sexuality of the characters, as discussed in chapter three, above. Jason, a black man, is "all cock." Mediyah, as we see below, is also a very sexual being. Both characters are exoticized, eroticized and are in danger of being possibly stereotypical representations of black sexuality. Eventually, however, the sexuality of the characters is transformed as Jason wins the Pecong and leaves Mediyah, causing her to displace her sexual energy into a violent response against her once-lover, as will be explored below.

Creon Pandit is Carter's manifestation of Creon. Creon Pandit is the local civic leader who also owns and runs the general store. His last name suggests "bandit," thus resonating the corruption and theft that mark Creon's rule as erstwhile mayor. It also suggests the role he will play in stealing Mediyah's man away from her.

Carter also introduces characters not found in Euripides's play. Cedric is Mediyah's twin brother, shown to be a model of ineffective manhood. Persis and Faustina are two sisters on Trankey Island who serve as chorus and messengers. As Cedric is the opposite of Jason in many ways, weak where Jason is strong, celibate where Jason is promiscuous, cerebral where Jason is unthinking, Persis and Faustina are the opposite of Mediyah and Granny Root, offering an alternative model of island women.

Faustina provides the link to both the African diaspora and the Afro-Asiatic origins of civilization. In an argument at the store, Creon Pandit calls Faustina a "Zulu," presumably intended as an insult, either for the darkness of her skin color, or suggesting that she is backwards, as Creon assumes people in Africa must be.[158] Creon is very much like Mama in *Raisin in the Sun*—disconnected from his own African roots and having grown up in an environment that encouraged the internalizing of the notion of European cultural superiority to Africa he is ignorant of the true nature of Africa and therefore contemptuous and dismissive towards it.

Faustina responds, "And who you callin' Zulu? We ancestor come here straight from Egypt!"[159] Creon responds that the crocodile comes from Egypt too, further insulting Faustina, while recognizing her dangerous nature. Faustina accepts Afrocentric classicism—the manifestation of the "Black Athena" paradigm in this play. She sees herself as having descended directly from Egyptians, a source of pride for her. Arguably, however, her identification with only Africa and rejection of the "Zulu" label indicates an identity rooted in Africa that is equally as problematic as Creon's formulation. Unlike Creon, she does not reject Africa entirely, but she looks to its ancient past for her immediate identity. She is arguably descended from Egypt, but she herself came, as did all the characters, as part of the Middle Passage. In holding Egypt and denying Zulu, she disconnects herself from the African diaspora and denies the reality of the middle passage. While this is a way of maintaining pride in one's heritage, it also ignores the historical reality and denies a connection to contemporary Africa.

At the center of the play, however, and the source of its title, is the Pecong, a contest of manhood, bravery, and creativity in which men duel with insults, not unlike the song duels of the Inuit, or "playing the dozens" in the African American community, also known as "sounding," woofing," or "signifying," and perhaps best understood in the popular mind as "your momma" jokes (though momma jokes are only one variation of a larger list of possible insult targets). In the Caribbean, the setting for the narrative, Calypso music, in fact, originated in part as a rhyming insult contest similar to the Pecong.[160] Peter Farb, in his analysis of verbal dueling in the book *Word Play*, notes that all of these verbal duels have several elements in common. They are, first and foremost, "an alternative to actual fighting," a way of proving one's manhood and engaging in competition without the risk of injury or death.[161] It should be noted that manhood is used accurately here, women do not fight Pecong in the play, and in many cultures that have verbal dueling it is a male-only activity. In their book *Cool Pose: The Dilemmas of Black Manhood in America*, Richard Majors and Janet Mancini Billson dedicate an entire chapter to the practice of "playing the dozens," noting that while some black women or white teens will occasionally engage in this behavior, it is primarily the province of black males, who use it as a way to establish identity, gain respect, avoid violence, entertain, and establish a social order.[162]

Another function of calypso, or playing the dozens, or the Pecong, for that matter is as "a training ground for adulthood."[163] Farb sees this training aspect especially important in the case of African Americans and calypso "fighters." Even more than its use as a tool for discovering boundaries and establishing personal identity, verbal dueling becomes a way to empower ones' self in an oppressive society:

> Virtually powerless in a white world, blacks discovered that one of the few ways they could fight back was verbally. Verbal battle against whites became more important than physical battle, where blacks have been outnumbered and outgunned.[164]

While we might take exception to Farb's construction of the social reality of African Americans (essentially correct, one might argue, if grossly oversimplified, and not taking into account other factors), the point is essentially true—from early minstrel show pieces to contemporary hip hop songs, verbal ability and the satirization and mocking of one's opponents (especially whites) are staples in African American performance.

In Carter's play the stage directions state, "*The Pecong is a contest in which each man insults the other. When one man does, the other will react as if he has been struck by a blow.*"[165] The two contestants attack each other's manhood, ancestry, health, sexual orientation, appearance, and morality in rhymed verse. Many of the verses concern the singer having sex with his opponent's mother. The winner is accorded many prizes and civic power. The loser may lose his life. All of which is very much in accord with the origins of Calypso and with playing the dozens. Majors and Billson observe that such formalized verbal aggression "becomes progressively nasty and pornographic, virtually every family member and every sexual act is woven into the verbal assault," which tends to focus very quickly on mothers.[166] Majors and Billson cite the absent father figure and the dominant mother figure in lower-income families, resulting in a closeness and appreciation of the sacrifices of one's mother, as a primary reason why mother-related insults become prevalent quickly in the contest. Rhyming is equally important in playing the dozens, as it "veil[s] and confound[s] meanings," making the pornographic sentiments more acceptable, also acting as a mnemonic device, and displaying one's prowess with language and, therefore, one's superiority.[167] Carter's creation is rooted in African American and Caribbean contests of verbal combat.

Pecong is the highlight of the Carnival, and is shaped by it. Carnival is a pre–Lenten celebration, consisting of masked revelers, historic re-enactments, dances, music, masquerades, and celebrations. Carnival allowed for challenges to authority within society, but in a limited fashion—controlling the outcome of contests such as Pecong.[168] The Carnival is also linked, metaphorically and thematically, with the Festival of Dionysus, as will be discussed in chapter five.

The Pecong is the center of the play, which means that Mediyah is not. Carter, by naming his play after the contest and not the heroine, as nearly every other playwright has, moves the focus from her to the verbal battle of Jason and Creon. We might further note that Carter's characters are all Caribbean of African descent, meaning that the conflict between black and white, present in almost every other adaptation, is not present here. *Pecong* is, on many levels, not about colonialism or revolution, or white European oppression of black Africans. It is not even a feminist representation of a woman empowering herself to strike back against a male oppressor. *Pecong* is about contests and battles, large and small. From both the titular fight between Creon and Jason and Cedric and Jason, which Jason wins, to the battle between Creon and Faustina for her identity, which she wins, to the battle between Jason and Mediyah over his faithlessness and desire for their children, the play concerns a fight between relative equals and the strategies employed to win.

Creon Pandit has won for four consecutive years, and if he beats his current opponent he will be named "Calabash for Life." Jason is his challenger. When Mediyah and Jason meet he is gathering materials in order to win the Pecong. He tells Mediyah that he must win, and she agrees to help. Like the mythic original, Jason is given a seemingly impossible task in the form of an unbeatable opponent (in the Argo myth, Jason had to yoke bulls that breathed fire and sew the teeth of a dragon he slew) that Mediyah helps him to defeat. Carter combines the Euripidean narrative of Creon enticing Jason into a union with his daughter while banishing Medea, and the quest for the Golden Fleece. Carter collapses all of Jason's male opponents into a single one: Creon Pandit is thus Creon, Aeetes, and guardians of the Golden Fleece all rolled into one. The Pecong is the Golden Fleece that Jason must win with the help of a woman.

Jason wins the contest. Sweet Bella, silent to this point, cries out "Jason! Jason!" as Jason announces that he loves Sweet Bella.[169] Creon Pandit announces that Jason and Sweet Bella will be married on the last day of Carnival, three days later. Creon Pandit has better reason to marry his daughter to Jason than did his Euripidean forebear—Jason is now the ruler of both Carnival and Trankey Island. In order to continue his own life of power, Creon needs to attach himself to the Pecong winner. As in the original, Jason also desires the marriage as it will heighten his legitimacy as ruler of a people different than his (he is from Togou Island) and will give him access to the economic power of Creon Bandit, store owner and wealthy man.

Carter subverts the character of Jason by having him win Pecong. Jason to this point has been, as his name suggests, "All cock"—driven by desire and known for his sexual and physical prowess. By winning Pecong he is shown to be creative, clever, intelligent, and linguistically dexterous. Much of the creativity is shown to be sexual in nature (he comments on the size of Creon's genitalia, Creon's choice of sexual partner, etc.), but the challenge to Jason remains an intellectual and creative one, not a physical and/or sexual one.

While Jason and Sweet Bella marry, Mediyah gives birth to twin boys, crying out, "I does curse you and before all here I swear I goin' have me vengeance!"[170] Mediyah then goes to see the spirit of Granny Root, telling her she hates Jason and wants revenge. Jason enters and confronts Mediyah, telling her he wants his sons. They are proof of his manhood and virility—his seed makes twin boys, and he wants possession of them.

Mediyah, like the original, is thus completely disenfranchised as Jason has now been accepted into the elite of the island: he has won Pecong, married the Calabash's daughter, and fathered twin boys—a sign of his potent manhood. Mediyah refuses Jason's request, uttering a long curse in verse in which she calls on the "God of Vengeance" to marry her since Jason would not:

> Sun, Moon, Star, hide you face and let through
> The God of Vengeance
> To Marry and consummate with me.[171]

The same life-energy and vitality she put into her sexual relations with Jason at the beginning of the play, she will now put into her relations with the God of Vengeance. She will turn her sexual power and energy against Jason to destroy him.

Like Demea, in Guy Butler's *Demea* (a South African adaptation of *Medea*, discussed in *Athenian Sun*), and the original Medea, Mediyah becomes a *theos*. Bernard M.W. Knox, in his analysis of Euripides's play concludes:

> The energy [Medea] had wasted on Jason was tempered to a deadly instrument to destroy him. It became a *theos*, relentless, merciless force, the unspeakable violence of the oppressed and betrayed, which, because it had been so long pent up, carries everything before it to destruction, even if it destroys also what it loves most.[172]

Medea's (and Mediyah's) revenge is an unstoppable violent force. Unlike Medea or Demea, however, Mediyah's vengeance is rooted first and foremost in her sexuality. She will marry *and consummate* with the "God of Vengeance." Just as her relationship with Jason was first and foremost as sexual one, so, too will be her vengeance. Medea's vengeance is not nearly as sexual in nature (if, indeed, it is at all), as Mediyah's is.

Mediyah, beginning her vengeance, in a show of regret, gives Jason a "night frock" for Sweet Bella. She also gives up the children, sending them to live with Jason and Bella. She tells the audience that, "He goin' to have the most long and slow life of remembrance."[173] She gives Persis and Faustina a concoction so that when they nurse the twins, the babies will die. After a brief interval, Persis and Faustina enter and give an almost exact duplicate of the messenger speech in Euripides's original. They report that the babies have died and when Creon Pandit and Jason went to see what was wrong, Sweet Bella, wearing the night frock, burst into flames. Creon and Jason jumped on Sweet Bella, they report, but Jason fell off the living pyre and watched father and daughter burn to death. Cedric, Mediyah's twin brother, hangs himself with grief. As they finish their report, Jason enters with a machete, come to kill Mediyah.

At first, he can only say his name repeatedly, and Mediyah curses and taunts him, calling him "Jason of Tougou, Master of Pecong."[174] He who won his status through his cleverness and his ability to use words can now only saw his name. Mediyah is the true master of Pecong; she has defeated Jason at his own game.

She reveals that her father is Damballah. As in Ferlita, Carter's play links the Medea-figure to voodoo in general and the *loa* Damballa. Similar to Euripides' Medea, Mediyah's divine ancestry allows her both to complete her vengeance and to escape punishment from those she has struck down. Mediyah and Granny Root mysteriously disappear after announcing that they will return to Meido Wood Island. It is the latter in which Carter differs from the Greek. Medea must go to Athens, being forever unable to return to her homeland. Carter shows Mediyah returning home, as his character never executed any family members or broke with a father. This difference is significant, as Medea reduced Jason to the same state he reduced her to: an individual without a home or community that would welcome him. In Carter's version, Medea can return home.

In the epilogue, Persis and Faustina announce to a passing group of revelers that, "Carnival over! It Lent and Carnival over!... Is time for all you 'semble here to low you eye and be austere. Go home! Go home! Until next year."[175] The lines clearly differentiate the periods between Carnival—the Dionysiac time of revelry and Lent, the Catholic period of preparation for Easter. Mediyah is a Carnival figure who has no place in the world of Lent. Lastly, the final lines remind us of the cyclical nature of the myth and the play: "until next year," meaning that the Calabash and the Carnival will come again, in spite of the tragedy that has occurred. Mediyah returns to Meido Wood Island, the masks and costumes are put away for a year, and neighbors behave normally again. But next year brings a new Carnival, and perhaps a return of the force that is Mediyah.

Ferlita and Carter both posit Medea-figures with voodoo powers and a relationship to Damballah. Carter makes Jason and Medea the same ethnicity, so missing from his play are all the colonial overtones present in almost every other adaptation considered in this chapter (the Medea Project being the other notable exception). Carter's play focuses on the battle of the sexes and the battle for sex. His play places primacy on the model of "Medea as abandoned wife" and "Medea as witch," whereas Father Ferlita's play also adds "Medea as outsider." More than any other adaptation, however, these two dwell on the supernatural aspect of Medea, focusing on her powers and her connections to the spiritual world. Emily A. McDermott claims that Euripides downplays the supernatural elements of the play until the very end, although the audience was surely familiar with her reputation as a witch.[176] These two adaptations begin with Medea's magical abilities, perhaps in part to remind the audience of her powers from the beginning, and partly to transculturate that aspect of the character and play into the new setting, but in doing so one must give that aspect primacy. One cannot have a Medea who suddenly picks up voodoo at the end of the play.

Other differences between these two are rooted in the conditions of their development. Carter was writing for professionals in the nineties, while Ferlita initially was writing for a Catholic college and a student audience and cast in the seventies, which is why Carter can and does focus on the sexuality of the characters and Ferlita less on the physical and more on the divine and spiritual. Ferlita also has a regional interest in New Orleans, where the play was both set and first performed. Carter's play was not performed in the Caribbean until 1994 (see chapter five). In both cases, however, the distance provided by time (in Ferlita's case) and geographic distance (in Carter's) allows the audience tragic vision.

We should also note that Magnuson and Ferlita, the European-American writers have written plays far more critical of colonial culture than Carter. Their plays engage the political realities of slavery, colonialism, and the survival of African culture in a way that Carter's does not. Carter, who, as an African American writer is in a position to be less political by virtue of his being closer to the material, chooses not to engage the political. Interestingly, the adaptation by the African American author follows the "Black Orpheus" paradigm the strongest. He is at the opposite of the spectrum from Silas Jones, whose work, considered next, is by far the strongest example of the "Black Athena" paradigm.

Additionally, Ferlita wrote a sequel of sorts to Black Medea based on Euripides' Hippolytus entitled The Twice-Born. Instead of Theseus, Ferlita posits Jerome, Comte D'Argonne (Jason) as the father-figure in another tragedy. Set in New Orleans in June of 1821, the play narrates the story of Hippolyte (Hippolytus) and his step-mother and Jerome's new wife Philippa (Phaedra). After the death of Croydon and his daughter Corinne, Jerome, unlike his Greek counterpart, remains in the city. He marries Croydon's other daughter, Philippa. Thus, the Phaedra-figure in this play is presented as Creon's daughter and the sister of Jason's unfortunate bride-to-be. In Greek mythology (and the original drama), Phaedra was the daughter of Minos and Pasiphae, sister of Ariadne, and wife of Theseus. Thus, Ferlita incorporates an entirely unrelated body of myth into the Medea narrative, effectively erasing the "real" myth of Phaedra. Jason was forced to flee Corinth after the Medea incident, but in Ferlita's second play he not only remains in the city, but is still welcomed into his new family, thus effectively undoing Medea's revenge. He still marries another and starts life anew in his new city.

The second problem caused by this new formulation is that if Hippolyte is Jerome's son from a previous relationship (in Greek mythology, his mother was Hippolyta, Queen of the Amazons and Theseus's first wife), why was he not mentioned by either Madeleine or Jerome in the first play—

she claims to have killed all his children, yet Hippolyte is obviously alive and well in *The Twice-Born*, which means that Madeleine's revenge is further undone, as Jerome already had a child who would carry on his name.

Before the play begins, Jerome was part of a plot to rescue Napoleon from St. Helena and bring him to New Orleans. The mission failed, and Jerome's ship supposedly sunk before it reached the port of Charleston. Before leaving, Jerome had arranged for Hippolyte to marry his stepmother's cousin Andrea. Hippolyte, however does not want to marry Andrea, preferring instead to go to seminary in Baltimore and become a Catholic priest. This formulation is a reflection of the Greek original, in which Hippolytus is devoted to Artemis, chaste goddess of the hunt, and thus chaste himself. In the prologue to Euripides' play, Aphrodite herself complains:

> He will none of the bed of love nor marriage,
> but honors Artemis, Zeus's daughter...
> But for his sins against me
> I shall punish Hippolytus this day. (14–15; 21–22)

It is Aphrodite that causes the tragedy of the house of Theseus, in revenge against Hippolytus's rejection of her.

In Ferlita's formulation, Artemis is replaced (albeit only in passing reference) with the Virgin Mary—Hippolyte wants to become a priest and devote his life to Mary. It is not Aphrodite's vengeance that is to be feared, however, but Madeleine's (Medea). In the second scene, Phillipa and Eulalie, her slave/nurse discuss Jerome's previous wife and the tragedy she caused. Philippa worries that her feelings for her stepson might somehow be Madeleine's doing, that she is "reaching all the way from Haiti" to curse and destroy Jerome's new wife and family.[177] Eulalie calls desire "poison," calling to mind the poisons that Madeleine used on Corinne and Croydon.[178] Like her Greek counterpart, Phillipa is attracted to, and possibly in love with, her stepson, but unlike her Greek counterpart, she is not the victim of the goddess of love, but possibly of her husband's first wife.

Jules Corbey, Philippa's cousin from New York, arrives with new of the search for Jerome. He reports that the ship has been found disabled, stripped, and empty of cargo and people. Jerome's bloody and torn shirt was found on board. His report seemingly confirms that Jerome has been lost at sea. Unlike a Greek messenger, however, Jules is a family member, and furthermore desires to marry Andrea, who has been promised to Hippolyte. Ferlita thus further complicates the already complex family dynamic of the original. Jules, angered at being denied his love, not because of

Hippolyte but because of Jerome's desires decides to kill Jerome, should he ever return home.

Hippolyte confesses his concerns to his old tutor, Père Cousineau, a priest who encourages him to pursue ordination. In addition to his desire to become a priest, Hippolyte is concerned that his own ethnic background would complicate both his marriage and his status as his father's heir. His birth mother came to Paris from Martinique, a French colony in the Caribbean. She was an actress whom Jerome met in Paris when he arrived there from Haiti to complete his education. She was of mixed race descent—her father was French, but her mother was "colored, a mulatto or a quadroon or some such melange," Hippolyte surmises.[179] He never knew his mother, and is even unsure of her exact parentage, which complicates his legal position, even his status as a free person or human being. Jerome want Hippolyte to marry, so that his name will continue—he sees this son as a potential heir should Philippa and he never have a son. Hippolyte's illegitimate and possibly mixed race origins, however, make him a bad candidate: "In fact, I couldn't be his son and heir—not legally, I mean—if I had even the slightest trace of African blood."[180] It is his father's penchant for being licentious that most disturbs his chaste son, however—Hippolyte believes his father to be given to sins of the flesh, and is determined not to be like him

Believing her husband dead, Philippa announces her love to her stepson, unlike the Greek original, in which it is the nurse who reveals her mistress's feelings. Instead, Ferlita has Eulalie pray to Erzuli Freda, the *vodun* loa of love, to allow the match. When Hippolyte refuses and flees, it is Eulalie who instructs her mistress to act as if Hippolyte attempted to rape her, going so far as to tear her dress as if she had been in a struggle.

As in the original, the husband returns alive and well. Jerome had been captured by the pirate Jean Lafitte, but was rescued by the United States Navy. He has returned to his family. Phillipa and Eulalie relate their version of the attempted rape. When Hippolyte is first approached by his father, the son rebukes Jerome. But Jerome turns on his son, accusing him of hypocrisy and lust. Jerome argues that these qualities come from his mother: "I should've known—your tainted blood, your *mother's* blood, there was no keeping it down."[181] Jerome, unable to accept his own philandering ways, sees his son as being "tainted" from having African blood. Jerome the hypocrite is also revealed to be Jerome the racist—if his son has acted lustfully, it must be because of his African origins, despite the fact that Jerome is the only one in either play who has demonstrated philandering capacities. Hippolyte runs out as Jerome disowns him.

Jerome then discovers a letter from Philippa revealing both her love and her lie. The fate that has been set in motion, however, from the beginning of the drama must now be played out. Hippolyte takes White Fury, Jerome's fastest and most powerful horse, and rides out into the night. Mistaking him for Jerome, Jules shoots Hippolyte, mortally wounding him. The body is brought in and Père Cousineau shrives Hippolyte, granting him absolution before he dies. Jerome compares the death of Hippolyte to the death of his sons by Madeleine, finally acknowledging his own responsibility in the events: "I used him, as I did my other sons, for my own selfish ends."[182] Jerome, at the end of the two-play cycle that tells his story, realizes that he is a user: someone who has used his family to further his own needs and desires. He cast off Madeleine, who helped him escape Haiti, and in doing so lost his sons. He neglected his older son and newer wife by going off on an imperialist mission. Rather than being a provider he left on an adventure, leaving wife and son behind, expecting his son to marry the woman of his choice in order to have children and carry on the D'Argonne family name, in the event that Jerome had no other children, and despite the fact that the son wanted to be a priest. It was Jerome's selfishness as a European aristocrat bound on a series of ill-advised colonialist and imperialist adventures that caused not one but two families of his to be destroyed.

As noted above, *The Twice-Born* collapses the Medea myth and the Phaedra myth into a single family narrative. In doing so, Medea's revenge is undone, as it is not a complete revenge. By the end of the second play, however, that revenge is restored. At the end of the play, Eulalie carries in the body of Philippa, who slit her wrists and stabbed herself when she learned what she had done. As in *Black Medea*, Jerome has lost an entire family: wife and son are now dead. Although Ferlita never returns to the idea expressed by Philippa in the second scene, that her attraction to Hippolyte might be Madeleine's curse, the notion is never fully dismissed either. One might read *The Twice- Born* as a further meditation on the idea of French colonial arrogance and racism, which translates into American arrogance and racism. Madeleine's African origins and Hippolyte's mixed race origins means they are not recognized as citizens, or even human beings under New Orleans law. Although *gens libre de couleur*, their thoughts, desires, and actions are secondary to the whims of Jerome, the white, European aristocrat. Whereas Madeleine is a full-blooded African, it is Hippolyte's mixed blood that is the focus of the second play.

The problem of "mixed blood" as explored in this play is that identity is not visible on the surface, as it is in people who are clearly black or white. One can't tell that Hippolyte is of mixed race descent from outward signs. He can "pass" for white, and "passing" is a source of anxiety for whites—it destabilizes the notion of racial identity. In a system that acknowledges but two categories—black and white—a third category, a blend of the first two is not permitted. Thus all who are of mixed race descent are placed in the "black category," but one cannot always tell. In the third chapter I discussed the "one drop" rule, and the fears surrounding miscegenation. Ferlita's second play engages these themes. Mixed blood is seen as being "tainted"– someone who appears white actually has African roots. If *Black Medea* is about fear of voodoo and revolution, then *The Twice-Born* is about the fear of taint and "passing."

Correcting Myth and History: Silas Jones's American Medea

Of all the plays and productions considered in this volume, Silas Jones's *American Medea* fits the "Black Athena" model best. Jones himself has been very vocal about the nature of the myth and why he chose to adapt the play. In an interview with Celia Wren, Jones stated that, "I have always thought that *Medea* was an insult to all women—a woman who killed her own children to spite her ex-lover."[183] His adaptation sets out to correct what he sees as a number of Eurocentric, patriarchal, racist versions of the story. Writing in a letter to the author, Jones states:

> The idea that Greece used the African Medea only to bring sympathy for the plight of their super-hero, Jason; and that this savage woman loved this Greek sailor boy so much that she killed her own flesh and blood to spite him has always galled me to the core. African women are nature's mother [sic].[184]

For Jones, as one can gather from the above quotation, Medea is not Greek, and never has been Greek. She is African. "Medea is an African legend promulgated by Greece," he writes, "It is **not** Greek, and I am sick of seeing white women playing the role of Medea" [emphasis his].[185] Jones takes a direct "Black Athena" stance: Medea is African, and the Greeks used her.

Jones sees the Argonaut myth as actually referring to commerce between Greece and Africa: "The dark continent was dark because Medea helped Jason steal the Golden Fleece, the light of Africa, the cloak of knowledge."[186] The Fleece was from Colchis, but Colchis is not in Georgia, it is a metaphor for Africa.

American Medea, written in 1995 was workshopped at the Mark Taper Forum in Los Angeles in 1995 and again at the Arena Stage in Washington, D.C. in 1996. Its most recent production, as of this writing, was in April of 2002 at Seattle's Northwest Asian-American Theatre. Excepts from the play were published in *The Best Stage Scenes of 1995,* but the entire script remains unpublished.[187]

American Medea is set after the American Revolution at the Mount Vernon estate of George Washington in Virginia. The steps of Mount Vernon and the front of the slaves' cabin serve as the *skene,* in front of which the action unfolds. Just as Magnuson's version is about 1968 America and not 1820 Africa, Jones's play is about 1995 America and not 1790 Virginia. The play carries with it a contemporary sensibility, verging at times on the anachronistic, all in the name of distancing the familiar and familiarizing the distant for the purposes of critiquing modern America. In doing so, Jones argues he has not written an adaptation: "I believe I have written not a Greek translation or version of their version, but rather an African and an American tragedy."[188]

The cast of characters has also been significantly altered. Medea is "an African of Ethiopian descent," from Colchis. Jason, a Greek, is now half her age—she is in her fifties, he is twenty-eight. He is described as "a California Golden Boy," an anachronism at best. Their two sons are biracial, but look different from each other. Imhotep, the older, is "Medea's black son." Alexander is "Medea's white son." The nurse is Greek (unlike the Euripidean original, where she, too, is from Colchis) and has been given a name: Helen. There is also an African American slave, a woman named Delaware. Instead of Creon, Jones gives the audience "Prince Whipple," Washington's personal slave and "our 1st 'Oreo,'" the latter a slang term for someone who is black on the outside but white on the inside. Interestingly, the cast also includes Set, the Egyptian god, force of evil, and "expatriated murderer of his god-brother Osiris." The slave trade has reawakened Set who has come to America in search of pain and suffering.

The play opens with the Nurses's lament, which in this case states the play's "Black Athena" model and Afrocentric point of view immediately, and is hardly a lament:

> I have prayed for understanding. Surely the universe is godless. Homer described them as 'the most just of men—the favorite of the gods.' 'They are the tallest, most beautiful and long-lived of the human races." They were talking about the inventors of writing, the calendar, architecture, astronomy, mathematics, religion, government—civilization itself.[189]

Helen, the Nurse, who is Greek, speaks of the Egyptians. The lament is not about the tragedy of Medea leaving her home to join Jason, at least not initially. Instead, she celebrates Egyptian achievement, arguing the Greeks share her opinion. She continues:

> The wisest Greek citizens—Pythagoras, Herodotus, Solon, Aristotle, Democratist (sic), Plato, Eudoxus, Diodorus—all traveled to Africa to become initiates in the School of Great Mysteries. The Delphi from which we Greeks got our most sacred Oracles was founded in Egypt by the Ethiopian dynasty. Socrates got his famous phrase, "Man know thyself" from the Delphi priestesses of Egypt. We Greeks regarded the Ethiopes— the burnt faces—as models of civilization.[190]

The reader and audience are given a crash course in Afrocentric classicism at the beginning of Jones's play: all Greek culture is derived from Egyptian. That which is the best of Greece is not Greek at all, but African. Jones frames his play from a very different perspective than any other adaptation, demonstrating his "Black Athena" paradigm for using Greek tragedy to prove the Africanness of it.

Helen confesses to envy African women, who unlike Greek women have complete freedom. "Theirs was a matriarchal society," she confesses, "and the marriage agreement stipulated that the man must obey the wife in all things."[191] In other words, African culture is the exact opposite of Greek, which completely reverses the lament of Medea later in the play that women have no power and wives live oppressed lives. The world that Medea was born to, states Helen, was "A world in which to be black and female was doubly auspicious."[192] Jones demonstrates the radically different hierarchy in Africa, as opposed to the disempowerment of women in general and non–European women especially in both ancient Greece and modern America.

The Nurse's lament actually begins in the middle of the prologue, in which Helen informs the audience that Jason seduced Medea, who stole the Fleece for him, killed her brother, and abandoned Africa. As no country would offer a black witch refuge, Jason took her to colonial America. Jason, a white male, has adjusted very well, while Medea is horrified at the enslavement of Africans. Helen's prologue concludes metatheatrically, noting, "The stage is set for some new kind of drama ... perhaps the first true African/American tragedy."[193] This last line is self-referential, acknowledging the tragedy of slavery while positing the play being performed as the first true African American tragedy as it is not assimilationist and it acknowledges the true history of Africa.

Scene one begins with Jason sending Helen to fetch Medea. That his wife has taken up residence in the slave quarters is of concern to him. Helen refers to Washington as "King George," which Jason half-heartedly corrects. She prophesies to him, "We're in for a tragedy of Greek proportions," maintaining the metatheatrical nature of the play.[194] As she exits, Imhotep and Alexander, Jason and Medea's sons, enter.

Jason calls them the "dynamic duo from Hell," an anachronistic sentiment that both comments on their rambunctiousness and not so subtly sites the play within a contemporary sensibility. The tragedy is not about colonial America, it is a contemporary mythic engagement of the history of Africans in America. Jason wrestles with his sons in a fatherly way.

They, too, call Washington "King George." Jason instructs them: "President. You must address him as president. Or general, he likes being called general."[195] Jones takes an irreverent approach to Washington, who is never seen on stage, and to whom Medea later refers as "America's pin-up patron saint."[196] Washington is "The Father of His Country" in the popular imagination, but Jones exposes the ugly truth behind the omnipresent heroic image of America's first president.

George Washington owned slaves. The fact that he freed them in his will makes him no less a hypocrite for fighting for freedom for white Americans while owning black Americans. Most presentations of Washington ignore this fact, as well as his behavior and policy towards Native Americans, especially the Iroquois. Nor was he the only so-called "Founding Father" to own slaves.

Patrick "Give me liberty, or give me death!" Henry owned slaves. Thomas Jefferson owned 175 slaves—human beings of African descent—when he wrote that "all men are created equal; that they are endowed by their creator with certain unalienable rights; that among these are life, liberty, and the pursuit of happiness." Jones's play, more so than any other work considered in this study, deals with the legacy of slavery and racism and how they have shaped American culture and discourse into the present day.

Jason tries to convince his sons of the greatness of America when the boys confess to being confused why the slaves are segregated from the whites and why, in a land of plenty, the African Americans have a poor diet. He explains:

> Democracy isn't always democratic. Sometimes it's aristocratic, sometimes it's plutocratic, even pseudocratic sometimes. Here it's Americratic—separate but equal, so to speak. (beat) It's a new world concept. (beat) Greece wasn't built overnight, you know! (beat) Right?[197]

Jason's argument does not convince his sons, and it demonstrates the hollowness of the ideal when compared with the reality. America celebrates ancient Athens as an inspiration—the original democracy. The reality is that in both cultures only members of the property-owning elite class of citizens had rights, including the right to vote and a voice in the system of governance. Women and non-white (non–Greek) men had no rights or privileges and were not considered citizens, and sometimes not even human.

Imhotep states that history has shown there is no shame in being a slave—Aesop, "the African-Greek slave who rose to prominence as the most respected fablist of all time," he cites as an example of a slave whose glory outshone his master's.[198] Jason's response is to change the terms of the discussion. "Greece is dead," he tells his sons, "Long live America."

He asks his sons how many Greeks are slaves. They tell him none. All of the slaves are African: "Ammon, Osiris, Isis, Hercules, Venus, Hecate, Circe," all of whom are "mother's people."[199] Alexander then asks if the gods of Africa have thus abandoned their people. Jason tells him that they have—the gods have all gone to Greece and Africa is now "godless," a play on both the Christian construction of Africa as a land of godless heathen and Greece as having stolen all of Africa's gods. Imhotep states that they have an obligation to care for the "savages" of Africa, picking up on his father's rhetoric. Alexander asks why the Africans let the Greeks steal their gods. "We didn't steal them," Jason responds, "we borrowed them, changed their names and then they were sacrificed."[200] Greece stole, used and destroyed the gods of ancient Egypt, just as America stole, used, and destroyed Africans.

Helen enters in a panic as Jason sends the children away. Helen has been informed that she, a servant to Medea for her whole life, must now live in Washington's manor and Medea has decided to live in the slave quarters. She is a princess and a sorceress, but she feels her place is with the other Africans. Jason observes, "That woman has the power to enslave the world, yet she's powerless to escape her blackness."[201] Jason recognizes the racial discrimination, but refuses to do anything about it. The scene concludes with Jason complaining, "The slave quarters ... I hate her when she's ironic," once again displaying a self-aware metatheatricality.[202]

In scene two we see Jones splitting the role of Creon. In one sense, the present through his absence Washington fulfils the role of Creon—he distrusts Medea and her powers. Other characters report his orders and commands, and he has decided to deport Medea and her children back to Africa. He has no daughter with which to entice Jason away from his wife, but as the "Father of the Country," he can tempt Jason with that child— American citizenship.

The other Creon character is Prince Whipple, who is Washington's personal slave and the "first Oreo." He appears in a powdered wig and tights. His language echoes that of whites, but he uses a good deal of malaprops and invented words and borders on the absurd. He orders Delaware, another African American slave, to be Medea's new nurse. She refuses and tells him that if Washington forces her to she will no longer visit his bed.

Whipple tells her to "debitchify your tongue," calls her a "contratious factorum" and states that the other slave women would be happy to "conjugate [Washington's] desire."[203] His favorite expression, repeated many times during the course of the play, is "Heavens to Caucasoids!" Delaware responds that Whipple is a slave just like her, so should not be putting on airs. "I servant, you slave," he tells her.

He explains that Helen can no longer be Medea's nurse because in America white women don't serve black women. Jason enters and sends Delaware to fetch Medea. While he waits, it is clear Prince Whipple is uncomfortable and uncertain how to behave. Jason casually asks if he is Washington's "belly warmer," and then sings a song implying that Washington uses Whipple for anal sex. Whipple retreats in shock and horror. Delaware returns to say Medea won't come, but that he can go to her. She then tells Jason that he is "one pretty dog" and that she "wouldn't mind you crossing my Delaware," thus providing the punchline for the earlier reference to her sharing Washington's bed.[204]

In the third scene, the audience finally meets Medea. She is in the slave quarters, tired, moaning and "dressed like a common slave." She comes outside in response to Jason's summons, calling him "my eternally youthful little love machine." She commands him, "Sit, you slut, and lie to your haggard wife."[205] The play presents another reversal from the Greek original—rather than the sexuality of Medea, it is the sexuality of Jason that becomes the focus.

She asks if their children are safe. Jason tells her that Washington is fond of Alexander, earning the reply, "That's goddamn white of him," turning the racist compliment into a slur of both Washington and European-Americans.[206] Jason and Medea argue about America—she argues that slave women suckle white children—their future masters: "The milk of Africa flows in their masters' bones yet they pay homage to Greece," she charges.[207] He tells her she looks like Medusa. "I have been feeling a little African lately," she states. "And I American," he responds.

Medea proclaims that Africa will rise, even as Jason proclaims its golden age over. She tells him she will leave him and he denies the possibility. "America is Jason's fate and loving Jason is Medea's," he brags.[208] "That's your version," she reassures him, "the tragic Greek version. You've had your plays, this is Medea's tragedy."

Medea also "plotted" the tragedy of the original. In one sense Medea serves as her own playwright, shaping the narrative to end the way she sees it, not as Jason and Creon have. Yet the reality is that playwright, actor, and majority of original audience all were men from the privileged class. Jones has Medea metatheatrically rewriting her own story so that it reflects the reality of Afrocentric classicism.

Medea warns Jason that she has sensed a powerful god lurking in America. "He has a plan for a bold new world order. Here destinies will be color-coded."[209] The prophesy refers both to the New World of America and to the phrase of President George Bush the first, invoked during the Gulf War to insinuate that nations will work together to overcome rogue states, but quickly interpreted to mean that America would throw its global weight around and expect other nations to fall in line—a new imperialism. The "color-coded" destinies is similar to the idea of fate as expressed in *Darker Face of the Earth*—that fate is not supernaturally determined, but rather shaped by social and cultural factors from birth, in this case, ethnicity.

Jason proclaims his love, but Medea tells him that he loved the Golden Fleece, not her. "Aunt Circe warned me: Beware of Gifts bearing Greeks," she puns.[210] As they reminisce about their early sex life she asks, "Had I been Greek, Jason, would you have screwed me so royally?"[211] Jones relies upon humor and irony throughout the script to indict the West for its behavior towards Africa and Africans. "I spoilt you," Medea tells Jason, she should have taught him his place in "the web of life" instead of allowing him to dwell on his own sense of importance. What Medea says to Jason, Jones says (on behalf of Egypt) to the west: you have made yourself the center when you are only one small part of the whole.

The Golden Fleece, she tells him, is actually the fabled "Cloak of Knowledge"—"the one who shoulders the cloak shall earn the right to mind the world," the legends say.[212] Jason had thought they had lost the Fleece in Corinth, but Medea explains that she lied to him and has had it all along. She plans on returning it to Africa, where it belongs and from whence it was stolen. Jason argues that she gave it to him and thus is, by rights, his. She counters that she gave him two sons—one he thought looked too African, so she gave him one "in his own image." The Fleece comes from the sacred ram of Ra, the Egyptian sun god, and belongs to Africa, not Greece. "Greece never claimed me; only blamed me, shamed me," she tells him.[213]

At the start of the next scene Helen again narrates the action. She claims she is a servant by class, not by race, but since Washington has freed her she does not know what to do. She also informs the audience that the slave ship "Salvation" (again, the name is ironic), which had been chartered to take Medea back to Africa sank off Barbados when its cargo of Ashanti slaves mutinied, set fire to the ship, and jumped "overboard into the mouths of waiting sharks."

Alexander spends all of his time with Washington. Imhotep spends all his time playing with slave children. They enter fighting and Helen separates them, telling them that brothers do not fight. Alexander denies Imhotep is his brother, claiming that they have different fathers. Alexander asserts that he is Greek. Helen tells them, "You are the sons of a Greek and an African," but Imhotep demands the Rite of Outcast. Alexander agrees and Helen is duty bound to witness. Alexander swears by Zeus, Imhotep swears by Osiris and they "release all blood ties" to each other.[214] Neither may claim the other as brother again.

In the following scene, Helen sneaks into the slave cabin at night to tell Medea about her children. She asks Medea why Medea does not use her powers, to which Medea informs her that Set is in America. She fears that he will work powerful evil if she uses her magic. The Rite of Outcast concerns her, and she decides she must act.

The sixth scene begins with Medea standing before the mansion of MountVernon yelling for Jason. A man appears in shadows at the entrance to the house and tells her to leave. She taunts him, calling him "boy". When he claims he is "the father of this country," she warns him to be careful what he wishes for.[215]

The man who claims to be Washington orders her back to her cabin. He informs her that Jason and Alexander have been made American citizens and will stay, and she and Imhotep must leave. Medea states that she will take both sons with her. Washington denies her that wish. He condemns her as a "Hamite" and tells her that slavery is "God's curse upon your race."[216] She calls him ignorant, a "second class savage," and asks him "who gave you the right to mind the world?"[217]

The man declares her private property and his slave. She waves her hand and he drops, revealing that it is Prince Whipple and not Washington. Sometimes those who work most strongly against the interests of African Americans, warns Jones, are other African Americans who have either bought into Eurocentrism or who see enslaving their people as a way of furthering themselves. Either way, such people are destructive and self-destructive.

Medea then addresses the audience in Jones's version of the warning to the women of the city:

> A gaggle of old white men in wigs
> With rouged cheeks ruled

All white men are equal.
And so they are. Sisters,
Beware, lest you fall prey to this
Perverse equality
Spawned by frail males in opportune times.[218]

Rather than an exhortation to disempowered wives of Athenian husbands, Jones's Medea warns women of color to beware of old men in drag dictating the terms of their lives. She curses America for making a whore of Africa and summons Set to wreak her revenge on the New World. She commands him to "Degreek the myth."

Set, the Egyptian god of evil and the night, the Egyptian Satan, is traditionally depicted as a scaled humanoid with the head of a jackal. In Jones's play his manifestation is described as:

> a monstrous creation ... an enormous deconstructed symbol of evil ancient and prophetic. He is a decadent, androgynous, obese boar hog with rings in his ears, red fishnet stockings, platform shoes, a steel cup bra and a mini skirt. His snout is lipstick red, his mane set in prink curlers, with eyelashes so long they obscure his beady red eyes. Standing erect, he is vulgarity incarnate.[219]

On one level, Set is not only the incarnation of evil and vulgarity, his dress is obviously designed to invoke female sexuality, thus making him the incarnation of evil sexuality. Set is the inverse of Medea. Whereas her sexuality is presented in the play as healthy and balanced, his is vulgar and obscene.

Set informs Prince Whipple that slave ships brought him from Egypt. The "Christians" of the slave trade freed him from the tomb where "Horus, the first Christ, son of Osiris" had buried him. The obscenity of the New World gave him power, and in return, he shares his blessings. He points out the pyramid and eye of Horus on the dollar bill and calls it "my promise."

Set pronounces a curse on America. A series of slides accompany his pronouncements, showing an ancient map, Presidents Reagan (called "the Prince of Smarm") and Bush the first (called "Left-handed Vice [who] routs reason"). When the signs that Set has prophesied come to pass, Set will rule America himself.

The next scene begins with Medea in a white ritual costume, "her face is painted white except for the eyes, which are painted red with the Egyptian hieroglyphic symbol for 'weep.'"[220] She screams for Jason, who enters and accuses her of using her magic on Prince Whipple who now believes he is Washington and that the events in the Book of Revelation are coming true. Medea tells him that America has become too much like Greece:

"The gods from Mount Olympus will sit atop Mount Rushmore," she proclaims, "This is the new Greece..."[221] She then informs him that she has decided to "make him a metaphor" in revenge for his betrayal.

He tells her to run, that Washington is sending troops to kill her. She laughs and tells him only one who loves her can kill her. She holds "the double pointed wisdom tooth of the Colchis hydra," an invention of Jones's found nowhere in Greek mythology. Jason seizes the weapon and tries to stab her with it. She stops his arm, predicting a dire future when African Americans will "baptize the streets" in the blood of "suicidal black boys," a reference to the continual violence and black on black crime in the eighties and nineties. Jones's play, written in 1995, traces the current state of race relations and the condition of the African American people as a tragedy rooted in the colonial beginnings of the country.

Jason stabs her and runs into the mansion. She removes the weapon, stands up and declares herself finally free. His wound did not kill her. Either he did not love her (which she said he did not) or she created a ruse of her own death so that she might be free to leave and fight against America. Alexander bursts in and seizing the weapon, stabs her as Imhotep enters from the mansion, announcing that Jason has opened the trunk wherein she keeps the Fleece.

Imhotep then stabs his brother with the tooth, killing him. Medea begs him to reverse the Rite of Outcast, and he embraces Alexander, the double-pointed weapon piercing his heart as well. Jones thus exonerates Medea of the crime of infanticide, of killing her own children. Instead, they kill each other, a metaphor for the state of race relations in America. Jones rejected the idea of an African mother murdering her own children, as noted above, so their deaths are no longer on her, nor are they part of her revenge on Jason. In a sense, this makes them more tragic, in the common sense, as their deaths are inadvertent to the main action.

Medea calls on Isis and Osiris to bring her into the afterworld. Helen enters, covers the children with a cloak, and, bidding Medea farewell, exits. Jason bursts in from the mansion, wearing the cloak. It has made him completely black—he is now an African American. Thus Jones transforms Medea's revenge from the murder of his new wife and old children (although his children do die) to metamorphosing him into a black man in colonial America. Having been given Medea's eternal youth and eternal life, he will live through slavery, Reconstruction, Jim Crow, segregation, the struggle for civil rights and the urban violence of the sixties through the nineties. As in Euripides, Medea's revenge is to reduce Jason to the state he reduced her to—in this case, a slave in America. He cries out "Eureka!" to the heavens as the stage goes dark.

Jones's play is a true model of the "Black Athena" paradigm. The play is used to assert the primacy of Egypt over Greece. America is presented as the "new Greece"—a nation state that sees itself as the center of the world and a people that have stolen what they have from Africa. Jones relies on humor and irony to critique contemporary America, Eurocentric classicism, and the abuse of Africa and Africans. He also uses these elements to deconstruct national myths. As Euripides deconstructed myths to critique Athenian society and to show the reality behind the heroic presentations of Sophocles and Aeschylus, Jones deconstructs Euripides to critique American society and show the reality behind the heroic myths of Washington and "All men are created equal."

Jones's play works as a corrective for the patriotic and heroic presentation of American history in the educational system, popular culture, and in our national self-portraits. As Nathan Huggins pointed out that the freedom of America that we celebrate was based on the unfreedom of others, Jones indicates that our legacy is not one of our ideals, but one of oppression and theft, one for which African Americans are still paying the price.

The world of colonial America that Jones presents on the stage still has reverberations in the present. As of this writing, major ongoing controversy over Thomas Jefferson and his legacy continues to make the news. In 1913 the Monticello Association was founded to preserve the grounds of the estate and the family cemetery, and connect Jefferson's descendants to each other. Its only membership qualification is direct descent from Thomas Jefferson. It currently has about 800 members. Only proven direct descendants of Thomas Jefferson may be buried in the cemetery at Monticello.

In 1998, DNA tests revealed that a male in Jefferson's family, possibly Thomas Jefferson himself, fathered a son by Jefferson's slave Sally Hemings, with whom Jefferson was alleged to have had an affair. African American descendants of Heming's last son contended that they are therefore, as direct descendants of Jefferson, entitled to be buried in Monticello Cemetery. While some members welcomed this branch of the family, a movement within the Monticello Association contended that Jefferson and Hemings were never lovers and commissioned another DNA study that "proved" via DNA testing in 2000 that Jefferson's younger brother Randolph Jefferson is the more likely father of Heming's last son.

By means of a compromise, the leaders of the Monticello Association proposed a plan "to create a separate but distinct heritage organization for descendants of Jefferson's slaves that could build its own burial plot."[222] Jefferson's African American descendants refer to such a plan as segregationist, and the "separate but distinct" description of the offered organization and cemetery is highly suggested of the "separate but equal" clause that allowed for segregation to continue in the United States until Brown vs the Board of Education struck down segregated schooling. David Works, a seventh generation grandson of Jefferson was quoted as saying, "It will be an equal partnership, not like we're the guys in the big house and they're the folks out in the field."[223] Unfortunately for Works, however, by creating a "separate but distinct heritage organization for descendants of Jefferson's slaves" with a separate but equal burial plot, that is exactly what it is like. The wording of the plan does not even concede Jefferson as the ancestor, but rather than being descended from "Jefferson's slaves" is the qualifying condition.

This condition, of course, raises the question of why a "separate but distinct" organization is needed for the descendants of Jefferson's slaves when no other such organizations or conditions exist for others linked to Jefferson. The white descendants of Randolph Jefferson, for example, cannot join the Monticello Association. Nor can the descendants of Jefferson's other relatives. In creating a "separate but distinct" organization, the Monticello Association tacitly admits that the descendants of Sally Heming's last son have a claim to the Jefferson heritage, but it is not as legitimate or equal to that of the white descendants. The world Jones presents on stage is sadly reflected in this controversy, and shows how far we have not progressed in two hundred years, as well as how the more we celebrate how much things have changed, the less likely it is that they have.

Women are Now in Charge: The Medea Project

In 1979 Idris Ackamoor founded Cultural Odyssey in San Francisco, an alternative performance and production company dedicated to the idea of the arts as social activism. In 1983 Rhodessa Jones, a singer, dancer, actress, writer, teacher, and director, joined as Co-Artistic Director of the company. During a 1989 residency at the San Francisco County Jail Jones developed the idea of working with female inmates to write and perform their own theatre pieces for fellow inmates and invited audiences. In 1992 the Medea Project: Theatre for Incarcerated Women had its first performance, which included an adaptation of the Medea story.

Rena Fraden chronicles the Medea Project in her book *Imagining Medea*. According to Fraden, the "key act of the Medea project" is "to make visible what has been repressed and oppressed," which is precisely what Medea herself did.[224] Medea, the outsider, the woman, the foreigner—all repressed, silenced groups in ancient Athens—made visible that repression through her terrible revenge and gave voice to the silenced.

During Jones's residency, she met a woman who had killed her own child. Reminded of Euripides' play, Jones brought the play in for the inmates to read. They would not open the book, let alone agree to mount the play. As Fraden reports, "Performing the classic in a classical way just was not going to work."[225]

Jones had planned on creating a piece of theatre to be written and performed by the inmates called *Reality is Just Outside the Window* and she wanted to include a version of the Medea story that incorporated the convicts' response to Jones's telling them the story and relating it to their lives. Fraden reports, "The Medea story is about a woman held subject and her struggle to break free."[226] They cite Medea's rage, her separation from family, her judgement by a society that sees her as criminal and barbaric, her self destructive and other-destructive behavior, the fact that she both sinned and was sinned against, and her giving into her passions as similarities between themselves and the Greek character.

With the input of Jones and the inmates, playwright Edris Cooper wrote *There Are Women Waiting: The Tragedy of Medea Jackson*, a brief adaptation of *Medea* that was part of the larger performance entitled *Reality is Just Outside the Window*, which also incorporated autobiographical pieces created by the inmates. As Tiffany Lopez summarizes, "Each Medea Project production results from a collaborative process that incorporates Greek mythology, hip-hop music, and autobiography."[227] The subsequent productions all invoke Greek myth. The second piece, 1993's *Food Taboos in the Land of the Dead* (whose title refers to a chapter in a book on mythology that Jones read) dealt with the myth of Persephone and Demeter. *Slouching Towards Armageddon: A Captive's Conversation/Observation on Race*, produced in 1999, originated in the myth of Pandora.[228]

Cooper states that she did not "attempt to reinvent anything other than putting the language in San Francisco street jargon."[229] She does not see her play as particularly Greek, noting "The adaptation became specifically African American and San Franciscan."[230] In the initial production, Cooper also played Medea.

The play within the performance is a comparatively short piece that follows Euripides' narrative fairly closely, leaving out the supernatural elements and transculturating the play to late twentieth century, lower class, urban San Francisco.[231] Medea and Jason are both African American, although the Creon character is white. The play is less about interracial struggle than it is centered on Medea and the choices she makes and the opportunities denied her by her gender, ethnicity, or situation.

The play opens with the cast singing "You Make Me Feel Like a Natural Woman." Medea, we are told by the Nurse, fell in love with Jason, quit going to school, got a job, gave up her kids, and spends all her money on him. Now he's sleeping with a white woman who is the daughter of their landlord.

Medea is first heard offstage, as in Euripides, and her speech, packed with obscenities and references to public figures with reputations for using and abusing women expresses the contempt she feels for her former lover:

> (Offstage) Motherfucking bastard! You Clarence Thomas, David Duke, Wilt Chamberlain, William Kennedy Smith-looking ass nigger! Son of a bitch motherfucker. I hope your dick falls off!

She enters complaining of Jason and his treatment of her. Cooper moves very quickly to Medea's imploring of the women in the audience:

> Y'all women; you know how it is. Look how we're treated. First of all, we always doing everything for our men and in return what do we get? Fucked! And most niggas feel that's payment. I did everything I was supposed to do. I cooked *dinner*. I cooked *rocks*. I even cooked in *bed*. But you know it's hard to find a good man with a job that won't beat you, that won't fuck around, and that'll be nice to your kids.

As Euripides' Medea talked to her audience in terms they would understand and recognize about the plight of women in their culture, so, too, does Cooper's Medea use the language and situations familiar to her audience.

Creon the landlord arrives and kicks Medea and her kids out of their house "cause you crazy, woman." He gives her one day "to get your kids and shit together" and get out. His daughter is the one sleeping with Jason. Medea, like her Greek forebear, tells the chorus that she will get Creon, his daughter, and Jason. "He done fucked with the wrong bitch now."

Aegeus enters, a drag queen who "got a sister I know who would be glad to hole up if you know what I mean." Like Euripides, the figure of the king (or in this case, queen) offers sanctuary. Again, the drag queen is a familiar and recognizable transculturation of the character into the San Francisco environment.

Medea gets "a beautiful teddy and a sexy g-string" that she laces with crystal meth, PCP, and heroin, all very strong street drugs that will most likely cause her to overdose and die. She sends her children to Jason with the gift, announcing that when they return "we are going to celebrate with some Jim Jones Koolaid," a reference that carries particular resonance in San Francisco as the People's Temple drew a large number of their converts, many of whom were lower-income African Americans from the San Francisco area.

The children return and the "sounds of hell" are heard swelling offstage. A news voiceover reports, "young, black teenagers are reported to be the oldest and the newest creature to be added to the endangered species list." Medea then kills the children, now represented by puppets, so that they will not "fall into the murderous hands of those that love them less than I do."" Many of the women working on the show had families on the outside, children who were motherless because of their incarceration. These women understood loving children so much that one would rather kill them than see them sent through Social Services. Like Morrison's *Beloved* or the historic Margaret Garner, Cooper interprets the killing of the children as an act of love.

The major change in Cooper's narrative, is that Medea does not escape. Indeed, in a theatre production in prison, she could not get away with her actions. A voiceover announces, "Medea Jackson, we have a warrant for your arrest" after Medea has thrown herself into the arms of the chorus. The chorus then begins to chant repeatedly, "She died like this."

Fraden sees this ending as having been created so that "a different beginning may be imagined. Women are now in charge of retelling the story."[232] Even in Silas Jones's pro-woman of color version, the play is ultimately being created by a man, just as in the Euripidean original. It is interesting that only in the two workings of Medea material by women—*Beloved* and *The Tragedy of Medea Jackson*—does Medea kill for love of the children rather than hatred of Jason. Ferlita, Magnuson, and Carter, after Euripides, posit revenge as the reason the children die. Jones has the children kill each other. Only Morrison and Cooper have the children die by the mother's hand in order to protect them.

Of course, *The Tragedy of Medea Jackson* is only one of the two uses that Jones and company make of the myth of Medea. The entire project is named after her, a way of recovering Medea from those male writers and siting the women in prison as Medeas themselves. Medea, in this case, is not a negative construction, as it was when *Harper's Weekly* invoked the Greek myth to indict Margaret Garner. Instead, Medea is a woman who, by virtue of her choices and situation, found herself criminalized, and, as Beah Richards indicated, needs to examine, evaluate, and recreate herself. Medea is a positive model for the reintegration of women prisoners into society, a model designed to ensure the chances of recidivism are low indeed.

The Tragedy of Medea Jackson, on the one hand, follows the "Black Orpheus" paradigm: Euripides' story is simply transculturated into contemporary San Francisco with the attendant language and character-type changes. Yet, as Fraden points out, "the pedagogical thrust of the Medea

Project is aimed at uncovering the connections between an individual and the system of power."[233] In that sense, the Medea Project follows the "Black Dionysus" paradigm—it uses the Greek myth to critique and question both the individual reasons why a woman is in prison and the socioeconomic and cultural indicators that also influence her life. Rather than entertainment, or an intellectual exercise, the Medea Project uses Greek myth and tragedy to empower oppressed and repressed women.

Fraden argues that "Jones's theatre, like the classical Greek, wants to make the audience the judge, reacting in horror to the violations of civilization and in sympathy with a critique of it."[234] Jones follows in the footsteps of Euripides, giving voice to the voiceless. Unlike Euripides, writing from a position of power, Jones works with the voiceless, so that the voice that is heard is not hers, but theirs.

E Pluribus Unum ... Medea

This chapter began with a consideration of the Margaret Garner case and concluded with an analysis of the Medea Project. In both cases, the focus is on women of color who have been criminalized by their actions in a context of oppression, but are much more the victims of white patriarchy and a system designed to keep black women subjugated. In both cases, it is the body of the woman of color, as Medea is embodied on stage, that becomes the focus and the means of overcoming the oppression.

In his analysis of Noble's painting, Albert Boime argues that the painting actually privileges Garner. He observes that the space is hers, and the white men are entering it. Her defiant gesture towards the bodies on the floor sets up an inverted triangle of bodies, slavers, and Garner whose action is one of empowerment and defiance: "The violation of her space sets into motion the exercise of her power to defeat the system of slavery by denying the slavers black bodies to oppress."[235] In this interpretation, Garner's tragedy is much like Medea's: not tragic at all in that she chooses to do what she does in defiance of those who would oppress her, and in doing so demonstrates great power.

The bodies of women involved on stage in the Medea Project are bodies that no longer belong to their owners. The San Francisco County Jail literally controls the bodies of the inmates—enclosing them in small cells, determining when and what they eat, when and how they exercise, etc. On stage, it is the physical presence of the inmate actresses that creates the performance, and, in doing so, draws attention to the inscribing of the body by prison and by stage. By creating with their bodies, the inmates also set in motion the exercise of power to defeat the system. Their voices no longer silenced, their bodies not bound by cells (but rather by the stage), the inmates can tell their own stories and take control of their lives, like the theatrical adaptations which present a character that takes control of her body and her life.

As with the motto on American currency, out of many emerges one Medea. Beginning in the mid-twentieth century, with the rise of feminist and postcolonialist cultures, Medea began to be seen as an empowered woman. As a result, though this chapter has explored numerous variations and seen numerous differences in the portrayal of Medea and her context, the ultimate result in often the same: a critique of Eurocentric colonialist culture which disempowers and disenfranchises women of color.

With the exception of *Pecong* and *The Tragedy of Medea Jackson*, which present both Jason and Medea as being of African descent, all other versions considered in this chapter present a white Jason and a black Medea. Indeed, part of what makes the tragedy so readily transculturated into an American context is that the two main characters are already of two different ethnicities. The male is of the ruling class, of the dominant culture, and in his home culture. Medea has been taken from her family and her culture, and lives a stranger in a foreign land that neither values nor respects her. The play is centered around a conflict of an outsider's seeming powerlessness against a seemingly all-powerful group of insider men, the revenge that oppression has caused bursting forth from the heroine once she has been pushed too far.

Even including *Pecong* and *Medea Jackson*, and thereby losing the racial conflict, all of the plays present women who resist being dominated by the men in their lives. Women who use language and violence as men do, and, in doing so, not only take control of their lives, but also avenge the wrongs that the men have done with them. Medea (in her original incarnation and all adaptations) is the original *Thema and Louise*, except she lives to celebrate her escape.

All Medeas from the modern period are, in a sense, revolutionaries. They take control of their situation and fight back against the white patriarchal culture. Magnuson's Medea, Ferlita's Medea, Silas Jones's Medea, and Rhodessa Jones's Medea all strike back against the men who would control them. Although their purposes all differ, their structures, characters, language, and narratives all significantly differ, all playwrights who adapt Euripides' play have one thing in common and that is Medea.

Medea is such a strong character that regardless of her exact geographical origins, her ethnicity, or her social level, she is a fairly static character, in that she does not change much from environment to environment. *Medea* is the most adapted play in the African Diaspora outside of the continent (on the continent it loses to *Antigone*, another play with a strong heroine who does not change much from adaptation to adaptation) and all Medeas are remarkably similar. Out of the many black Medeas on the stages of America, one dominant model emerges: a strong, empowered woman who stands against racism and sexism and fights by any means necessary to gain justice.

5

Mediterranean/Caribbean, or Odysseus Looks for Home

Where are your monuments, your battles, martyrs?
Where is your tribal memory? Sirs,
in the grey vault. The sea. The sea
has locked them up. The sea is History.

Derek Walcott
"The Sea is History"

Ocean, who is the source of all.

Homer
The Iliad
Book XIV: 246

He who commands the sea has command of everything.

Themistocles

In his survey of Caribbean literature in *African Forum*, West Indian author George Lamming argues that West Indian (English-speaking Carribbea) society is in a state of transition, learning to define itself as a complete culture "in a context of diluted slavery." This context is not unlike the legacy of slavery in the United States, which continues to not only profoundly impact the lives of millions, but remains a point of contention in national discourse.[1]

Lamming further argues, however, that it is not only Africa that Caribbean writers must look to, but also to North and South America and the peoples of African descent living there. The Caribbean, he claims, must "be understood in relationship to the development of civilization in the Americas."[2] Thus, although a chapter on Caribbean theatre may seem initially out of place in a book on African American theatre and the way in which Greek cultural material has been used in reference to African-America, there are actually several reasons why this book closes with a chapter linking Caribbean use of Greek myth, epic, and tragedy to the larger topic.

As I started the survey of African American Greek tragedy with an exploration of cultural continuity between Africa and America, the Caribbean is a part of the larger Americas that made up the western corner of the "Triangular Trade." Scholars such as Paul Gilroy and Joseph Roach have demonstrated the strong links in the so-called "Black Atlantic." As Gilroy indicates, "A new structure of cultural exchange has now been built up across the imperial networks which once played to the triangular trade of sugar, slaves, and capital."[3] The Black Atlantic is a "transcultural, international formation" consisting of the United Kingdom, Africa, the Caribbean, Brazil, and North America, which constitutes the majority of African diaspora culture in the world.[4] As the nations and cultures of the Caribbean are an integral part of this cultural formation, I would be remiss in ignoring its similar use of Greek cultural material when considering African American practice.

As noted above, the shared experience of slavery gives African Americans and African-Caribbeans not only a similar history but also a shared sense of identity. Both groups are of African descent, but living outside the Motherland. Both groups have suffered a rupture with their individual and cultural pasts, leading to a lost sense of identity. The individual and collective struggles of the Caribbean people of color are in many ways the same as those of African Americans.

Furthermore, beginning in the 1960s American and Caribbean reciprocal cultural exchanges have grown, in part due to a recognition of common grounds and origins and in part because of a more mobile population that now shares roots or communities in both locations. The theatre has not lagged behind in these exchanges.

The universities, schools, amateur and professional theatre groups in the Caribbean look to both African-America and Africa for material to present on stage. The University of the Virgin Islands Little Theatre, for example, has presented numerous plays by African American authors, such as Douglas Turner Ward's *Day of Absence* in 1971, James Baldwin's *The Amen Corner* in 1974, and August Wilson's *Fences* in 1997. Plays by Soyinka and Fugard have also been presented by the Little Theatre, in addition to western classics and indigenous drama.

David Edgecomb, playwright, director, and Director of the Reichhold Center for the Arts at the University of the Virgin Islands in St. Thomas argues that insularity is the "malady that continues to plague Caribbean theatre."[5] Edgecomb is one of a growing number of theatre artists committed to developing a Pan-Caribbean theatre. Among his five suggestions to improve Caribbean theatre he includes the encouragement of serious, critical evaluation of theatre in the Caribbean.[6] This chapter is, therefore, in part, a response to that call.

Lastly, in 1992 Caribbean poet and playwright Derek Walcott, who divides his time between Boston and Saint Lucia and whose plays have been extensively presented in the United States, won the Nobel Prize for Literature. Walcott, throughout his entire career, has employed Greek epic, myth, and tragedy as source material and has voiced strong opinions about the use of Greek (and other Eurocentric) material by writers of African descent. His importance and significance as a playwright demand analysis and discussion in any consideration of Greek tragedy and the African diaspora.

This chapter begins with an analysis of the hybrid nature of Caribbean culture and Caribbean identity. Then, production and adaptation of Greek tragedies in the Caribbean are considered, including exploring the major themes of exile and odyssey/homecoming and the importance of the sea in linking the two cultures of ancient Greece and twentieth-century Caribbean. Lastly, in a separate section, Derek Walcott's use of Greek material is considered.

Poseidon, Odysseus, and Caribbean Greek Tragedy

To speak of "The Caribbean" is to assign common qualities and to speak of a homogeneity which does not take into account the huge differences in culture(s) both within and without the geographical region. The islands of the Caribbean make up a two thousand mile arc in a tropical sea with a variety of cultures intermingling in different amounts dependant on location and history. Indigenous cultures (and the peoples who created them) remain present: Taino, Siboney, Carib, and Arawak, to name but a few, still have a cultural presence despite the best attempts of the colonizers to eliminate indigenous culture. The "intrusion of European culture and peoples" during the colonial period brought in the languages, cultures, economies, and genes of the Spanish, French, English, and Dutch, who also brought with them as slaves individuals (and attendant cultures, languages, beliefs, etc.) from a number of African nations, including the Ashanti, the Congo, the Yoruba, the Ibo, and others from the west coast of Africa.[7] This polyglot of influence and origin has produced shifting cultures in the Caribbean, unstable and in flux, the product of many influences. We should note that European powers and African and indigenous peoples' powerlessness during the colonial years led to an unequal distribution of economic, social, and political power after independence. This inequality continues to profoundly shape the choices (or lack thereof) that develop Caribbean culture. The legacy of colonialism privileges the European aspects of Caribbean culture, including and especially the choice of language (English, Spanish, and French) and the forms of performance.

Despite this, perhaps even more than in the rest of the Americas, the Caribbean people have maintained contact with African cultural survivals as part of a larger *bricolage* of culture. This *bricolage* extends to every part of Caribbean life: arts, language, religion, and material culture. Even in Cuba, where the government of Fidel Castro (unofficially) discourages religious practice, seventy percent of the citizens practice some form of *Santeria*. This local religion is similar to *voudun* which has at its core the Yoruba-based Orisha tradition and combines elements of Christianity (specifically Catholicism) with the practices of Orisha worship and, as Masland and Larmer explain, "speaks to their deeper Cuban identity."[8] As "Cuban identity" is constructed from a combination of Spanish Catholicism, Yoruban practice, and indigenous sacred sites and beliefs, one can see it as representative of the complex and multi-origin nature of Caribbean culture. We may (indeed, we must) critique the colonial capitalist culture that imposed slavery and Catholicism on both Africans ripped from their homelands to be imported for slavery and indigenous Caribbean peoples also forced to work and evicted from their land for the enrichment of the European imperialists. However, it was this terrible history that has resulted in the *bricolage* culture.

As Stuart Hall notes in his essay "Cultural Identity and Diaspora," the Caribbean identity is formed from a variety of presences: African, European, indigenous American, and even the presence of Chinese, Indian, and Lebanese identities/cultures.[9] To further complicate the issue, the Caribbean is also a place of absences of these same presences and a place of displacement: Arawaks, Caribs, and other Amerind peoples have been displaced, and in some cases literally eradicated by the colonizers and colonial culture, but also by the cultures of the enslaved.[10] We must also beware against assuming a homogeneity of identity, culture, and experience among Caribbean peoples, even on an existential ground: "common history—transportation, slavery, colonization—...does not constitute a common origin," warns Hall.[11] Instead, we should note the shifting points of origin and the shifting contemporary boundaries of Caribbean culture and identity.

The people(s) of the Caribbean have a variety of possible cultural identities and thus no one set cultural identity.

Hall himself identifies Derrida's notion of *différance* (suspending the world (and the word) between "differ" and "defer," and thus allowing for the "infinite postponement of meaning"), as being particularly apt for the Caribbean, in which no one cultural identity maintains hold, as the blend of cultures is constant and unstable.[12] Thus, there are diverse origins, even within the diverse origins of the Caribbean peoples. While difference can be used for exploitive purposes—for example, the physical and cultural differences between Europeans and Africans being used as justification by the Europeans to enslave Africans—difference is also the product of a variety of sources, which creates strengths—for example, the more genetic sources an individual has the stronger the immune system, whereas inbreeding prompts weakness.

Judy Stone identifies five streams within contemporary Caribbean drama: social realism (plays that reflect the social and economic reality of the working classes), popular theatre (plays by and for the people, including all manner of folk plays), total theatre (including musical extravaganzas and Carnival), classical theatre (plays which adapt western classics to Caribbean settings), and ritual theatre (plays that either employ or are part of religious rituals, such as public rites of *Santeria/voudon*/Obeah, Catholic processions, etc.).[13] The borders that delineate the differences between these types of drama can be, and frequently are, blurred. Much like Caribbean cultural identity is unstable and in flux, shifting between different axes, so, too, can Caribbean drama move back and forth between these (arbitrary) divisions. For the purposes of this study, the fourth category, or "classical" drama is of concern.

In the category of "plays that adapt Western classics to Caribbean settings," there are the inevitable adaptations of Shakespeare and Molière, as well as adaptations of less common source material such as Synge (Mustapha Matura's *The Playboy of the West Indies*), Tirso de Molina (Walcott's *The Joker of Seville*), and many others. In all of these plays a synthesis exists between Western, African, and indigenous cultures, even down to the language of adaptation. As Morgan Dalphinis observes, "While the vocabulary of Caribbean literature is from European languages, the language structures in which this vocabulary is used is of African origins."[14] Much like the Homerically-inspired drama of various African American playwrights such as Ifa Bayeza, Dalphinis connects Homer with the griots of Africa in demonstrating the orality of Caribbean literature, noting the similar tension in the West Indies between orature and literature which can also be seen in both Homeric Greece and colonial Africa.[15] Many Caribbean writers find connections between their lands, histories, and cultures and the myths, epics, and tragedies of the Greeks. It is the primacy of the sea and the culture derived from and created by living near it (fishing, shipping, piracy, travel, etc.) that creates a strong link between mythic, tragic Greece and the modern Caribbean.

The peoples of the Peloponesian archipelago and the various isles of the Caribbean both understand the many moods and aspects of the ocean: the savagery of storms that can wipe entire villages off the map, the provider that gives food, work, transportation, and all things needed for life, an unpredictable ally, and an unpredictable enemy. Life and death reside in its depths. The sea isolates one island from another, yet draws all islands together in a sense of community. In any island culture, from Caribbean to Mediterranean islands, the sea plays an important role in the art, music, literature and theatre.

In Greek mythology, the three major gods were the king of the sky, Zeus, the king of the underworld, Hades, and the king of the sea, Poseidon; the sea god is given primacy together with his two brothers of sky and underworld. Though not more powerful than Zeus, Poseidon is known to flout his brother's will and send sea monsters and storms to punish and attack even the children of "the Father of the Gods." Poseidon is said to have created the horse. His love affairs and offspring are almost as prodigious, if not as famous or celebrated, as those of Zeus are. He backed the Greeks during the Trojan War, giving them assistance. So it is no wonder that Poseidon is one of the most important of gods to the Greeks, and his influence and the importance of his realm is seen in epic, myth, and drama.

The Odyssey essentially tells of the ten-year sea voyage of Odysseus, who ranges over the Mediterranean until returning to the little island of Ithaca in the Ionian Sea. Homer's epic enumerates all the wonders and the horrors of the ocean. Erick A. Havelock, in his study of the orality of Greek literature, observes that The Iliad and The Odyssey are "a running report upon the nomos and ethos of the Greek maritime complex."[16] Charles Van Doren argues that the soundscape of The Iliad is "clashing arms and the screams of wounded men," but The Odyssey is filled with the "cries of sea birds," and whereas the former evokes night, the time in the latter is "high noon, with the sun shining and the little waves of the sea lapping against a white beach."[17]

Entire sections of The Iliad are simply lists of ships and their contents. Likewise, the books of The Odyssey are taken up with information about the sea and Greek sea practice:

> No look-out,
> nobody saw the island dead ahead,

> nor even the great landward rolling billow
> that took us in: we found ourselves in shallows,
> keels grazing shore: so furled our sails
> and disembarked where low ripples broke.[18]

The imagery is that of a seascape, the language that of sailors and fishermen, the intended audience one familiar with the dangers of the coast where land meets ocean and with seafaring.

Not only epics, but many Greek myths are rooted in sea voyages and the omnipresence of the ocean: Jason and the Argonauts, the black ship which came to Athens every seven years from Crete to bring victims to the Minotaur, King Aegeus throwing himself into the sea which now bears his name. When Heracles (himself one of the Argonauts) prepared for his famous twelve labors, Poseidon gave him a horse, and watched over him during the several sea journeys undertaken to complete the labors. Heracles also rescued Hesione from a sea monster, as Perseus did with Andromeda. Perseus also gave the throne of Polydectes to the kind fisherman Dictys, who had rescued Perseus and his mother Danae from the sea. These are but a handful of myths chosen at random which demonstrate that the adventures of the heroes of Greek mythology take place with a background of the sea, and that fishermen, watercraft, and the daily interaction with the ocean is of great significance in the myths.

Tragedy, too, reflects the primacy of the ocean. From Oceanus and the chorus of his daughters questioning Prometheus in Aeschylus's play, to the island of Lemnos on which Philoctetes has been marooned and a chorus of sailors joins in the attempt to convince him to go to Troy in Sophocles's play, from the watchman of the opening of *Agamemnon* waiting for the beacon that will tell him the war is over and the fleet is returning to Theseus calling upon Poseidon's vengeance and the report of the sea monster that carried it out in Euripides's *Hippolytus*, from the destruction of the Persian fleet in *Persians* to the actual presence on stage of Poseidon in *Trojan Women*, when the play opens with the sea god and Athena agree to a truce at the end of the Trojan War that will make the homecoming of the Greeks as difficult as possible, Greek tragedy is as much centered on the sea as are myth and epic. Thetis, the sea-goddess appears in *Andromache*. *Iphigenia at Aulis* concerns the need to sacrifice Agamemnon's daughter on the coast of Boeotia in order to bring favorable winds for sea travel to Troy. The satyr play *Cyclops*, one of only two extant plays based on an episode directly from Homer, features Odysseus and the sailors who accompany him to the cave of Polyphemus.[19] Another chorus of sailors, this time from Salamis, is found in Sophocles's *Ajax*. The chorus of daughters of Danaus in the Aeschylus' *Suppliants* are ordered to board the ship of the Herald of Aegyptus or be dragged there by their hair. They had already fled by sea to Argos where they are given sanctuary. The ocean provides settings, characters, choruses, themes, and material culture of seafaring to be used on the stage by the tragedians. Greek tragedy, myth, and epic are rooted in a culture that itself is rooted in the ocean.

The cultures of the Caribbean, being located on a series of islands located in a two thousand mile long belt of the ocean, are certainly comparable in many ways to that of ancient Greece. The very name given to the cultures of these islands, "Caribbean," is taken not from the islands themselves but from the sea which surrounds them. Caribbean writing is rooted in the economic and cultural realities of living on an island in a group of islands in the middle of a vast ocean. The rhythm of Caribbean culture is the rhythm of waves. The ocean is source material and setting. From calypso music to the poems of Derek Walcott to the novels of George Lamming to the souvenirs offered up to tourists in the shops of the Caribbean, the ocean and the human activities associated with it are at the center.

In particular, there are two recurrent and connected ocean-related themes in Caribbean literature and drama that also play a prominent role in ancient Greek culture as well: exile and odyssey. The former is the idea of being sent away from the community and separated from the place of one's origins. The latter is the idea of searching, with the implication (thanks to Homer) of a lengthy journey involved, for that home.

The Greeks considered exile to be one of the most horrific punishments that can be visited on one. Oedipus, when his pollution is discovered, is exiled. Orestes, Heracles, Medea, Jason, Theseus, and many other mythic figures faced exile at various points in their lives; sent away or voluntarily leaving their place of origin. Exile separates one from family, society, culture, way of life, worldview, and, in short, one's entire universe. To be in a state of exile is to be a perpetual outsider, living away from one's true home.

Exile is a major theme in Caribbean literature, primarily because of the African diaspora. Gareth Griffiths, in his book *A Double Exile*, argues that people of African descent in the Caribbean are worse off than their African counterparts as, "The African was colonized, the West Indian was enslaved."[20] The Africans, who were also victims of European imperialism, economic, political, and cultural oppression and forced labor were, argues Griffiths, spared the ultimate rupture of being separated from the Motherland. While exploited and oppressed, they remained connected to the land of their people. Those Africans taken to the Caribbean are oppressed in every manner that the Africans are, but are further oppressed by separation from the Motherland. Though taught to speak European languages and learn European literatures, they are, because of racism, not fully assimilated and embraced within the European tradition. Thus, argues Griffiths, the West Indian of African descent is forced into a "double exile," "exiled culturally from the sources and traditions of that language [English], and linguistically from the landscapes and people they write about."[21] Coming from a culture that is rooted in both Europe and Africa, yet not allowed to fully be a part of either culture, Griffiths claims to be living in exile from both, an expatriate in his own nation.

West Indian novelist George Lamming, on the other hand, entitled his collection of essays on Caribbean literature and life *The Pleasure of Exile*, in which he argues that the distance which exile affords allows the artist to see more clearly the cultures from which he is descended and exiled. Exile allows the artist to better see from where he came and the difference between home and new dwelling place. Given that, however, Lamming is in agreement with Griffiths that the West Indian shares the colonial situation with the African, but the former is "wholly severed from the cradle of a continuous culture and tradition" in a way that the latter is not.[22] In his survey of Caribbean literature Lamming further argues that, although there are similarities in American and Caribbean cultural constructions, most white Americans are descended from people who chose to leave their homeland, and who now live in a European-based culture, speaking a European language, but the West Indian, forcibly exiled and descended from slaves, is separated from the cultures that created his or hers.

In fairness, Edward Said posits that the Caribbean is not alone: "Modern Western culture is in large part the work of exiles, émigrés, refugees."[23] Although, like Lamming, Said differentiates types of exile based on the cause and specific situation—exile is not the same if it is a matter of choice as opposed to enforced from without.[24]

The counter to exile, contends Said, is nationalism, specifically the creation of a national identity that posits individual and collective identity rooted in shared values, history, and experiences in the same locale. "Nationalism," he pronounces, "is an assertion of belonging in and to a place, a people, a heritage. It affirms the home created by a community of language, culture, and customs, and, by so doing, it fends off exile..."[25] In other words, the creation of a communal or national identity erases exile, positing the new locale as "home." In the postcolonial era, assertions of Caribbean culture and Caribbean identity have begun to move away from the notion of exile and creating a uniquely Caribbean culture, or a culture that is part of a larger diaspora continuum.[26]

The notion of odyssey, connected as it is with a long journey that is in essence an attempt to return home, is linked with the notion of exile. If exile is the condition of existing apart from one's home, odyssey is the counter, as it is the journey back from exile to home. Homer's *Odyssey* begins (in the Fitzgerald translation):

> Sing in me, Muse, and through me tell the story
> of that man skilled in all ways of contending,
> the wanderer, harried for years on end,
> after he plundered the stronghold
> of the proud heart of Troy.
> He saw the townlands
> and learned the minds of many distant men,
> and weathered many bitter nights and days
> in his deep heart at sea, while he fought only
> to save his life, to bring his shipmates home.[27]

This opening suggests the lengthy wandering that must be endured to return home as well as the physically and emotionally exhausting nature of the journey. Also of import is the fact that he "learned the minds of many distant men," suggesting that an odyssey involves the encounter of foreigners and foreign cultures, and learning the ways of those cultures. Odysseus, in his journey home, learned of many other lands and peoples. We might term him the original exchange student, spending only part of the ten year voyage actually at sea, many of the years were spent living among different people. However, the reader is constantly reminded by Homer that, "Homeward you think we must be sailing/to our own land."[28] In other words, although the voyager encounters many cultures in his journey, the journey is always one moving towards a home.

Said, after Lukács, contends that *The Odyssey* is a product of an established society: "Classical epics...emanate from settled cultures in which values are clear, identities stable, life unchanging."[29] Odysseus returns home—his exile ends as his odyssey does, with a return to Ithaca and his family. This fact may be the reason why *The Odyssey* serves as an anchor for the writings of Derek Walcott, who has turned to Homer's epic twice as source material for a major work. *Omeros*, an epic poem in its own right, deconstructs and reconstructs Homer's works in the Caribbean, forming a metaphoric journey of a Caribbean man to his home—Africa. *The Odyssey* is a stage adaptation of Homer's epic that utilizes Caribbean culture to create a new frame of reference for the Greek narrative. Both of these texts will be considered below.

Homer's poem serves as the model for Caribbean writing because it shows the hero returning home from exile. In this sense the poem serves as diaspora identity wish-fulfillment—the hero, from a stable society whose values are unquestioned journeys for many years but eventually returns home. *The Odyssey* proves there is an end to exile, which makes it appealing. The seascape that serves as setting and material culture of the poem ensures a smoother transition into the cultural codes of another seafaring culture.

In terms of the production and presentation of Greek tragedy in the islands, it is primarily the universities and the amateur groups that present Greek tragedies, although several important professional productions and adaptations have been mounted by professional companies as well. As in Africa and the United States, it is often the universities that serve as the site for development of the less commercial, more political dramas that explore the relationship between Europe, America, Africa, and the Caribbean.

While Derek Walcott's own adaptations are dealt with separately below, it should be noted that under his guidance at the Trinidad Theatre Workshop and under the guidance of Errol Hill at the University of the West Indies a number of Caribbean playwrights have adapted Greek tragedies into West Indian settings. In 1970 Dennis Scott adapted the Clytemnestra legend as outlined in *The Oresteia* into *The Crime of Annabel Patterson*. In *The Pan Beaters*, the very title of which suggests Pan, the Greek satyr god who was associated with Dionysus, Stephan Landrigan set the story of *Phaedra* in Trinidad. Derek Walcott's twin brother Roderick Walcott, a playwright and director in his own right, took over the St. Lucia Arts Guild a year after Derek founded it. Roderick directed *Oedipus Rex* among several other western classics during his tenure. Kendel Hippolyte reports that under Roderick Walcott "the group followed a two-track program of acquainting itself and its audience with the old and modern classics of western drama while nurturing the St. Lucian and Caribbean drama."[30] While the choice of western material might be read critically as legacy of colonialism privileging European culture over African or indigenous cultures, as well as an arts economy that privileges the known European art work over the unknown indigenous drama, Roderick Walcott's "balanced policy" placed the development of indigenous drama in a position as equal in importance to the presentation of Western classics.[31] Doing so does privilege western drama as the standard by which the developing drama will be measured, and thus is very much a product of the colonial system. Yet this policy also asserts the importance of both developing one's own drama and engaging in one's own cultural heritage. Walcott was claiming a Western heritage just as much, if not more so, than simply and unquestioningly accepting the primacy of western culture. In other words, the "balanced policy" of Walcott is also a balance between "Black Orpheus" (European model) and "Black Athena" (reclamation of one's own property).

The Spanish-speaking Caribbean has also enjoyed several adaptations of Greek tragedy. José Triana, the Cuban playwright, wrote *Medea en el espejo* (*Medea in the Mirror*) in 1960, following it with *La muerte del 'eque* (*The Death of the Strong Man*) in 1963. Banham, Hill, and Woodyard note that, "both contain elements of classical Greek tragic figures integrated into a lower-class Cuban environment..."[32] Likewise, Héctor Incháustegui Cabral, poet, playwright, essayist and novelist of the Dominican Republic, turned to Greek material for his trilogy *Miedo en un pu'ado de polvo* (*Fear in a Handful of Dust*), which incorporates material from three different Greek tragedies.[33]

Similarly to the other producing organizations, the University of the Virgin Islands' Little Theatre in St. Thomas has been active in both developing indigenous drama and engaging European and American drama, including Greek tragedy. UVI Theatre presented Jean Anouihl's adaptation of *Antigone* in 1987 and even presented a production of Steve Carter's *Pecong*, the adaptation of *Medea* set in the Caribbean discussed in the previous chapter, to acclaim in November of 1994. As in other cases, these theatrical experiments are driven by a small group of individuals such as playwright David Edgecomb and teacher/director Rosary E. Harper, who serve in the same manner as Walcott and Hill before them. Teachers are often also the makers of culture, just as in Africa where Ola Rotimi, Wole Soyinka, Femi Osofisan, Efua Sutherland, and many others teach at university, write plays, direct, and write scholarly and critically about indigenous and international theatre.

In addition to the University of the Virgin Islands, the University of the West Indies, with its three campuses has enjoyed several significant productions of Greek tragedy as well. In the fifties a major production of *Oedipus Rex* was mounted with a young Jamaican actress named Mavis Arscott, who would later become very well known under her married name Mavis Lee Wah, playing Jocasta and the actor regarded as one of the best in the Anglophone Caribbean, Slade Hopkinson, playing Tiresias.[34] Hopkinson went on to direct Euripides' *The Trojan Women* in the sixties at St. George's college in Trinidad.[35] Even on the secondary school level, Greek tragedy was occasionally performed. Belinda Scott directed a group of students in Sophocles' *Electra* for the 1987 secondary schools drama festival.[36] One might argue that these performances indicate the continued influence of colonialist education and the privileging of European culture. On the other hand, many of these plays were presented in part of a larger context of world drama, including indigenous plays.

The sense of exile is also present in the works of Edward Kamau Brathwaite, the Barbadian poet and essayist who also lived and taught in Ghana for several years. "The most significant feature of West Indian life and imagination since Emancipation has been its sense of rootlessness, of not belonging to the landscape."[37] Brathwaite's own adaptation of the *Antigone* of Sophocles, *Odale's Choice*, is analyzed at length in *The Athenian Sun in an African Sky*, but there are a few points about it worth mentioning here.[38]

Odale's Choice was written and performed with a student cast at Mfantsiman Secondary School in Saltpond, Ghana in June of 1962. That year was one of strong theatrical linkage between Ghana, the Caribbean, and ancient Greece. In addition to Brathwaite's play, the Theatre Club in Accra sponsored *Antigone in Haiti*, yet another rewriting of Sophocles's play set on the Caribbean island during a slave revolt.[39] In this period, both African and Caribbean nations, feeling a sense of similarity, looked to each other as former colonial states, often of the same imperialist powers, with a common colonial language, experiencing the same joy at independence, but also the same "nervous condition" from being formerly colonized and experiencing cultural disruption, and in a similar situation in their histories and development. This sense of commonality was often reflected in the theatre and drama of the period, particularly in West Africa, from which a great deal of the Africans who were taken to the New World came.

Brathwaite, Gilbert and Tomkins claim, was in Ghana on a "mission to find in Africa an 'authentic' ancestral homeland for West Indians of African origin..."[40] The non-specific ethnicity of the characters in *Odale's Choice* reflect a Caribbean more than an African sensibility. As most West Indians of African origin cannot claim a specific nation, specific culture, or specific group, all Africa becomes the homeland. An absence of a concrete, traceable connection results in the creation of a connection to the whole, or an adaptive group. Like Walcott's Africa, discussed below, Brathwaite's is an imaginary one, even though the play was written and performed in Ghana. The play, with its non-specific setting is a unique piece in Greco-African adaptation that reflects both the search for an African identity by the author and the context of the newly independent nation of Ghana. Brathwaite, returning to African in search of an identity and therefore living in exile from his home in Barbados, is therefore still living in a double exile, albeit a new one—he is newly rooted in an African culture where he is still an outsider (he is, after all, not an indigenous Ghanaian) but also away from the culture, land, and society into which he was born.

Brathwaite occupies a unique position as both outsider and insider. As a teacher, he is an authority figure, and one who is connected to his African context. In 1962 Ghana was still a newly independent nation attempting to create its own national identity. Brathwaite found his African identity while teaching in Ghana. *Odale's Choice* is a Caribbean play for an African audience in which both author and audience are seeking to define a new cultural/individual/historical identity. Commonality is found in the experience, as defined in the adaptation of *Antigone*, of resistance to an oppressive state. As Antigone stood against Creon, as Odale's choice was to disobey Creon and bury her brother, so, too do Ghanaians and Caribbeans alike need to make the choice to resist oppression.

Like Brathwaite, Derek Walcott is a teacher, playwright, poet, and essayist looking for a Caribbean identity. Unlike Brathwaite, Walcott does not reject the European sources of his culture in favor of the African ones, rather seeing the Caribbean as the culmination of so many cultures, including those of Europe. Walcott, like Brathwaite, sees Greek material as a source for his own writing. Unlike Brathwaite, however, Walcott does not simply take Greek dramaturgy and reset it in African or Caribbean settings. Instead he reworks and transforms the material into a reflection of the history, identity, and culture of his Caribbean.

The Homer of the West Indies: Derek Walcott

Derek Walcott, Nobel Laureate for literature, university professor, actor, poet, playwright, and Caribbean writer *par excellence*, calls himself "a mulatto of style."[41] By this he means that he blends old and new worlds, Africa, Europe and the Americas, that his works are of mixed-race descent, metaphorically speaking, resulting in a synthesis. Tejumola Olaniyan claims that synthesis "is a process of continuous experimentation," and Walcott has spent a considerable amount of his career as a writer experimenting with the blend of European language, Caribbean sensibility, African identity and connections, and West Indian imagery.[42] Walcott also draws heavily on European drama and literature for his own plays. Whether adapting entire plays or merely making allusions or referencing a particular work through its form, plot, characters, language, or structure, Walcott is never far from the western canon. He has used Shakespeare and other Jacobean dramatists, Synge, Tirso de Molina, Molière, and, most often, the Greek tragedians as raw materials for the construction of his own dramas. Although many postcolonial scholars and artists criticize Walcott for seemingly favoring Western culture over African in his blends, Olaniyan finds "an enabling cultural identity" in Walcott's use of "conscious and controlled eclecticism."[43] As noted in the first chapter, Olaniyan still argues that Walcott's use of Greek material is a "thoroughly ideological" choice that makes his work different, less revolutionary, and arguably more rooted in colonial culture than, for example, Silas Jones's or even Jim Magnuson's plays, and argues that Walcott's choice, while not negative in and of itself, can be thoroughly colonialist if not a part of artistic creation that is thoroughly self aware and thoroughly self-interrogative. In other words, Olaniyan finds Walcott problematic in his unquestioned acceptance of Western source material that indicates a "universalist and aristocratic notion of form and literary greatness."[44] Walcott is "an accomplished craftsman who is able to turn challenge into great creative resource" and he "writes so well" of the neocolonial problems of Carribea, yet his recourse to and privileging of Western sources can and do subordinate black culture.[45]

Walcott, however, sees, in the words of Olaniyan, many "cultural tributaries that feed the Caribbean."[46] The metaphor is apt: just as one cannot separate out the waters that combine from many rivers to make up a sea, so, too, does Walcott not focus on a single cultural flow in his own individual and communal cultural background. Walcott's stance is that Caribbean identity is the result of a blend of cultures, therefore the Caribbean artist is free to consciously control and shape the individual cultural influences in his own particular work. The end result will be truly Caribbean.

It is the sea that links the Greeks to the Caribbean in Walcott's writing. As the poem that opened this chapter, "The Sea is History," states, the sea is not only history, it is "tribal memory."[47] The sea is a vault that "locks up" everything that constitutes a culture. Locking up can contain and isolate, but it can also preserve and maintain. The sea is a link that connects the Caribbean to the Americas and both to Africa. The sea connects the tribes separated by the African diaspora and serves as a collective "tribal memory" for all peoples of African descent.

The idea of exile, as discussed above, as a shared state for people of African descent, creates a common experience that is inextricably linked to the tribal memory of the sea. Robert D. Hamner argues in his analysis of *Omeros* that Walcott's poem "the African diaspora has generated a sense of nationality bound together primarily by the shared state of exile."[48] Exile, combined with "the urgency of homecoming," what I have termed odyssey, mark the two main themes in Walcott's stage adaptation of *The Odyssey* according to Stone.[49] In a larger sense, however, these are the themes of much of Walcott's work and certainly all of his Greek-related material.

Walcott's affinity for Greek material is related to a sense of identity that he believes he shares with ancient Greece. Walcott constructs an ancient Greece that is remarkably similar to the islands of the Caribbean in the postcolonial era. "The Greeks were the niggers of the Mediterranean," he stated in an interview.[50] He posits the Greeks as an oppressed, seafaring culture that had to fight to maintain their identity, their freedom, and their culture against the Persians, the Carthaginians, the Romans, and other empires that sought to conquer them. Walcott's Greeks had to fight to achieve cultural and social greatness in the face of imperialist threats throughout its golden age.

Walcott is, of course, ignoring the historical fact that Athens, too, became an imperial power that conquered much of the surrounding area and defeated both the Persians and the Carthaginians. For Walcott, the Greeks are the equivalent of the people of the Caribbean. As The Odyssey is a model for returning home, so, too, Walcott's construction of Greek history is a model for rising to greatness after achieving independence from imperial powers.

In his Greco-Caribbean plays and poems Walcott engages in what Edward Said calls "imaginative geography and history."[51] He is not bound in the poem Omeros or in plays such as The Odyssey or The Isle is Full of Noises by the confines of the actual globe or the actual Caribbean. In Omeros characters can journey from St. Lucia to Africa in a small boat, and coastlines reshape themselves to fit Walcott's needs. History, as presented in his plays is less reflective of actual Caribbean history than a Greco-Caribbean history, in which the events of Greek mythology are played out on the contemporary or recent beaches, forests, and cities of the West Indies.[52]

Walcott's early work was influenced by Greek tragedy and he returned to Greek material, including epic and myth, again and again in his later years. Walcott was born on St. Lucia in 1930. In 1946, at the age of 16, he wrote his first play Flight and Sanctuary which was never staged—a "verse play with a chorus," based on Greek models.[53] At this period of his development as a writer he also used to write and declaim for his schoolmates "marathon poems on Greek heroes," according to Judy Stone.[54] Therefore it is no wonder that in later life he would continue by taking Greek source material and not merely recontextualizing it but using it as a springboard for his own mythic and dramatic writing.

He denies that his practice is to parallel or overlay Greek originals in Caribbean settings. Walcott states, "I don't use my work as a sort of referential this-equals-that, this is supposed to be that in black, or whatever."[55] Walcott denies that his work follows a "Black Orpheus" model. His work is not a recontextualization of Greek tragedy and epic, but is inspired by and interacts with Greek material. Oliver Taplin, in his analysis of Omeros, for example, sees "no straight parallels, no one-to-one correspondences" with the Homeric original, "yet," he concludes, "Walcott's poem is still...infused and suffused with Homer."[56]

If his work is not of the "Black Orpheus" paradigm, can it be considered to be of the "Black Athena" paradigm? Nowhere in any of his writings, either creative or critical, does Walcott espouse anything resembling Afrocentric classicism. For Walcott, Greece is the cornerstone of Western civilization and not of African origins. Thus, on the surface, he rejects "Black Athena" just as he did "Black Orpheus." If one considers his earlier comment, however, that the Greeks were the "niggers of the Mediterranean," then a different type of identification is established: not "the Greeks were African," but "the Greeks were just like me—the product of resistance to imperialism in a sea-based culture." Rather than attempt to establish an historical link (epistemological) between ancient Africa and ancient Greece, Walcott's formulation establishes a link of cultural identification (ontological). For Walcott, the Greeks do not actually need to be influenced by Africa in order for him to identify with them. As noted above, Walcott does not merely construct a Caribbean influenced by the Greeks in his writing, he also constructs an ancient Greece influenced by the Caribbean. For Walcott, the Greeks aren't African—they are Caribbean-like.

Is this construction "Black Dionysus?" Olaniyan would say no. Although Walcott is identifying with the Greeks on his terms, not on theirs, he is still privileging the European over the genuinely African. In doing so, however, he is appropriating the Greek identity in order to subsume it into his own. While not postcolonial or post-Afrocentric, such a strategy avoids the accusation of simply accepting European superiority. Instead, it sets up a model whereby the use of Greek material becomes an appropriation not from a dominant culture, but from another cultural equal. Walcott, in this sense, equates ancient Greece not only with the Caribbean, but also with Africa, with whom cultural exchange is presumably not tinged with colonialist inequality. Walcott, in his own way, Africanizes the Greeks.

In 1957 Walcott returned to Greek material to write the play *Ione*. Stone writes, "He created an original myth of classical dimensions, using classical themes and classical characters, constructing his drama true to the classical unities of time, place, and action, and couching his dialogue in the classical language at which he excelled..."[57] The names of the characters are Francophone adaptations of figures from Greek myth and history: Helène, Achille, Alexandre, Diogene, Ione, etc. First performed in 1957 in Jamaica, St. Lucia, and Trinidad, followed by a student performance at the Edinburgh Festival, the play tells the story of two tragic island families, "hill tribes," who have been feuding over land for generations.[58] Achille kills Diogene when he finds him in bed with Achille's wife Hélène, who is subsequently stoned for her part in the adultery. Ione, Hélène's older sister, is pregnant by a visiting American, and the play concludes with the American returning to the United States and Ione killing herself out of grief.

Norman Rae, in his critical study of the play, calls it "an academic exercise, awkward in its Aristotelian conventions."[59] The play is a classic study in the (mis)conception of the Greek idea of fate: "All events are preordained and what must come must inevitably come."[60] Although scholars criticize the play for its fixation on the "outward conventions of classical theatre,"[61] and the awkwardness of the language,[62] the play achieved popular success in the Caribbean and reviewers at the time hailed the production for its powerful presentation of emotion and its easy transition of classical conceits into the historical Caribbean.[63] Although an early work, *Ione* already demonstrates all of the qualities that would be in evidence in *Omeros* and *The Odyssey*: blending of Greek, African, and European cultures, the sense of realistic mythic history, the use of multiple levels of intertextuality and reference, and the refusal to allow the source material to dominate the new creation.

Walcott's next venture to Athens via the Caribbean was in the late 1970s when he began adapting the story of Philoctetes. The resultant play, *The Island Is Full of Noises*, by its title invokes Shakespeare's *The Tempest*, with which the play also intertextually interacts, but it is Sophocles' play which forms the source for the text. Performed 1982 in Hartford, Connecticut, the play adapts the story of the wounded hero whose bite from a snake refused to heal and caused him to cry out so disturbingly and smelled so horrific that the Greeks marooned him on an island on the way to Troy. Robinson, a "foul smelling hermit" on the fictional isle of Santa Marta, is the target of a campaign to remove him from the beach by "Prime Minister Papa." But those who would remove this man are foiled, not by the bow of Heracles, as in the original, but by a speargun. Taking as its satirical subject the overriding concern of Caribbean governments for the tourist economy at the expense of the indigenous people, Walcott's play is not a parallel of Sophocles, but rather takes its plot and premise as a starting point for exploring the corrupting influence not only of colonialism, but of the former colonizers even after independence. Judy Stone sees the play as "a metaphor for political corruption," which results in "a joltingly uncomfortable play."[64]

Walcott combines the plot of a Greek tragedy, African mythology, Caribbean sensibility, the imagery and terminology of Christianity, and the language of the colonizer to critique corruption at the local level, but also on the international level. Where *Ione* embraced classical convention for its own sake, Walcott used classical material in *The Isle* to indict Caribbean politicians and governments that value westerners more than their own constituents. Stone reports that *The Isle* was Walcott's "most intense exploration to date of the colonial cultural conundrum that had vexed him since childhood."⁶⁵ We might argue that *The Isle* is proto-*Black Dionysus*. Walcott used Greek material, but unlike *Ione*, combined it with indigenous culture to indict both colonial culture and social and political issues in the Caribbean. He would not use Greek material in a way this overtly political again.

Albert Ashaolu observes that even when not directly adapting Greek material to the Caribbean, Walcott relies upon the Greek tragedies for references, allegories, and dramaturgical models. In his study of Walcott's *Ti-Jean and His Brothers*, one of Walcott's most popular plays, Ashaolu demonstrates how Greek references occur throughout the play. After sneezing, a character who is a frog says, "Aeschylus me," instead of, "Bless me," a direct reference to the *Frogs* of Aristophanes as well as Aeschylus himself. And, as Ashaolu writes, "by invoking the name of Aeschylus, the Frog has elevated itself from the low status of a mere folktale animal to that of an inspired poet-narrator with a vision."⁶⁶

Ashaolu's interpretation is problematic. On the one hand, the Frog is a substitute for Walcott, who by calling attention to the process of invention and creation of the tale-teller simultaneously mocks himself and elevates himself: he is a lowly frog, but he is also the "inspired poet-narrator," which means there is no difference between himself and the poet-dramatists of the Greeks. The lowly frog is also the equal of Aeschylus. The problem with this interpretation of the passage is that it elevates Aeschylus over the "mere folktale," thereby privileging European over African culture. Why is a folktale "mere"? Why is the creator of Greek tragedy "an inspired poet-narrator with a vision," and the teller of folktales not? Aeschylus becomes the measure by which all narrators must be measured.

It might be better argued that in this passage Walcott uses the Greek references subversively. It is the folktale Frog who knows Aeschylus and can make witty reference to him that works on several levels. Aeschylus is not a "poet-narrator with a vision" but the punchline of a joke that one understands only if one gets the reference. The reference privileges those with classical knowledge, but does not privilege Aeschylus. Instead, by engaging in witty wordplay with his name, Walcott proves himself the superior creator. Walcott perceives Aeschylus as an element of culture from one more cultural stream that flows into the Caribbean, something to be used as a joke and then left behind. It is this sort of playfulness with the material that elevates Walcott, not merely "invoking the name." It is this sort of playfulness that begins to move Walcott into a "Black Dionysus" paradigm.

Most recently, Walcott dramatized and adapted Homer's *Odyssey*, premiering in 1992 in Stratford-upon-Avon at the Royal Shakespeare Company's The Other Place. The location and premiering organization, director (the RSC's Artistic Director Trevor Nunn), and predominantly white European cast, including Ron Cook, who is white, as Odysseus, problematize understanding *The Odyssey* as a Caribbean play, or even as a play rooted in the African diaspora. It is almost as if Walcott, while remaining tied to the body that is Caribbean culture, has chosen to sail up the stream of European culture that empties into the sea, rooting *The Odyssey* much more firmly in British waters than Caribbean.

That being said, Walcott's play is very much a soundscape, as Homer's original was suggested to be above. The text calls for the play to begin and end with the sound of waves. This *Odyssey* demonstrates that what links Homer, the Greeks, the Caribbean and Walcott is the ocean. In performance, one is never allowed to forget the presence of the sea. Sea birds cry, storms break, waves roll and crash in the background as Odysseus encounters fantastic beings, angry gods, and challenges natural and supernatural, in his attempt to return to Ithaca. The sea is replaced, however, in Hades with the literal and metaphoric sounds of the underground. As Odysseus journeys to the underworld, the sights, sounds, and winds of the London subway greet him. The spirits of Hades are homeless vagabonds, the winds that toss them are generated by rushing trains, bringing more dead to the underworld, but also linking modern urban world with Greek afterlife. Simultaneously, Walcott is able both to satirize the modern urban dweller who rides the subway to work—they are dead, in Walcott's world, and to imply that the dead have no contact with the sea—the only time in the play when we are not aware of the ocean is when the action is in the urban underworld. The sea is, quite literally, life.

Homer is brought onstage in the form of "Blind Billy Blue," a name that conjures bards, blues singers, the blue of the ocean, the sightlessness of the original Homer, and the multiple sources of culture which will shape this *Odyssey*. Blind Billy Blue is identified only as "a singer" in the *dramatis personae*. Like Homer and legendary bluesmen, he is a singer of tales. His words create worlds. It is he who will shape this narrative; not the original Homer, but a blind singer who might serve in a more modern fashion. Like the Frog of *Ti-Jean*, Blind Billy Blue is yet another "mulatto of style" who stands for the poet, and therefore for Walcott himself.

Blind Billy Blue tells the audience that he is

Gone sing about that man because his stories please us,
Who saw trials and tempests for ten years after Troy.
I'm Blind Billy Blue, my main man's sea-smart Odysseus,
Who the God of the Sea drove crazy and tried to destroy.[67]

In the first four lines of the play Walcott establishes that Odysseus is "sea-smart," that he knows the ocean, yet has made an enemy of the "God of the Sea." Like the Greek original, Walcott introduces the theme of the paradoxical nature of the sea: it is friend and enemy, it ushers in life and death, it separates and brings together. The sea is what keeps Odysseus from home, but it is also the medium by which he can and will travel home. The water separates and isolates the different islands, yet the same ocean that touches Ogygia, Aeaea, and Troy also touches Ithaca.

Out of necessity for creating a two to three hour stage play out of a several thousand-line epic, Walcott cuts some material and combines and collapses other things. Circe, for example, is not found on her mythological island of Aeaea, but on an island named Calypso, where Carnival is being celebrated. But in Greek mythology, Calypso was not an island, but a nymph who lived on the island of Ogygia. Walcott uses the name of Calypso, a significant figure in the *Odyssey*, to suggest the unrelated calypso—the music of Trinidad and Tobago.

In Greek myth Calypso was a daughter of Atlas, or, in some myths a daughter of Oceanus and Thetis, both sea gods. Odysseus was shipwrecked on her island and, according to Hesiod, during his seven year stay with her sired two sons. The etymology of her name includes the Greek word meaning "the concealer" or "the hidden."

Completely unrelated to the Greek word is the Caribbean word "calypso," describing a kind of music that developed in Trinidad and spread throughout the islands, especially to Barbados and Jamaica. The origin of the term is highly debated, but the most popular theory is that it comes from the West African term "kaiso," meaning a shout of encouragement.[68] Calypso developed out of African music that early Trinidadian slaves were allowed to sing in the fields when talking was forbidden them. It was developed at the end of the nineteenth and beginning of the twentieth centuries by lower class Trinidadians into a music of the people. Satirical in nature, these topical songs were usually improvised initially, but through the growth of calypso culture have become one of the dominant musical forms of the Caribbean, along with Reggae.

Walcott uses the name of Homer's nymph to suggest the unrelated (although spelled exactly the same) music form of the Caribbean. The nymph with whom Odysseus falls in love becomes the island that celebrates carnival. In scene ten of act one, after having escaped the Cyclops, Odysseus and his men arrive on a beautiful beach where they hear drumming. The men have no desire to leave, even though, as Odysseus argues "my longing for home is as strong as theirs."[69]

A chorus of revelers wearing animal masks enters, singing of Carnival:

The island of Calypso	Bacchanal
Aeaea	And carnival
Ai-ee-o	Is the place to go[70]

Although the actual name is given (Aeaea) as part of the rhythmic chant, Calypso is identified as the island that is "the place to go." Carnival is the pre-Lenten celebration that occurs throughout the Caribbean, Brazil, and New Orleans. In one sense, it is not a place that one can go, but a time and a particular celebration. The line, however, may also be invoking a suggestion of how commercialized and tourist-driven Carnival has become.

Carnival began over two hundred years ago in Catholic colonies. It has since grown and developed and now is considered a form of indigenous celebration. We might consider Carnival a form of the Festival of Dionysus. Bands of masked revelers and costumed dancers engage in parades and performances. Beginning in the nineteenth century, Carnival featured historic reenactments and masquerades based on myth and folktales.[71] Christopher Dunn reports that, "Carnival symbolism often references the Dionysian celebrations of ancient Greece..."[72] Like the City Dionysia, Carnival is a time of religious, social, and cultural celebration. In other words, Dionysus and his worship is already symbolically engaged and referenced by Carnival. It is part religious festival, part civic celebration, and part performance (often with contests and competitions). One might make the argument that Walcott is acknowledging the bond between the two in this scene.

Circe's home is a brothel, where Odysseus's men become pig-men and only Odysseus and his lieutenant Eurylochus remain unenthralled. Circe gives the men a "powerful weed" that "metamorphosizes" them, and her music is "pounding with the odours of rutting."[73] Modern audiences would recognize the former as not merely a reference to the herbs that Circe used to turn the men into swine in the original but also as a reference to marijuana, whose use in the islands, as part of Rastafari culture, and whose promotion is found in many reggae songs (the music "pounding with the odours of rutting") is well known in popular culture. The enthralling party of Circe during carnival is presented as a raucous party with reggae and marijuana.

After a night spent together, with Odysseus safe from the spells of Circe because of the moly Athena gave him, Circe awakes to tell Odysseus he must journey to the aforementioned underworld. It is only by going to the land of the dead that he can return home. Odysseus, agreeing, dresses in an admiral's uniform and joins Circe in an obeah ceremony.

For the second time (the first is in *Omeros*, analyzed below), Walcott combines Greek and *voudon* pantheons. "Shango dancers" light candles, draw a chalk circle on the ground, and swing a sacrificial rooster as the priests perform the ritual that will open the way to the underworld. They chant:

Shango	Go down to hell
Zeus	Sprinkle water
Who see us	Erzulie
Man go	Athena
Name Odysseus	Maman d'l'Eau
Go down	River Daughter
Go down	Shango
Ogun	Zeus
Erzulie	All who see us[74]

Walcott distinctively links the ancient Olympians with the *loa* of the Caribbean. Rather than privileging either, he creates one larger pantheon in which all gods are equal, much like his model for Caribbean culture. Shango, Ogun and Erzulie are exactly the same as Zeus and Athena as they are "all who see us." To pray to one set of gods alone would have no efficacy in Walcott's world—both Greek and African are needed, just as in Walcott's writing both European and African sources are needed.

The larger theme of Walcott's version, as in the Greek original, is homecoming. At the close of the play, Blind Billy Blue confirms that not only is he not Homer, but that he is both aware of Homer and of the history of adaptations of *The Odyssey*:

> Since that first blind singer, others will sing down the ages
> Of the heart in its harbor, then long years after Troy, after Troy.[75]

Blind Billy Blue is simply the most recent in a series of singers to sing of the "sea-smart man" who found his way home, whose heart found "its harbor." Walcott's *Odyssey* is not *The Odyssey*, it is a retelling, and example of stage orature—an oral epic that became a literary epic and continues to inspire oral performance. Walcott's *Odyssey* regards itself as simply the next in a series of retellings of the homecoming by, to, and from the sea.

Walcott and his creations the Frog and Blind Billy Blue are connected to the world of Greek culture as they all see themselves as the natural inheritors of all culture. Others have come before, they create now, and others will come after. In an interview with Leif Sjoberg in 1983, Walcott laid claim to his inheritance:

> Whatever happened before me is mine, the guilt is mine, the grandeur and horror were mine. Roman, Greek, African, all mine, veined in me, more alive than marble, bleeding and drying up. Literature reopens wounds more deeply than history does.[76]

As with Brathwaite's choice to identify with all of Africa, Walcott goes one step further by identifying with the entire world, or at least all Europe, the Americas, and Africa. With this legacy, however, comes responsibility ("the guilt is mine") and the arduous task of reopening wounds that have not healed. In many ways, Walcott is claiming postcolonial postmodernism as his culture: he freely blends cultures without considering context or source. He mines myth because he believes all myths are his to mine.

The purpose of literature is to open up old wounds. Walcott sees literature as more real than history, or at least as more powerful than history. One "opens old wounds" in order to cause more damage or in order to heal them properly. The rift in Caribbean identity can be healed, argues Walcott, not by history, or by adapting an Afrocentric stance, but by opening and exploring that wound and then allowing it to close up. Once an old wound is opened, metaphorically speaking, one must stitch it back together, tying the two sides of the wound together until they grow together seamlessly. Literature opens the wound and heals it, under Walcott's vision.

Although it is an epic poem and not a play, Walcott's *Omeros* deserves mention here as a "creolized version" of Homer's epics.[77] According to Brucker, *Omeros* "is homage, meant to capture the whole experience of the people of the Caribbean" through the plots of Homer.[78] Taplin sees it as "profoundly Homeric and undoubtedly epic," "infused and suffused with Homer," although varying greatly in the "relative complexity and...degree of explicitness" of his intertextual interactions.[79] *Omeros* is arguably Walcott's most studied, most written about work.

The lengthy narrative poem tells the story of the Caribbean fisherman Achille, who returns to the village in Africa where his ancestor was captured by slavers in the eighteenth century. It is in this work that Walcott explicitly locates "home" as Africa. The work is full of references to the works of Homer as well as various Greek tragedies. A blind ex-merchant seaman tells stories, and is equated with Homer. Hector is the name of a taxi driver who is killed in a car crash. Philoctete is a fisherman cut by a rusty anchor. He is forced to leave the sea and clean pig pens and farm yams because the wound will not heal. After Hector's death, he is cured.

Yet Walcott claims never to have read Homer: "As a narrative thing, the poem is not like a rewrite of The Iliad. I don't know The Iliad and I don't know The Odyssey. I've never read them."[80] Tongue may have been in cheek, or Walcott may have been exaggerating, or there may be some other explanation. Walcott said this before his own adaptation of The Odyssey (so he may have read it by the time of this writing), but we can read his statement as similar to his expression in Taplin that his work is not a recontextualization of Homer's epics in the Caribbean, but a work in its own right. Walcott does not want his work perceived as a "rewriting" of a Greek original or an adaptation that simply resets someone else's work into his cultural milieu. Walcott is not a translator or adapter, he is, like Homer himself, a transformer. He takes cultural material and transforms it into a new form with new foci. Walcott takes the marginal figures of the epic, those who have been swept aside by history, those who are exiled in the very work of literature that creates them, and centers them, bringing them home. He does not put Homer's poems in a new cultural frame; he uses Homer's frame as a way to view his own culture and the people of that culture. He freely combines Greek and African cultures as they are both his.

In Omeros Walcott most strongly links Africa and Greece. For example, to describe a hurricane which Achille's boat encounters, he writes, "the abrupt Shango drums/made Neptune rock in the cave."[81] Shango is the god of thunder for several West African ethnic groups, most specifically the Yoruba, and in Caribbean vodun and obeah. Neptune is the Latin name of Poseidon, the Greco-Roman god of the sea. In this image, Walcott links the pantheons of Greece and Africa. Both sets of gods coexist for him, and both gods are equals in Walcott's world, where the Greeks are the "niggers of the Mediterranean" and "Roman, Greek, and Africa" are "all [his]." In Walcott's world, all cultures are equal and all cultures are his.

Robert D. Hamner calls Omeros "the epic of the dispossessed," because, as he states, "each of its protagonists is a castaway in one sense or another," castaway meaning both person marooned or in exile and person who has been cast away—displaced by society.[82] Walcott's interest in the poem is not in the grand figures of the war, or even in the battles at Troy. It is, instead, in what Hamner calls "marginal individuals," the dispossessed—those not possessed by any land or culture and who possess nothing themselves.[83] By using the names of Greek heroes for dispossessed people Walcott creates an empowering inversion. Mythic figures are reduced from their mythic stature and made to seem common and everyday. Conversely, the lives of simple, common, everyday people are therefore elevated to the status of myth.

Walcott himself has said, "Many assume that we live in a world of myths which are constantly replaced with new myths...I believe myths are unkillable. Either man is a myth or he is a piece of dirt. I prefer the former view."[84] Walcott takes those who colonialism and the economic realities of postcolonial life in the Caribbean would equate with the piece of dirt and makes them myths. Rather than creating new myths, Walcott utilizes old ones, both African and European, to elevate the status of the West Indian. In this sense his work, from earlier works like *The Isle Is Full of Noise* through *Omeros* to *The Odyssey* are all part of a larger enterprise in which Greek myth, epic, and tragedy is used to elevate and celebrate the Caribbean identity, hybrid as it is. Derek Walcott's writing displays elements of the "Black Athena" model, not by claiming Greece, and not by identifying the Caribbean as similar to Greece, but by identifying Greece as similar to the Caribbean. The Caribbean becomes the measure by which the Greeks are measured. The cultural material of Europe and Africa being open to him, Walcott uses Greek material partly in a "Black Dionysian" paradigm—he uses Greek culture to interrogate his own sense of identity. He uses the material uncritically, however, accepting European culture without questioning the society that produced it, which is what prevents him from being fully within the "Black Dionysus" paradigm. He does not parallel the originals either, however, but uses them as raw material to develop truly Caribbean works.

John Figueroa concurs with Hamner's assessment, observing:

> In *Omeros* the grand names are given to simple folk some of whom had the kind of problems the noble heroes had in Homer's poems... But what is common to Homer and *Omeros* is not only struggle and coming to terms with death and violence and separation from home, but the sea, the loud sounding *poluphloisboiothalasseesie* and its moods and sounds.[85]

In other words, while the guiding themes of exile and homecoming are present in *Omeros*, the two loudest sounds in this soundscape are the voices of the marginalized and the sounds of the sea. The roar in *Omeros* is not of battle, but of waves. This much is shared between Homer and Walcott. To the waves, however, and in place of the voices of gods and heroes, Walcott adds the voices of unkillable, reborn myths: the exiled castaways of the Caribbean.

The sea is history, but it is also myth, and home. The sea is the voice of a marginalized people. Literature reopens wounds deeper than history can, but the sea can wash those wounds clean and reshaping myths can heal them. Once healed, Philoctetes and Odysseus, and all dispossessed will be brought home again.

Conclusion: Black Dionysus, or Athenian-African American Theatre

"It is tedious to tell again tales already plainly told."

Homer
Odyssey
Book XII: 208

I concluded *The Athenian Sun in an African Sky* with a report on an experimental student production of the *Hippolytus* of Euripides in South Africa in 1998. Using this production as an example, I prophesied that African theatre, like all theatre, was rapidly developing through hybridization, "hybrids of hybrids of hybrids" which had both international and indigenous roots were the norm for late twentieth century African theatre. The same holds true in the African Diaspora.

In March of 1998, roughly the same time as the South African production described above, another, unrelated student-created piece of experimental theatre was mounted at the Carnegie Mellon University School of Drama in the United States. Written and directed by undergraduate theatre student Russell Kaplan, *Ulysses Runs the Voodoo Down* was a multi-media, experimental piece of physical theatre that told the story of *The Odyssey* utilizing "the exploratory nature of Jazz music," according to Kaplan.[1] The title was suggested by the Miles Davis song "Miles Runs the Voodoo Down," itself an example of fusion. Fusion is a kind of music which, as the name suggests, blends elements of jazz, rock, and funk, all three of which are musical styles initially developed by African Americans and then appropriated and further developed by European Americans, until finally they have become part of a global culture (I have been in jazz clubs in Europe, Africa, America, and Japan, for example). All three forms are uniquely American, but have become internationalized.

In the case of "Ulysses Runs the Voodoo Down," the writer/director

231

attempted to use fusion music to structure the narrative of Homer's epic and provide a modern American context through which to tell the story of Ulysses. Eleven actors and a nine-piece jazz band performed the piece, while an unseen, miked narrator spoke the lines of the text, formed from a combination of the Fitzgerald translation of Homer and some Beat poets. The actors did not speak, but danced and moved to the music and spoken text. The set was limited to chairs, tables, and three screens upon which images were projected to suggest locale or theme: images of stars or an island, sketches of jazz instruments, images which suggested the jazz world. For example, in the scene in Hades, when Odysseus meets the ghost of Tiresias, a picture of a steaming coffee mug was projected. The underworld of Homer became the beatnik underworld of a basement coffeehouse, with all of the shades in "shades"—sunglasses—and berets, snapping their fingers in appreciation of the music or poetry. Tiresias was presented as an old hipster who recites his prophesies as beat poems, referencing not only Homer but other, famous beat poems. For example, he recites, "I saw the best minds of my generation destroyed by cattle," referring not only to the incident in *The Iliad* when Ajax, mad with rage and grief, slaughters cattle instead of his fellow Greeks, but also to the opening line of Alan Ginsberg's *Howl*, considered by some to be the defining poem of the beat culture.

Odysseus, played by African American actor Tyrone Mitchell, journeys home to Ithaca through the world of Jazz. Kaplan notes that *The Odyssey* is "the ultimate journey tale," and that jazz is the ultimate exploratory music form, in which improvisation is as important as classical structure. Just as Miles can "run the voodoo down," i.e. play a piece of music to its fullest, so, too, can Odysseus play life like a jazz instrument: improvisational, following a basic structure with much room for exploration and personal creation, full of sound and emotion, finding both the highs and the lows in the attempt to "bring it home," i.e. finish.

Kaplan argues that his production was full of hybrid forms. Jazz is a musical hybrid that links Africa and America. Theatre is a hybrid form, linking text to performance. Translations of Homer are hybrid forms, breeding a new text out of a classic narrative and contemporary American English. Even the title of "Ulysses Runs the Voodoo Down," uses the Roman name of the character, not the Greek, reminding the audience of the transcultural blend which they are receiving. In short, "Ulysses Runs the Voodoo Down" is a hybrid of hybrids, a cross-cultural form that blends other cross-cultural forms.

I noted in *Athenian Sun*, and have continued to argue in this volume, that it was in the universities where many successful productions of multicultural Greek tragedy began. Universities can afford to be experimental, and those who work in their theatre departments tend to look for connections between cultures as part of the larger project of education. Both the South African and the American productions noted here were created by students. In both cases, students of different ethnic and economic backgrounds worked together to create pieces based on classical Greek texts, but were informed by a multicultural, multi-media, multi-performance point of view. Faculty members as well, create and develop modern productions based on Greek originals, but that reflect contemporary issue, not just of race and ethnicity, but of gender, sexual orientation, and political and social issues of concern to the community.

The danger, however, is in the prioritization of the material. Whereas universities can be more liberal in their work than most commercial theatres, concerns of tenure, sensitivity to the community that comprises the audience (especially at state schools funded in part by public money and even private institutions worried about alumni donations), censure and censorship are dangers that may limit more controversial productions. More radical black theatre artists would further argue that for every Greek play, even an Afrocentric-sensitive adaptation, there is one less opportunity to engage African American drama. Adaptations can be a double-edged sword as they allow a living playwright's work to be staged, but there is a danger of the prioritization of material rooted in European classics demonstrating a continued bias in favor of the West. On the positive side, debate leads to inquiry, which, it is to be hoped, might open up students', faculty's and audience's minds to the larger issues that this very work has engaged.

There are different ways of contextualizing these plays. They are dramatic texts. They are theatrical productions. In either case, the product is the result of culture workers making "culture." We can contextualize the plays as texts that engage the larger issue of representation, race relations and issues of identity. The plays can be considered for their contextualization of American history as well as how they use Greek material to that end. In fairness to the playwrights, it is easy to critique, harder to create.

We live in the age of the hyphen: African-American, Euro-American, Afro-Asiatic, Afro-Caribbean, Caribbean-American, etc. This theatre might be termed "Athenian-African American," as a summary of its major influences. The Theatre is where the issues of the hyphen can be explored and represented. Theatre first and foremost deals with community—whereas reading is a solo act, a private one, and, in fairness, the creating of drama (writing) is a private act—performance is a social act, both actor and audience are needed for the art to exist. Therefore, theatre artists have a tremendous responsibility from the Egyptians through the Greeks through Africa, Europe, and America to engage history as it relates to the audience.

Black Dionysus is a god who is transformative—his theatre is a creative force, a revolutionary force, a confrontational force that can reshape
the world and the way we look at it. I noted above that it is in the universities that many productions of Greek tragedy occur, and where many experimental works of theatre are engaged. It is perhaps the province of students
to engage other cultures and attempt to transcend ethnic and cultural
boundaries, as such is their experience in the classroom every day. In *Race
Matters*, Cornell West observes that

> ...when white and black kids buy the same Billboard hits and laud the
> same athletic heroes the result is often a shared cultural space where some
> humane interaction takes place.[2]

We should note, however, that this "shared cultural space" is not "universal" but arises from specific cultural origins, whether hip-hop music or
Larry Byrd's and Michael Jordan's skills and constructed identities as professional basketball players in the NBA. While the "humane interaction"
is of key importance, and shared cultural space helps us to better understand ourselves and each other, and perhaps even move beyond simplistic
and stereotypical representations of the Other, the reality remains that
"shared space" is all too often the appropriation of African American culture by mainstream (read Euro-American) culture. Positive engagement by
all ethnicities can result, but so can cultural colonialism.

The role of the theatre is perhaps to force the questions beyond the
"shared cultural space": to force the "white kids buying the same Billboard
hits" to question the socio-economic forces that have created and developed African American culture and that privileges classical Greek and Euro-
American culture, and the "black kids buying the same Billboard hits" to
question the same from their position. It is the role of Black Dionysus, the
spirit of Greek theatre infused with Egyptian models and developed by
multicultural theatre artists for multicultural audiences, therefore, to
encourage us to share cultural space as well as to consider and question
the nature and origins of that culture and that space, and to correct social,
economic, and political imbalances, and, lastly, to reflect both the best and
the worst of what we as human beings and what we as Americans can be.

Humani Nihil Alienum.
(Nothing human is alien to me.)

Terrence

Humanity is my tribe.

Ola Rotimi

Notes

Introduction

1. White 46.
2. Loewen 58.
3. Loewen 58.
4. Weatherford 12.
5. Hill, "Black Theatre into the Mainstream" 81.
6. Hill, "Mainstream" 95.
7. Taplin, *Greek Fire* 4.
8. Taplin, *Greek Fire* iv.
9. Tatlow 78.
10. Tatlow 77.
11. Tatlow 2–3.
12. Gilroy, *Small Acts* 1–2.
13. See George M. Fredrickson, *Black Liberation* and *White Supremacy*.
14. Lowen 136.
15. Douglas Turner Ward. Lecture. Schaeffer Theatre, Bates College, Lewiston. 15 February 1989.

Chapter 1

1. DuBois 136–7.
2. Taplin, "Derek Walcott" 312.
3. Sartre 137.
4. Sartre 137.
5. Sartre 126.
6. Sartre 128.
7. Fanon, *Black Masks* 132.
8. Simawe, "Introduction." *Black Orpheus* xii.
9. Benson ix. Much of the historical information about *Black Orpheus* comes from Benson's excellent history of that publication.
10. Benson 13.
11. Benson 24.
12. Benson 26.
13. Ottley vii.
14. Ottley vii.
15. Huggins lxxv.
16. Huggins 3, 26–7.
17. Huggins lxxi, lxxiv.
18. Book I, 1–3.
19. Woods xviii.
20. Quoted in Tuttle 1072.
21. See the shooting script with an introduction by Pasolini for his thoughts on this project and why he made the choices he did.
22. Greene 149.
23. Quoted in Greene 129.
24. Sharply-Whiting 7.
25. Gilman, "Black Bodies" 231.
26. Sharpley-Whiting 10.
27. West 119.
28. West 119.
29. West 125–130.
30. West 126.
31. Sharpley-Whiting 21–2. Sharpley-Whiting also translates the script of the melodrama in its entirety in an appendix. A simple, didactic one act, its sole purpose is, as Sharpley-Whiting states, to strip the "primitive savage" of sex appeal and reassert European ideals of beauty as superior (34).
32. Sharpley-Whiting 33.
33. Quoted in Sharpley-Whiting 36.
34. In Sharpley-Whiting 161.
35. Sharpley-Whiting 40.
36. Parks, *Venus* in *Theatre Forum* 72.

37. Quoted in Sellar, "Shape of the Past" 36.

38. Sellar, "Making History" 38.

39. Sellar, "Shape of the Past" 36.

40. Quoted in Tetrel B6.

41. Bernal, *Black Athena Volume I* 30.

42. Berlinerblau 15–17.

43. Jones, *Black Zeus* 5.

44. Jones, *Black Zeus* 2.

45. Williams 6.

46. Williams 6.

47. Williams 7.

48. See Wetmore 24–30 for links between Homer and griots in Africa.

49. Quoted in Rubin E1.

50. Quoted in Williams 7. Davis is also one of the three original founders of the Non-Traditional Casting Project, discussed in chapter 3.

51. Quoted in Williams 7.

52. Bharucha, *Politics* 2.

53. Olaniyan 115.

54. See Larlham 76.

55. Hall 24.

56. Mercer 33, 37.

57. Mercer 37.

58. The phrase and idea are Angela Y. Davis's, concerning the perception of "multiculturalism" 47.

59. McDonald, *Ancient Sun* 75.

60. Patrice Pavis, introduction to "Somebody's Other: Disorientations in the Cultural Politics of Our Times" in *The Intercultural Performance Reader* 196–7.

Chapter 2

1. Wilson and Goldfarb 71.

2. Wilson and Goldfarb 71. Their definition is "An Afrocentric approach to history suggests that scholars explore the African origins of many accomplishments usually credited to European cultures" (71), itself a reductive and simplistic definition of the approach that casts Afrocentrism solely in terms of African response to Europe, rather than a methodology in its own right with its own approach. This definition also casts Afrocentrism solely in terms of "scholarly exploration," rather than an active political methodology. Wilson and Goldfarb, by and large, attempt to avoid ideology in their text, but in doing so privilege Eurocentrism and maintain the West as the center of theatre history.

3. Wilson and Goldfarb 71. See also Walter E. Forehand, *Terence* (Boston: Twayne, 1985).

4. Lefkowitz, *Not Out of Africa* 27.

5. Bernal, *Black Athena Writes Back* 14.

6. Bernal, *Black Athena Writes Back* 376.

7. Bernal, *Black Athena Writes Back* 393.

8. Bernal, *Black Athena Writes Back* 11.

9. James 7.

10. See the works by Diop, Asante, Jones and Obenga which trace the origins of Greek culture, primarily through linguistics, accounts by ancient historians, and cultural similarities.

11. Asante, *Kemet, Afrocentricity and Knowledge* 47.

12. Jones, *Profiles in Black Heritage* xiii.

13. Jones, *Profiles in Black Heritage* xvii.

14. Jones, *The Black Diaspora* 1.

15. Jones, *The Black Diaspora* 36.

16. Jones. *The African Diaspora* 31.

17. Snowden 48.

18. Lefkowitz, *Not out of Africa* 159.

19. Roth 314.

20. Roth 315.

21. Roth 315.

22. Roth 319.

23. Roth 318.

24. Patterson 29.

25. Patterson 30.

26. Patterson 30.

27. Patterson 30.

28. Asante, *The Afrocentric Ideal* 99.

29. Roach 211.

30. Blake 29.

31. Taken from title page of Blake's book (Columbus: O.H. Miller, 1857).

32. Asante, *The Afrocentric Idea* 149.

33. Tatlow 120.

34. Cartledge 102.

35. Snowden 63.

35. Silas Jones 20.

37. Diop 336–7.

38. Harrison 28.

39. Bernal, *Black Athena Volume I* 65.

40. Brockett 3rd ed. 12.

41. Brockett and Hildy, 8th ed. 10.

42. Molette and Molette 40.

43. Molette and Molette 40.
44. Asante, *The Afrocentric Ideal* 185.
45. Harrison 8.
46. Harrison 10.
47. Bernal, *Black Athena Volume II* 32.
48. Simon, "The Gospel Untruth" 96.
49. Bharucha, *Theatre and the World* 240.
50. Bharucha, *Theatre and the World* 8.

Chapter 3

1. Vernant 238.
2. Vernant 237.
3. Walton, *Greek Theatre Practice* 11.
4. Vernant 242.
5. Vernant 240.
6. Vernant 242.
7. Vernant 242.
8. Vernant 243.
9. McDonald, *Ancient Sun* 86.
10. Walton, *Greek Theatre Practice* 5.
11. Gilula 12.
12. See Hartigan, *Greek Tragedy on the American Stage*, Walcott, *Living Greek Theatre*, McDonald, *Sing Sorrow*, McDonald, *Ancient Sun*, Smethurst, *Artistry*, Diamond, "The Floating World," and Wetmore, *Athenian Sun* for detailed surveys of recent Greek adaptations.
13. See Hartigan, *Greek Tragedy on the American Stage*.
14. Green 1.
15. Beacham 37.
16. Beacham 37.
17. Quoted in McDonald, *Ancient Sun* 93.
18. Green 31.
19. Hatch and Abdullah 31.
20. Hill, *Shakespeare* 189.
21. Hill, *Shakespeare* xxi. See also Banham, Hill, and Woodyard 234.
22. Pao 15. Angela Pao, after the Non-Traditional Casting Project, a national organization started "to increase the participation of ethnic, female, and disabled artists in the performing arts in ways that are not token or stereotypical" (Andrea Wolper, "What Is the Non-Traditional Casting Project?" *Back Stage* 23 February 1990, 27A, quoted in Pao 2), actually identifies four types of non-traditional casting:

Colorblind casting—"actors are cast without regard to their race or ethnicity; the best actor is cast in the role."
Societal casting—"ethnic and female actors are cast in roles they perform in society as a whole."
Conceptual casting—"an ethnic actor is cast in a role to give the play greater resonance."
Cross-cultural casting—"the entire world of the play is translated to a different culture."
(These definitions are taken from the NTCP's pamphlet "What Is Non-Traditional Casting?" quoted in Pao 2). The last three categories are variations within African American Adaptations of Greek tragedy, and, in fact, are usually part of the same production concept: actors of color are conceptually cast in productions or adaptations that move the world of the play to one in which African Americans or Africans are playing the roles that they perform within that society as a whole. For example, Rita Dove's play *The Darker Face of the Earth* moves Sophocles' *Oedipus Rex* to 19th century South Carolina, in which the character Augustus (Oedipus) is a slave, and thus must be cast as an African American in keeping with the concept, the societal role of African Americans in South Carolina at the time, and the world of the play. Thus, as the last three categories of the NTCP overlap, for purposes of this study, only two categories shall be considered: "Colorblind" and "Conceptual."
23. C. John Herrington, "Introduction." *Prometheus Bound* 8.
24. Durant 384.
25. Herrington 12.
26. Herrington 12.
27. *Prometheus Bound* 55. (I use page number instead of line number here as the description is the translators' handiwork, not from the Greek original).
28. Bernstein 13.
29. The translators kept the last line in Greek. It translates to, "You see me, how I suffer unjust things!" In production, when Prometheus called out the line, only those who knew Greek knew what he was saying. An informal poll of audience members indicated that most who saw the show assumed that Prometheus said something in an African language, which further indicates

how ethnicity of the actor and an Afrocentric mise-en-scène can generate meaning for
the audience, or at the very least lead them
to a series of assumptions.
    30. The information on audience recep-
tion comes from Tom Mikotowicz, who
notes that one night during the Washington
run only 18 people were in the 1100 seats of
the Eisenhower Theatre at the Kennedy
Center (89).
    31. Quoted in McDonald, *Ancient Sun*
80.
    32. Quoted in McDonald, *Ancient Sun*
82.
    33. Quoted in McDonald, *Ancient Sun*
82.
    34. Quoted in McDonald, *Ancient Sun*
79.
    35. Walton, *Living Greek Theatre* 69.
    36. Quoted in McDonald, *Ancient Sun*
94.
    37. McDonald, *Ancient Sun* 81. She does
state that the box represents madness,
"among other things." Considering the
other signifiers of the production, however,
the box seems much more to trap, contain
and limit Ajax, than to define his insanity.
    38. Quoted in Bartow 281.
    39. Shewey 270.
    40. Quoted in McDonald, *Ancient Sun*
16.
    41. McDonald, *Ancient Sun* 77.
    42. See the section on Black Venus in
chapter 2 and sexuality as a focus in adaptations in the section entitled "Shifting
Contexts and Cultural Codes."
    43. Quoted in McDonald, *Ancient Sun*
85.
    44. Shewey 271. Shewey also writes that
Athena uses her microphone "like a disco
deity," connecting the Greek goddess to the
dance and music movement, many of whose
singers were African American (270).
    45. Gill 160.
    46. Hill, *Shakespeare* 172.
    47. Gill 10.
    48. See Hill's *Shakespeare in Sable*, which
includes analyses of many black college productions of Shakespeare.
    49. Gill 10.
    50. Hill, *Shakespeare* 58.
    51. Sun 88.
    52. Pao 12.
    53. Sun 88.

    54. Wilson, *Ground* 26.
    55. Wilson, *Ground* 29.
    56. Wilson, *Ground* 30–31.
    57. Wilson, *Ground* 28.
    58. Hatch, "Here Comes Everybody"
148.
    59. Wetmore 35–9.
    60. See Weber 27–35.
    61. Fleurant 10.
    62. Davis 8.
    63. Davis 11.
    64. Levine 152.
    65. Epskamp and de Geus 145–6.
    66. West 119.
    67. West 119.
    68. See Zeitlin, *Playing the Other: Gender
and Society in Classical Greek Literature.* Also
see the essay "The Dynamics of Misogyny:
Myth and Myth Making in the *Oresteia.*
    69. For a full history of the identification
based on ancestry and "black blood," see
Keith Irvine, *The Rise of the Colored Races.*
    70. Newman 1320.
    71. Jordan 174.
    72. Quoted in "African Odyssey Interac-
tive." Kennedy Center for the Performing
Arts homepage. 24 November 1998.
    73. Hatch and Abdullah 115.
    74. *Dionysus in 69* n.p.
    75. Aguiar 119.
    76. Aguiar 119.
    77. Overbeck, "The Life" 25.
    78. Woods, "From the Dramaturg."
    79. Quoted in Stein 195.
    80. Quoted in Stein 195.
    81. Stein 194 and Overbeck, "The Life"
35.
    82. Kennedy, "Electra" 115. In *Adrienne
Kennedy in One Act.*
    83. Kennedy, "Electra" 135.
    84. Walton, *Living Greek Theatre* 144.
    85. Kennedy, "Electra" 139.
    86. Kennedy, "Electra" 139.
    87. Emily Townsend Vermuele, "Intro-
duction to *Electra.*" 3 (in *Complete Greek
Tragedies*).
    88. Kennedy, "Orestes" 147. In *Adrienne
Kennedy in One Act.*
    89. Quoted in Bryant-Jackson and Over-
beck, "Interview" 9.
    90. See Wetmore 103–120 for an analy-
sis of this adaptation.
    91. Wilson, "From the Artistic Director"
7.

92. Pensak 10–11. Interestingly , for a seemingly Afrocentric production, the program demonstrates a strong Eurocentric bias. Under a section entitled "The House of Cadmus, The Tragedy of Thebes" the program lists ten other adaptations of *Oedipus Rex*, all European. Not a single African adaptation is mentioned on the list, or even anywhere in the program despite there being several of them, some quite well known, such as the aforementioned *The Gods Are Not to Blame*.

93. Sources: World Heath Organization and UNAIDS as quoted in Weiss, "War on Disease," Klesius, "Search for a Cure," and Bartholet, "The Plague Years."

94. Bartholet 35. See also Ellen Cose for a debate on the role African Americans can and should play in combating AIDS in Africa.

95. See Simon Watney, "Missionary Positions: AIDS, 'Africa,' and Race.

96. Hartigan F5.

97. The author spoke with several people from the Hartford Stage, who would only confirm that Kennedy was the Text Consultant. No one indicated whether Kennedy had ever written her own adaptation which was rejected, or if she had been engaged from the beginning to simply adapt the Fitts and Fitzgerald translation. The latter is not out of the realm of possibility as Kennedy had already used the Arrowsmith translation of *Orestes* to develop her version, as explored earlier in the chapter.

98. Hartigan F5.
99. Weber G15.
100. Weber G15.
101. Smith, *Intercultural* 40–41.
102. Breuer, "Acknowledgments." *Gospel at Colonus* ix.
103. Breuer, "Acknowledgments" ix.
104. D'Aponte 102.
105. Burdine 73.
106. Burdine 81.
107. Burdine 81.
108. Coppenger 80.
109. Levine 175.
110. Taplin, *Greek Fire* 60.
111. Burdine 80.
112. Brustein 28.
113. Simon 96.
114. Fitzgerald, "Preface" *Gospel at Colonus* xii.
115. McDonald, *Sing Sorrow* 160.

116. McDonald, *Sing Sorrow* 163.
117. Koger 23–4.
118. Koger 24.
119. D'Aponte 109.
120. McDonald, *Sing Sorrow* 175.
121. Quoted in Rabkin 48.
122. Koger 23; D'Aponte 109; Kramer 73.
123. Quoted in Levine 174.
124. See Goines, "Gospel Music and Black Consciousness" and Spenser, *Protest and Praise: Sacred Music of Black Religion* for extended studies of the nature, purpose, and effect of Gospel music, individually and collectively on its singers and audiences.
125. Gill 200.
126. Disch 690.
127. Coppenger 77.
128. Interestingly, Ivan M. Linforth argues that despite the presence of the material culture of Greek religion and the references to oracles, the Eumenides, and the gods, as well as the final miracle, *Oedipus at Colonus* is not a very religious play. He concludes that the play is not nearly as religious as much extant Sophocles or Aeschylus. Breuer and Telson might well have constructed a religious musical on one of the least religious plays in the Greek canon.
129. Daniel 2.
130. Daniel 3.
131. Jenkins 152.
132. Weaver 59.
133. Spenser 225, 227–243.
134. Breuer 4.
135. Southern 464.
136. Breuer 4–5.
137. McDonald, *Sing Sorrow* 175.
138. Linforth 184.
139. Breuer 6.
140. Breuer 11.
141. Breuer 17.
142. Breuer 24.
143. Breuer 29.
144. Breuer 36.
145. Breuer 37.
146. Breuer 43; Fitzgerald 145.
147. Coppenger 78.
148. Breuer 45.
149. Breuer 49.
150. Breuer 49.
151. Breuer 51.
152. Breuer 53.
153. Fitzgerald 170.

154. Earl F. Miller, "Note on Performance," *Gospel at Colonus* xiv.
155. Southern 608.
156. Simon 96.
157. Kramer 74.
158. Green 65.
159. Quoted in McDowell 156.
160. Quoted in McDowell 159.
161. Quoted in McDowell 159.
162. Dove 19. All quotations, unless otherwise indicated, come from the third
revised edition of the text.
163. Dove 27.
164. Dove 21.
165. Quoted in interview on "African
Odyssey Interactive." Kennedy Center for
the Performing Arts Homepage. 24 November 1998.
166. Dove 38.
167. Dove 43.
168. Dove 44.
169. Dove 47.
170. Dove 51.
171. The one thing that all of these plays
have in common, in particular those set in
the more recent past, is that the characters
are ignorant of the direct link they have to
myth. For al of his mythical references,
Augustus never refers to Oedipus or sees
himself as Oedipus. Likewise, as will be seen
in chapter four, missing from all plays with
characters named "Medea" is the sense of
the mythic Medea. Nowhere in Jim Magnuson's *African Medea*, set in nineteenth
century Africa, do the characters of Jason
and Medea refer to their mythic antecedents
or recognize themselves in Greek myth. In
other words, the only part of the classical
world that is unreferenced in these plays by
the characters themselves is the specific
myth or tragedy that is being adapted.
172. Dove 64.
173. Dove 71–2.
174. Dove 78.
175. Dove 79.
176. Dove 20.
177. Dove 83.
178. Dove 83.
179. Dove 86.
180. Dove 87.
181. Dove 118.
182. Dove 120.
183. Dove 141.
184. See Vernant, "Oedipus without the

Complex" in *Myth and Tragedy in Ancient
Greece.*
185. Dove 143.
186. Dove 144.
187. Dove, "Oedipus in America," *Darker
Face of the Earth* theatrical program. 10.
188. "Oedipus in America" 12.
189. "Oedipus in America" 18.
190. Quoted in McDowell 188.
191. Liston 67.
192. See Duboys.
193. Vernant 116.
194. Kennedy Center program 5.
195. Quoted in "African Odyssey Interactive." Kennedy Center for the Performing
Arts Homepage. 24 November 1998.

Chapter 4

1. Translated by Frederick Ahl.
2. Furth 53–4.
3. Weisenburger 228.
4. Furth argues that the production
"may even have directly inspired Noble to
retell the Margaret Garner story" (53), but
this idea is mere conjecture—there exists no
evidence to either support or disprove the
theory that the production in any way
influenced Noble, or that he even saw it.
The Modern Medea was *Harper's Weekly*'s title
for the lithograph based on Noble's painting entitled *Margaret Garner.*
5. This narrative is based on those
constructed by Weisenbuger, Boime (51),
and Furth (37–38).
6. Furth 39.
7. Boime 49.
8. The small version is now owned by
Proctor and Gamble, Inc., and is on display
in Cincinnati. A private collector currently
owns the larger painting.
9. Boime 51.
10. "The Modern Medea" 318.
11. Weisenburger 8.
12. Weisenburger 61.
13. Weisenburger 77.
14. Quoted in Weisenberger 202.
15. Furth 46.
16. Furth 39–40.
17. Furth 46.
18. Gilman, *Difference* 132–6.
19. Numbers quoted in Gilman, *Difference* 137, as is the following information.

20. Quoted in Gilman, *Difference* 138.
21. Gilman, *Difference* 138.
22. Weisenburger 228.
23. Cornell 194.
24. Cornell 194.
25. Blondell 152–3.
26. Knox 273.
27. See DuBois, *Centaurs and Amazons* 115.
28. Herodotus 2.104.
29. Bell 293.
30. "Introduction to The Medea" in *The Complete Greek Tragedies: Euripides* I. 56.
31. Knox 274, Blondell 163.
32. Rabinowitz 125.
33. DuBois, *Centaurs and Amazons* 119.
34. Rabinowitz 137.
35. Burnett 195–6.
36. Rabinowitz 143.
37. McDermott 45.
38. Anderson 87.
39. Quoted in Bondanella 277–8.
40. See chapter 4 in Wetmore for an analysis of the play.
41. Banning 43.
42. Celia Wren, "In Medea Res." *American Theatre*. 19.4 (April 2002): 22–25, 60–61.
43. Macintosh 3.
44. McDonald, "Medea as Politician and Diva: Riding the Dragon into the Future" 301–2.
45. McDonald, "Medea" 302.
46. Where McDonald's argument falls apart is when she argues that "Medea illustrates what happens in every revolution: when the oppressed come to power they often perpetuate the abuses they have suffered" (302). She further notes, after Said that "Medea exerted her imperial will over her victims" (n302). I believe that McDonald is wrong. Medea never "comes to power," she performs a violent act and then leaves forever. Furthermore, most postcolonialist scholars would argue that the colonized cannot have an "imperial will." Fanon would argue, correctly so that, as colonialism is violence, Medea's violent response grows out of the wrongs done to her—she has no "imperial will" to exert. Lastly, not every revolution results in continued abuse. Even in recent history the revolutionary changes in Eastern Europe and South Africa have been carried out with a minimum of perpetuation of abuse.

47. Corti 180–1. See also Jahnn, *Medea*, which contains the text in the original German and Jahnn, *Medea: Ein Theatrebuch von Manfred Weber*, also in German, and containing essays and a photohistory of significant productions of Jahnn's play.
48. Jahnn, *Medea* 5.
49. See *Medea: Ein Theatrebuch von Manfred Weber* for a survey and photographs of these productions.
50. Quoted in Gill 23.
51. Hatch and Abdullah 57.
52. Cullen 9, 15.
53. Cullen 3.
54. Rice 336.
55. Rice 336.
56. Corti 193.
57. Quoted in Sharp 9.
58. Quoted in Sharp 9.
59. Quoted in Istel.
60. Holman.
61. Quoted in Istel.
62. Blondell 155.
63. Wolfe 27.
64. Wolfe 27.
65. Wolfe 28.
66. In satirizing Shange, Wolfe has the Lady in Plaid remark "And she cried for her sister in Detroit / Who knew, as she, that their souls belonged / in ancient temples on the Nile," right before Medea enters (26). Wolfe juxtaposes the Afrocentric, "Black Athena" connection to the ancient world of the Lady in Plaid with the over-the-top histrionic posing of Medea Jones, a firm devotee of the "Black Orpheus" model—the universality of the Greeks. Although not targets escape unscathed, and Wolfe obviously fondly satirizes both of these stereotypes equally, it is interesting to note that he does present both views side by side in the same scene.
67. The author is in debt to Jim Magnuson for providing additional personal and production background information via email. Email to Author. 4 June 2002.
68. Magnuson, Email to Author. 4 June 2002.
69. Magnuson, "African Medea" 155.
70. Magnuson 155.
71. Magnuson 162.
72. Magnuson 157.
73. Magnuson 156; 163.
74. Magnuson 155.

75. Magnuson 157.
76. Magnuson 159.
77. Magnuson 161.
78. Magnuson 163.
79. Magnuson 163.
80. Magnuson 165.
81. Magnuson 167.
82. Magnuson 170.
83. See Fanon, *The Wretched of the Earth* for the extended argument.
84. Magnuson 173.
85. For an interesting analysis of the Evans case, in which it is argued that the police were entirely to blame for the incident, perhaps even engineering it, see Wecht, Curriden, and Wecht chapter 4. Chapter 5 in the same book deals with a police shootout with the Black Panthers in Chicago for which the Panthers were blamed, but Wecht et al. argue the police were the only ones firing. Such incidents in the late sixties and early seventies only fueled the distrust between the white mainstream and African Americans and the revolutionary fervor of the time.
86. Magnuson. Email to the author. 4 June 2002.
87. Magnuson, "African Medea" 178.
88. Magnuson 180–1.
89. Magnuson. Email to the author. 4 June 2004.
90. See Fanon, *Wretched of the Earth* for a full analysis of this phenomenon.
91. Magnuson. Email to author. 4 June 2002.
92. Gurr 140.
93. Jeyifo 26.
94. Magnuson. Email to the author. 4 June 2002.
95. Magnuson, "African Medea" 183.
96. Magnuson 183.
97. Fanon, *Wretched* 309.
98. Magnuson 187.
99. Magnuson 187.
100. Magnuson 190.
101. Magnuson 190.
102. Magnuson 190.
103. Magnuson 190.
104. See, for example, George Fredrickson's constructions of similarities between the freedom struggles of blacks in the United States and South Africa in *Black Liberation*. Fredrickson gives an excellent comparison of the Black Power and Black

Consciousness movements in chapter 7.
105. Fredrickson, *Black Liberation* 296.
106. Fredrickson, *Black Liberation* 297.
107. See Davidson and Ramsay. São Tomé and Príncipe, the other Portuguese colony on the West coast of Africa had a brief resistance movement in the early 1950s which was stopped by the Batepa Massacre in 1953 when several hundred laborers were killed by the Portuguese. An armed resistance therefore did not emerge until 1972, after Magnuson's play, and independence was achieved in 1975 (See Ramsay 88). Thus, this particular revolution is not included in the list of those referenced by African Medea.
108. Ramsay 145.
109. Ramsay 145, 265.
110. Ramsay 145.
111. Ramsay 41.
112. Ramsay 41–2.
113. Magnuson. Email to the author, 4 June 2002.
114. Magnuson. Email to the author. 4 June 2002.
115. Ferlita. Email to the author, 2 March 2002.
116. "Playwright's Note" in the original production program. Email to the author. 15 April 2002. All of the information on the original impetus for creation and the development of the play comes from E-interviews with Father Ferlita himself.
117. The author is again in debt to Father Ferlita for this extended production history. Email to the author. 3 May 2002.
118. Mission Statement and Company History from the New Federal Theatre homepage: (http://metrobase.com/newfederal/index.htm).
119. The author is in debt to Father Ernest Ferlita for providing a copy of the text. Rights and information about the play can be gained from Father Ferlita (Loyola University—New Orleans, 6363 St. Charles Ave., New Orleans, LA 70118-6195. Email: ferlita@loyno.edu).
120. Thompson, "Kongo" 150.
121. Ferlita, *Black Medea* 4.
122. Ferlita, *Black Medea* 5.
123. Ferlita, *Black Medea* 6.
124. Ferlita, *Black Medea* 7.
125. See Tallant's *Voodoo in New Orleans*, Mulira's article in Holloway, and

Jacobs and Kaslow for in-depth studies of Damballah and New Orleans voodoo. See especially Mulira's article for the lyrics of songs in the worship of Damballah that link Dahomey, Haiti, and New Orleans (44–47).

126. Pinn 38.
127. Metraux 332.
128. Mulira 34.
129. Mulira 35.
130. Ferlita, Black Medea 8.
131. Ferlita, Black Medea 8.
132. Ferlita, Black Medea 9.
133. Ferlita, Black Medea 9.
134. Ferlita, Black Medea 10.
135. See Duboys.
136. Ferlita, Black Medea 10.
137. Ferlita, Black Medea 11.
138. Mulira 36-7.
139. Tallant 9.
140. Mulira 36.
141. Roach 208.
142. Ferlita, Black Medea 17.
143. Ferlita, Black Medea 23.
144. Ferlita, Black Medea 28.
145. Ferlita, Black Medea 15, 18, 31.
146. Ferlita, Black Medea 46.
147. Ferlita, Black Medea 46.
148. Ferlita, Black Medea 66.
149. Ferlita, Black Medea 71.
150. See reviews by Ahlgren, Winn, Klein, and Kingston.
151. Klein, "Pecong" 12NJ11.
152. Carter 21.
153. Carter 21.
154. Carter 24.
155. Carter 25.
156. Carter 41.
157. Carter 46.
158. Carter 14.
159. Carter 14.
160. Farb 108.
161. Farb 110.
162. Majors and Billson 91– 102.
163. Farb 110.
164. Farb 111.
165. Carter 59.
166. Majors and Billson 93; 95.
167. Majors and Bilson 95-6.
168. Dunn 376.
169. Carter 67.
170. Carter 69.
171. Carter 77.
172. Knox 292-3.
173. Carter 79.

174. Carter 85.
175. Carter 88.
176. McDermott 9.
177. Ferlita, Twice-Born 13.
178. Ferlita, Twice-Born 17.
179. Ferlita, Twice-Born 31.
180. Ferlita, Twice-Born 40.
181. Ferlita, Twice-Born 75.
182. Ferlita, Twice-Born 87.
183. Quoted in Wren 25.
184. Letter to the author, 21 April 2001. The author must note, however, that this remark is the first he has ever heard of the interpretation that the Greeks used Medea to get sympathy for Jason. Most Eurocentric classicists do not see Jason in a sympathetic light at all, and certainly in Euripides he does not come across as such. Even as the reader/audience is horrified at Medea's actions, Jason is not the recipient of our sympathy.
185. Letter to the author, 21 April 2001.
186. Quoted in Wren 25.
187. The author is in debt to Silas Jones for the use of his unpublished manuscript. Rights and information about the play are available from Mr. Jones (642 Burnside Ave., Los Angeles, CA 90036).
188. Letter to the author, 21 April 2001.
189. Silas Jones, American Medea 1.
190. Silas Jones 1.
191. Silas Jones 1.
192. Silas Jones 1.
193. Silas Jones 3.
194. Silas Jones 4.
195. Silas Jones 6.
196. Silas Jones 18.
197. Silas Jones 6.
198. Silas Jones 6.
199. Silas Jones 7.
200. Silas Jones 8.
210. Silas Jones 10.
202. Silas Jones 10.
203. Silas Jones 11.
204. Silas Jones 15.
205. Silas Jones 16.
206. Silas Jones 17.
207. Silas Jones 18.
208. Silas Jones 20.
209. Silas Jones 20.
210. Silas Jones 21.
211. Silas Jones 22.
212. Silas Jones 24.
213. Silas Jones 27.

214. Silas Jones 33.
215. Silas Jones 41.
216. Silas Jones 42.
217. Silas Jones 43.
218. Silas Jones 44.
219. Silas Jones 46.
220. Silas Jones 50.
221. Silas Jones 52.
222. Kahn A5. Much of the information about the Monticello Association is also from this article.
223. Quoted in Kahn A5.
224. Fraden 1.
225. Fraden 42.
226. Fraden 48.
227. Lopez 39.
228. Fraden 72.
229. Quoted in Fraden 55.
230. Quoted in Fraden 56.
231. Cooper's script is the property of Cultural Odyssey, which allowed the text of *The Tragedy of Medea Jackson* to be reproduced in Fraden's *Imagining Medea* (56–64). The original manuscript has not been published, and I am grateful to Rhodessa Jones, Jeannie Gerber, and Cultural Odyssey (762 Fulton Street, Suite 306, San Francisco CA 94102) for the use of a copy of the play.
232. Fraden 64.
233. Fraden 70.
234. Fraden 2.
235. Boime 51–52.

Chapter 5

1. Lamming, "Caribbean Literature" 33. The legacy of slavery remains to this day a point of contention in national debate in the United States, particularly when it comes to the issue of reparations. Within recent years discussions were held in the media, the halls of government, in the classroom, and on the street on whether or not it was appropriate for President Clinton to apologize for slavery. A backlash against affirmative action has grown in the past decade. Despite progress in civil rights and race relations, the legacy of slavery, many feel has still left the African American community at a socio-economic and cultural disadvantage and the topic remains a divisive and challenging one.

2. Lamming, "Caribbean Literature" 33.
3. Gilroy, *There Ain't No Black in the Union Jack* 157.
4. Gilroy, *Black Atlantic* 4.
5. Edgecomb, "Introduction" 9.
6. Edgecomb, "Introduction" 12. The other four are to provide wages for artists and technicians, who too often are called upon to be volunteer labor, to develop trained personnel in all areas of theatre, to build well-equipped, practical facilities, and to create and maintain effective theatre programs including audience development and children's theatre etc. (9–12).
7. Brathwaite, History 6–7.
8. Masland and Larimer 42.
9. Hall 230.
10. Hall 235.
11. Hall 228.
12. Hall 229.
13. Stone xi.
14. Dalphinis 159.
15. Dalphinis 173.
16. Havelock 263.
17. Van Doren 231.
18. *Odyssey* Book IX: 156–161.
19. Cyclops is based on an episode in Book IX of *The Odyssey*. The other play is Euripides's *Rhesus*, taken from Book X of *The Iliad*. Other plays deal with episodes mentioned in passing in the epics, but only these two dramatize episodes presented in detail in the epics.
20. Griffiths 79.
21. Griffiths 9.
22. Lamming, *Pleasure* 34.
23. Said 357.
24. Said 362–3.
25. Said 359.
26. See the writings of Paul Gilroy, Stuart Hall, David Edgecomb, and Judy Stone.
27. Book I: 1–10.
28. Book X: 620–1.
29. Said, 363.
30. Hippolyte ix.
31. A "balanced policy" is Hippolyte's assessment of Walcott's program, ix.
32. Banham, Hill, and Woodyard 167.
33. Banham, Hill, and Woodyard 172.
34. Banham, Hill, and Woodyard 191, 211.
35. Banham, Hill, and Woodyard 192.
36. Banham, Hill, and Woodyard 231.

37. Brathwaite, "Timehri" 29.
38. See Wetmore, chapter 6 "African Antigones," the section entitled "Antigone in Exile 1." 176–181.
39. Sutherland 55.
40. Gilbert and Tompkins 42.
41. Quoted in Crow 21.
42. Olaniyan 102.
43. Olaniyan 114.
44. Olaniyan 115.
45. Olaniyan 113, 115.
46. Olaniyan 113.
47. Walcott, Collected Poems 364.
48. Hamner, Epic 80.
49. Stone 140.
50. Quoted in Brown and Johnson 216.
51. See Williams and Chrisman; Said, Orientalism 49.
52. Olaniyan, in fact, titles his chapter on Walcott "Islands of History at a Rendezvous with a Muse" (93). One of Olaniyan's main criticisms of Walcott is Walcott's privileging of the construction of history as myth, as opposed to history as politics or, in Walcott's terminology "history as time." Walcott sees those who insist that Africa replace the West as the center of Caribbean culture, poets who rely on history as politics, as limiting, whereas his own figuration of multiple cultural streams feeding Caribbean culture is more enabling. Olaniyan sees this as a problematic and overly simplistic response. See Olaniyan and Walcott's essay "The Muse of History."
53. Stone 93.
54. Stone 93.
55. Quoted in Taplin, "Derek Walcott" 312.
56. Taplin, "Derek Walcott" 316.
57. Stone 100.
58. Stone 101.
59. Rae 114.
60. Rae 113.
61. Rae 113.

62. Stone 114.
63. Grimes 116.
64. Stone 133–134.
65. Stone 133.
66. Ashaolu 119.
67. Walcott, Odyssey 1.
68. For a complete discussion of the etymology, morphology, and history of calypso the reader is directed towards the anonymous essay on Calypso on the world music website entitled Global Village Idiot (http://www.globalvillageidiot.net/calypso.htm). For more on the history and cultural significance of calypso music, especially in relation to anticolonial culture, see Lashley and the relevant chapter (Chapter 8) in Manuel, Bilby, and Largey.
69. Walcott, Odyssey 73.
70. Walcott, Odyssey 75.
71. Banham, Hill, and Woodyard 245.
72. Dunn 376.
73. Walcott, Odyssey 76.
74. Walcott, Odyssey 87–8.
75. Walcott, Odyssey 160.
76. Quoted in Baer 84–5.
77. Hamner, Epic 1.
78. Brucker 396.
79. Taplin, "Derek Walcott" 312, 316, 317.
80. Quoted in Baer 173.
81. Walcott, Omeros 52.
82. Hamner, Epic 2.
83. Hamner, Epic 15.
84. Quoted in Baer 84.
85. Figueroa 212.

Conclusion

1. Russell Kaplan, in an interview with the author, 12 September 1998.
2. West, Race Matters 121.

Works Cited

Aeschylus. *Prometheus Bound*. Trans. James Scully and C. John Herington. Oxford: Oxford University Press, 1975.

Aguiar, Marian. "Apollo Theatre." Appiah and Gates 119.

Ahlgren, Calvin. "A Tropical Twist on Medea Legend." *San Francisco Chronicle* 17 October 1993: 39.

Aidoo, Ama Ata. *The Dilemma of a Ghost and Anowa*. Ibadan: Longman, 1980.

Anderson, Lisa M. *Mammies No More: The Changing Image of Black Women on Stage and Screen*. Lanham: Rowman & Littlefield, 1997.

Apollodorus. *Gods and Heroes of the Greeks: The Library of Apollodorus*. Ed. Trans. Michael Simpson. Amherst: University of Massachusettes Press, 1976.

Appiah, Kwame, and Henry Louis Gates, Jr., eds. *Africana*. New York: Basic Civitas, 1999.

Appunti per un Orestiade africana. Dir. Pier Paolo Passolini. Idi Cinematografica, 1970. VHS. Mystic Fire Video, 1989.

Asante, Molefe Kete. *The Afrocentric Idea*. Rev. ed. Philadelphia: Temple University Press, 1998.

_____. *Kemet, Afrocentricity, and Knowledge*. Trenton: Africa World Press, 1990.

Ashaolu, Albert. "Allegory in *Ti-Jean and His Brothers*." Hamner *Critical* 118–124.

Baer, William. ed. *Conversations with Derek Walcott*. Jackson: University of Mississippi Press, 1996.

Banham, Martin, Errol Hill, and George Woodyard, eds. *The Cambridge Guide to African and Caribbean Theatre*. Cambridge: Cambridge University Press, 1992.

Banning, Yvonne. "Speaking Silences: Images of Cultural Differences and Gender in Fleishman and Reznek's *Medea*." *South African Theatre As/And Intervention*. Eds. Marcia Blumberg and Dennis Walder. Atlanta: Rodopi, 1999. 41–77.

Bartholet, Jeffrey. "The Plague Years." *Newsweek*. 17 January 2000: 32–37.

Barton, John. *Tantalus: Ten New Plays*. London: Oberon, 2000.

Bartow, Arthur. *The Director's Voice*. New York: Theatre Communications Group, 1988.

Beacham, Richard. "John Barton Directs the Greeks." *Theatre* 11 (1980) 37–42.

Beier, Ulli, ed. *Black Orpheus: An Anthology of New African and African American Stories*. New York: McGraw-Hill, 1967.

_____. *Political Spider: An Anthology of Stories from Black Orpheus*. London: Heinemann, 1969.

Bell, Robert E. *Women of Classical Mythology*. Oxford: Oxford University Press, 1991.

Benson, Peter. *Black Orpheus, Transition, and Modern Cultural Awakening in Africa*. Berkeley: University of California Press, 1986.

Benston, Kimberly W. "The Aesthetics of Modern Black Drama: From Mimesis to Mithexis." Hill 61–78.

Berlinerblau, Jacques. *Heresy in the University*. New Brunswick: Rutgers University Press, 1999.

Bernal, Martin. *Black Athena: Volume I: The Fabrication of Ancient Greece 1785–1985*. London: Free Association, 1987.

_____. *Black Athena: Volume II: The Archeological and Documentary Evidence*. New Brunswick: Rutgers University Press, 1991.

_____. *Black Athena Writes Back: Martin Bernal Responds to His Critics*. Ed. David Chioni Moore. Durham: Duke University Press, 2001.

Bernstein, Hilda. *No. 46—Steve Biko*. London: International Defense and Aid Fund, 1978.

Bharucha, Rustom. *The Politics of Cultural Practice*. Hanover: Weslyan University Press, 2000.

_____. "Somebody's Other: Disorientations in the Cultural Politics of Our Times." *The Intercultural Performance Reader*. Ed. Patrice Pavis. London: Routledge, 1996. 196–212.

_____. *Theatre and the World: Performance and the Politics of Culture*. London: Routledge, 1993.

Black Orpheus. (*Orfeu Negro*). Dir. Marcel Camus. Writ. Jacques Voit. Lopert Films, 1958. VHS Janus Films, 1988.

Blake, W.O. *The History of Slavery and the Slave Trade, Ancient and Modern*. Columbus: O.H. Miller, 1857.

Blondell, Ruby. "Introduction to *Medea*." *Women on the Edge*. Eds Ruby Blondell, Mary-Kay Gamel, Nancy Sorkin Rabinowitz, and Bella Zweig. New York: Routledge, 1999.

Boime, Albert. "Burgoo and Bourgeois: Thomas Noble's Images of Black People" *Thomas Satterwhite Noble, 1835–1907*. James D. Birchfield, Albert Boime, and William J. Hennesey. Lexington: University of Kentucky Art Museum, 1988.

Bondanella, Peter. *Italian Cinema: From Neorealism to the Present*. 3rd ed. New York: Continuum, 2001.

Branch, William, ed. *Crosswinds: Black dramatists in the Diaspora*. Bloomington: Indiana University Press, 1993.

Brathwaite, Edward Kamau. *History of the Voice*. London: New Beacon Books, 1984.

_____. *Odale's Choice*. London: Evans Brothers, 1983.

_____. "Timehri." *Is Massa Day Dead? Black Moods in the Caribbean*. Ed. Orde Coombs. New York: Anchor, 1974. 28–44.

Breuer, Lee. *The Gospel at Colonus*. New York: TCG, 1989.

Brockett, Oscar. *History of the Theatre*. 3rd ed. Boston: Allyn and Bacon, 1977.

_____ and Franklin J. Hildy. *History of the Theatre*. 8th ed. Boston: Allyn and Bacon, 1999.

Brown, Robert, and Cheryl Johnson. "An Interview with Derek Walcott." *Cream City Review* 14.2 (1990): 209–23.

Bruckner, D.J.R. "A Poem in Homage to an Unwanted Man." In Hamner *Critical* 396–399.

Brustein, Robert. "On Theatre: Transcultural Blends." *New Republic* 198 (April 25,1988): 28–29.

Bryant-Jackson, Paul K. and Lois More Overbeck. "Adrienne Kennedy: An Interview." In Bryant-Jackson and Overbeck, *Intersecting* 3–12.

____, and ____, eds. *Intersecting Boundaries: The Theatre of Adrienne Kennedy*. Minneapolis: University of Minnesota Press, 1992.

Burdine, Walter. "Let the Theatre Say 'Amen'." *Black American Literature Forum* 25(1991): 73–82.

Burnett, Anne Pippin. *Revenge in Attic and Later Tragedy*. Berkeley: University of California Press, 1998.

Cable, Mary. *Black Odyssey: The Case of the Slave Ship Amistad*. New York: Penguin, 1971.

Carter, Angela. *Black Venus's Tale*. London: Next Editions, 1980.

____. *Burning Your Boats: The Collected Short Stories*. New York: Henry Holt, 1995.

Carter, Steve. *Pecong*. New York: Broadway Play, 1993.

Cartledge, Paul. "Classical Studies." *Encyclopedia of Social and Cultural Anthropology*. Eds. Alan Barnard and Jonathan Spencer. New York: Routledge, 1996. 100–102.

Clauss, James J., and Sarah Iles Johnston, eds. *Medea: Essays on Medea in Myth, Literature, Philosophy, and Art*. Princeton: Princeton University Press, 1997.

Coppenger, Royston. "Theatre in Brooklyn: Lee Breuer's *Gospel*." *Theatre* 15 (1984): 71–80.

Cornell, Drucilla. *Beyond Accommodation: Ethical Feminism, Reeconstruction, and the, Law*. New York: Routledge, 1991.

Corti, Lillian. *The Myth of Medea and the Murder of Children*. Westport: Greenwood, 1998.

Cose, Ellen. "A Cause That Crosses the Color Line." *Newsweek* 17 January 2000: 49.

Crow, Brian, and Chris Banfield. *An Introduction to Post-Colonial Theatre*. Cambridge: Cambridge University Press, 1996.

Cullen, Countee. *The Medea and Some Poems*. New York: Harper & Brothers, 1935.

Dalphinis, Morgan. *Caribbean and African Languages: Social History, Language,Literature and Education*. London: Karia Press, 1985.

Daniel, Walter C. *Images of the Preacher in Afro-American Literature*. Washington D.C.: University Press of America, 1981.

D'Aponte, Mimi Gisolfi. "*The Gospel at Colonus* and Other Black Morality Plays." *Black American Literature Forum* 25 (1991) 101–113.

Davidson, Basil. *Modern Africa: A Social and Political History*. 3rd ed. London: Longman, 1994.

Davis, Angela Y. "Gender, Class, and Multiculturalism: Rethinking 'Race' Politics." *Mapping Multiculturalism*. Eds. Avery F. Gordon and Christopher Newfield. Minneapolis: University of Minnesota Press, 1996.

Davis, Rod. *American Voodoo: Journey into a Hidden World*. Denton: University of North Texas Press, 1998.

Diamond, Catherine. "The Floating World of Nouveau Chinoiserie: Asian Orientalist Productions of Greek Tragedy." *New Theatre Quarterly* XV.2 58 (May 1999): 142–164.

Diop, Cheikh Anta. *Civilization or Barbarism*. Trans. Yaa Lengi meema Ngemi. Eds.

Harold J. Salemson and Marjolijn de Jager. New York: Lawrence Hill, 1991.

Disch, Thomas M. "Theatre." *The Nation* 14 May 1988: 689–90.

Dove, Rita. *The Darker Face of the Earth.* Brownsville: Storyline Press, 1994.

_____. *The Darker Face of the Earth.* 3rd. ed. Ashland: Storyline Press, 2000.

DuBois, Page. *Centaurs and Amazons.* Ann Arbor: University of Michigan Press, 1982.

DuBois, W.E.B. *The Souls of Black Folk.* New York: The Modern Library, 1996.

Duboys, J. *Recueils de Reglements, Edits, Declarations et Arrêts, Concernant le Commerce, l'Administration de la Justice et la Police des Colonies Françaises de l'Amérique et le Engagés, avec le Code Noir et l'Addition Audit Code.* Paris: Chez les Libraries Associez, 1744. Reprinted as "Code Noir of Louisiana" Trans. Douglas Slawson. National University Website. Internet. 1997. 4 June 2002. <http://www.ac-amiens.fr/college60/delaunay_gouvieux/codenen. htm>.

Dunn, Christopher. "Carnivals in Latin America and the Caribbean." Appiah and Gates 376–381.

Durant, Will. *The Life of Greece.* New York: Simon and Schuster, 1939.

Edgecomb, David. "Introduction: 'Always Make Sure They Pay You': Towards the Building of a Vibrant Pan-Caribbean Theatre." *Contemporary Drama of the Caribbean.* Eds. Erika J. Waters and David Edgecomb. Kingshill: Caribbean Writer, 2001.

Fanon, Franz. *Black Skin White Masks.* Trans. Charles Lam Markmann. New York: Grove, 1967.

_____. *The Wretched of the Earth.* Trans. Constance Farrington. New York: Grove, 1963.

Farb, Peter. *Word Play.* New York: Alfred A. Knopf, 1974.

Farr, James Barker. *Black Odyssey: The Seafaring Traditions of Afro-Americans.* New York: Peter Lang, 1989.

Ferguson, Russell, Martha Gever, Trinh T. Minh-ha, and Cornel West, eds. *Out There: Maginalization and Contemporary Culture.* New York: New Museum of Contemporary Art, 1990.

Ferlita, Ernest. *Black Medea.* Unpublished play, 1990.

_____. Email to the author. 2 March 2002.

_____. Email to the author. 15 April 2002.

_____. Email to the author. 3 May 2002.

_____. "Playwright's Note." *Black Medea* Program.. Marquette Theatre. Loyola University, 1976.

_____. *The Twice-Born.* Unpublished play, n.d.

Figueroa, John. "Omeros." *In the Art of Derek Walcott.* Ed. Stewart Brown. Chester-Springs: Dufour, 1991.

Fleurant, Gerdès. *Dancing Spirits: Rhythms and Rituals of Haitian Vodun, The Radu Rite.* Westport: Greenwood, 1996.

Fraden, Rena. *Imagining Medea: Rhodessa Jones and Theatre for Incarcerated Women.* Chapel Hill: University of North Carolina Press, 2001.

Fredrickson, George M. *Black Liberation.* New York: Oxford University Press, 1995.

_____. *White Supremacy.* New York: Oxford University Press, 1981.

Furth, Leslie. "'The Modern Medea' and Race Matters: Thomas Satterwhite Noble's *Margaret Garner.*" *American Art* 12.2 (1998): 37–57.

Gilbert, Helen, and Joanne Tompkins. *Post-Colonial Drama.* New York: Routledge,

1996.

Gill, Glenda E. *No Surrender! No Retreat! African-American Pioneer Performers of Twentieth Century American Theatre.* New York: St. Martin's, 2000.

Gilman, Sander L. "Black Bodies, White Bodies: Toward an Iconography of Female Sexuality in Late Nineteenth Century Art, Medicine, and Literature." In *"Race," Writing, and Difference.* Ed. Henry Louis Gates, Jr. Chicago: University of Chicago Press, 1985.

_____. *Difference and Pathology: Stereotypes of Sexuality, Race, and Madness.* Ithaca: Cornell University Press, 1985.

Gilroy, Paul. *The Black Atlantic.* Cambridge: Harvard University Press, 1993.

_____. *Small Acts.* London: Serpent's Tail, 1993.

_____. *There Ain't No Black in the Union Jack: The Cultural Politics of Race and Nation.* Chicago: University of Chicago Press, 1987.

Gilula, Dwora. "Greek Drama in Rome: Some Aspects of Cultural Transposition." In *The Play out of Context.* Eds. Hann Scolnicov and Peter Holland. Cambridge: Cambridge University Press 1989. 99–109.

Goines, Leonard. "Gospel Music and the Black Consciousness." Internet. 11 January 2002. <http://artemis.austine.edu/acad/HWC22/Greek/Gospel/gospel-music.html>.

Green, Amy S. *The Revisionist Stage.* Cambridge: Cambridge University Press, 1994.

Greene, Naomi. *Pier Paolo Pasolini: Cinema as Heresy.* Princeton: Princeton University Press, 1990.

Grene, David, and Richmond Lattimore, eds. *The Complete Greek Tragedies.* 1960. 2nd ed. 9 vols. Chicago: Chicago University Press, 1991.

Griffiths, Gareth. *A Double Exile.* London: Marion Boyers, 1978.

Grimes, John. "Company of Players Win Praise for *Ione.*" In Hamner *Critical* 116–117.

Gross, Paul R., Norman Levitt, and Martin W. Lewis, eds. *The Flight from Science and Reason.* New York: New York Academy of Sciences, 1996.

Gurr, Andrew. "Third World Drama: Soyinka and Tragedy." In *Critical Perspectives on Wole Soyinka.* Ed. James Gibbs. Washington, D.C.: Three Continents, 1980. 139–146.

Haley, Alex. *Roots.* Garden City: Doubleday, 1976.

Hall, Peter. *Exposed by the Mask.* New York: Theatre Communications Group, 2000.

Hall, Stuart. "Cultural Identity and Diaspora." In *Identity: Community, Culture, Difference.* Ed. Jonathan Rutherford. London: Lawrence and Wishart, 1990. 222–237.

Hamner, Robert D. *Epic of the Dispossessed: Derek Walcott's Omeros.* Columbia: University of Missouri Press, 1997.

_____. ed. *Critical Perspectives on Derek Walcott.* Washington: Three Continents, 1993.

Harrison, Paul Carter. *The Drama of Nommo.* New York: Grove, 1972.

Hartigan, Kalista V. *Greek Tragedy on the American Stage.* Westport, CT: Greenwood, 1995.

Hartigan, Patti. "Hartford's *Oedipus* opts for pride over passion." *Boston Globe.* 24 January 2001: F5.

Hatch, James V. "Here Comes Everybody: Scholarship and Black Theatre History" *Interpreting the Theatrical Past.* Eds. Tom Postlewait and Bruce McConachie. Iowa City: University of Iowa Press, 1989. 148–165.

_____. "Some African Influences on the Afro-American Theatre." In Hill "Pulpit"

13–29.

_____ and Omanii Abdullah. *Black Playwrights, 1823–1977: An Annotated Anthology of Plays*. New York: R.R. Bowker, 1977.

Hay, Samuel A. *African-American Theatre: An Historical and Critical Analysis*. Cambridge: Cambridge University Press, 1994.

Hill, Anthony D. "The Pulpit and Grease Paint: The Influence of Black Church Ritual on Black Theatre." *Black American Literature Forum* 25 (Spring 1991): 113–120.

Hill, Errol. "Shakespeare in Sable." Amherst: University of Massachusetts Press, 1984.

Hill, Holly. "Black Theatre into the Mainstream." In *Contemporary American Theatre*. Ed. Bruce King. New York: St. Martin's, 1991. 81–96.

Hippolyte, Kendel. "Introduction." In *The Benjy Trilogy*. Roderick Walcott. Kingston: Ian Randle, 2000.

Holloway, Joseph E., ed. *Africanisms in American Culture*. Bloomington: Indiana University Press, 1990.

Holman, Curt. "One Bad Mother: *Medea* at the Alliance." Internet. 23 May 1998. *Creative Loafing*. 18 April 2002. <http:www.creative_loafing.com/acrn. lanta/newstand/052398/a_artsd.htm>.

Homer. *The Illiad*. Trans. Richmond Lattimore. Chicago: University of Chicago Press, 1951.

_____. *The Odyssey*. Trans. Robert Fitzgerald. New York: Vintage, 1990.

Huggins, Nathan Irvin. *Black Odyssey: The Afro-American Ordeal in Slavery*. New York: Vintage, 1997.

Istel, John. "From Sitcom Mom to a Woman of Scorn" *The Atlantic Online*. May 1998. 18 April 2002. <http://www.theatlantic.com/ae/98May/98maydt.htm>.

Irvine, Keith. *The Rise of the Colored Races*. New York: W.W. Norton, 1970.

Jacobs, Claude F., and Kaslow, Andrew J. *The Spiritual Churches of New Orleans: Origins, Beliefs, and Rituals of an African-American Religion*. Knoxville: University of Tennessee Press, 1985.

Jahnn, Hans Henny. *Medea*. Frankfurt am Main: Europäische Verlagsanstalt, 1959.

_____. *Medea: Ein Theaterbuch von Manfred Weber*. Berlin: Edition Hentrich, 1989.

James, George G.M. *Stolen Legacy*. Nashville: James C. Winston, 1954.

Jenkins, Ulysses Duke. *Ancient African Religion and the African-American Church*. Jacksonville: Flame International, 1978.

Jeyifo, Biodun. *The Truthful Lie*. London: New Beacon, 1985.

Jones, Edward L. *The Black Diaspora: Colonization of Colored People*. Seattle: Edward L. Jones, 1989.

_____. *Black Zeus: African Mythology and History*. Seattle: Edward L. Jones, 1972.

_____. *Profiles in Black Heritage*. Seattle: Edward L. Jones, 1972.

Jones, Silas. *American Medea*. Unpublished play, 1995.

_____. Letter to the author. 21 April 2002.

Jordan, Winthrop. *White Over Black: American Attitudes Towards the Negro, 1550–1812*. Chapel Hill: University of North Carolina Press, 1968.

Kahn, Chris. "Jefferson Family Feud Heads for Final Vote." *Columbus Dispatch*. 5 May 2002. A5.

Kennedy, Adrienne. *Adrienne Kennedy in One Act*. Minneapolis: University of Minnesota Press, 1988.

Kennedy Center for Performing Arts. "Oedipus in America." *Stagebill* November 1997: 13–37.

Kingston, Jeremy. "*Pecong, Tricycle.*" London *Times* 2 October 1991.

Klein, Alvin. "*Pecong*: Medea's Tale Retold." *New York Times* New Jersey ed. 26 April 1992: 12NJ11.

Klesius, Michael. "Search for a Cure." *National Geographic* 201.2 (February 2002): 32–43.

Knox. Bernard M.W., "The *Medea* of Euripides." In *Oxford Readings in Greek Tragedy.* Ed. Erich Segal. Oxford: Oxford University Press, 1983: 272–293.

Koger, Alicia Kae. "Dramaturgical Criticism: A Case History of *The Gospel at Colonus.*" *Theatre Topics* 1 (1997): 23–35.

Kramer, Mimi. "Say Catharsis, Somebody." *The New Yorker* (4 April 1998): 73–4.

Kyrkland, Willy. *Medea fra Mbongo.* Copenhagen: Forening for Boghaandvaerk, 1970.

Lamming, George. "Caribbean Literature: The Black Rock of Africa." *Africa Forum* 1:4 (1966): 32–52.

_____. *The Pleasure of Exile.* Ann Arbor: University of Michigan Press, 1960.

Lancaster, Kurt. "Theatrical Deconstructionists: The Social 'Gests' of Peter Sellars's *Ajax* and Robert Wilson's *Einstein on the Beach.*" *Modern Drama* XLIII.3 (2000): 461–468.

Larlham, Peter. *Black Theatre, Dance, and Ritual in South Africa.* Ann Arbor: UMI Research, 1985.

Lashley, Leroy. "Decades of Change in Calypso Culture" *Culture and Mass Communication in the Caribbean.* Ed. Humphrey A. Regis. Gainesville: University Press of Florida, 2001. 83–93.

Lefkowitz, Mary R. "Influential Women." In *Images of Women in Antiquity.* Eds. A. Cameron and A. Kuhrt. Detroit: Wayne State University Press, 1983.

_____. "Introduction." In Lefkowitz and Rogers 1–11.

_____. *Not Out of Africa.* New York: New Republic, 1996.

_____. *Women in Greek Myth.* Baltimore: Johns Hopkins University Press, 1986.

_____ and Guy MacLean Rogers, eds. *Black Athena Revisited.* Chapel Hill: University of North Carolina Press, 1996.

Levine, Lawrence W. *Black Culture and Black Consciousness.* New York: Oxford University Press, 1977.

Levine, Molly Myerowitz, ed. *Arethusa: The Challenge of "Black Athena."* Baltimore: Johns Hopkins University Press, 1989.

_____. *The Opening of the American Mind.* Boston: Beacon, 1996.

Linforth, Ivan M. *Religion and Drama in Oedipus at Colonus.* University of California Publications in Classical Philology. 14.4 (1951): 75–192. Reprint: Berkeley: University of California Press, 1951.

Liston, William T. "The Darker Face of the Earth: Review." *Theatre Journal* 49 (1997): 65–7.

Loewen, James W. *Lies My Teacher Told Me.* New York: New Press, 1995.

Lopez, Tiffany Ann. "Prison Break." *American Theatre* 19.3 (March 2002): 39–40.

Macintosh, Fiona. "Introduction." In *Medea in Performance, 1500–2000.* Eds. Edith Hall, Fiona Macintosh, and Oliver Taplin. Oxford: Legenda, 2000.

Magnuson, Jim. "African Medea." In *New American Plays Volume Four.* Ed. William M. Hoffman. New York: Hill and Wang, 1971. 151–190.

_____. Email to the author. 4 June 2002.

Majors, Richard and Janet Mancini Billson. *Cool Pose: The Dilemmas of Black Manhood in America*. New York: Touchstone, 1992.

Manning, Kenneth R. *Black Apollo of Science: The Life of Ernest Everett Just*. Oxford: Oxford University Press, 1983.

Manuel, Peter, Kenneth Bilby and Michael Largey. *Caribbean Currents: Caribbean Music from Rumba to Reggae*. Philadelphia: Temple University Press, 1995.

Masland, Tom, and Brook Larmer. "Cuba's Real Religion." *Newsweek* 19 January 1998: 42.

McDermott, Emily A. *Euripides' Medea: The Incarnation of Disorder*. University Park: Pennsylvania State University Press, 1989.

McDonald, Marianne. *Ancient Sun, Modern Light*. New York: Columbia University Press, 1992.

_____. "Medea as Politician and Diva: Riding the Dragon into the Future." In Claus and Johnston 297–323.

_____. *Sing Sorrow: Classics, History, and Heroines in Opera*. Westport, CT: Greenwood, 2001.

McDowell, Robert. "An Interview with Rita Dove." In *Darker Face of the Earth* 3rd. ed. Rita Dove. Ashland: Storyline, 2000. 153–163.

Mercer, Kobena. "Interculturality Is Ordinary." In *Intercultural Arts Education and Municipal Policy*. Ed. Ria Lavrijsen. Amsterdam: Royal Tropical Institute of the Netherlands, 1997. 33–44.

Metraux, Alfred. *Voodoo in Haiti*. New York: Schocken Books, 1982.

Mikotowicz, Tom. "Director Peter Sellars: Bridging the Modern and Postmodern Theatre." *Theatre Topics* 1.1 (1991): 87–98. "The Modern Medea." *Harper's Weekly* 11 (18 May 1867): 318.

Mollette, Carleton W., and Barbara J. Molette. *Black Theatre: Premise and Presentation*. 2nd rev. ed. Bristol: Wyndham Hall, 1992.

Morrison, Toni. *Beloved*. New York: Plume, 1987.

_____. *Playing in the Dark*. Cambridge: Harvard University Press, 1992.

Mulira, Jessie Gaston. "The Case of Voodoo in New Orleans." Holloway 34–68.

New Federal Theatre New York Website. Internet. 18 February 2002. <http://metrobase.com/newfederal/index.htm>.

Newman, Richard. "Miscegenation." Appiah and Gates 1320.

Olaniyan, Tejumola. *Scars of Conquest / Masks of Resistance*. Oxford: Oxford University Press, 1995.

Ottley, Roi. *Black Odyssey: The Story of the Negro in America*. New York: Charles Sribner's Sons, 1948.

Overbeck, Lois More. "The Life of the Work: A Preliminary Sketch." In Bryant-Jackson and Overbeck, *Intersecting* 21–41.

Parks, Suzan-Lori. *Venus*. New York: Theatre Communications Group, 1997.

_____. "Venus." *Theatre Forum*. 9 (Summer/Fall 1996): 40–72.

Panger, Daniel. *Black Ulysses*. Athens: Ohio University Press, 1982.

Pao, Angela C. "Recasting Race: Casting Practice and Racial Formations." *Theatre Survey* 41.2 (2000): 1–21.

Pasolini, Pier Paolo. *Oedipus Rex*. Trans. John Matthews. London: Lorrimer, 1971.

Patterson, Orlando. "Rethinking Black History" *Africa Report*. 17:9 (1972): 29–31.

Performance Group. *Dionysus in 69*. Ed. Richard Schechner. New York: Farrar,

Straus, and Giroux, 1970.

Pensak, Sherry, ed. *Oedipus Rex* theatre program. Hartford: Hartford Stage, Jan. 11–Feb. 11, 2001.

Pinn, Anthony B. *Varieties of African-American Religious Experience*. Minneapolis: Fortress, 1998.

Rabinowitz, Nancy Sorkin. *Anxiety Veiled: Euripides and the Traffic in Women*. Ithaca: Cornell University Press, 1993.

Rabkin, Gerald. "Lee Breuer on *The Gospel at Colonus*." *Performing Arts Journal* 22 (1989): 48–51.

Rae, Norman. "*Ione*: Colourful But Academic." In Hamner *Critical* 113–115.

Ramsay, F. Jeffress. *Africa*. 6th ed. Guilford: Dushkin, 1995.

Rice, Philip Blair. "Euripides in Harlem." *The Nation*. 141 (18 September 1935): 336.

Roach, Joseph. *Cities of the Dead: Circum-Atlantic Performance*. New York: Columbia University Press, 1996.

Roth, Ann Macy. "Building Bridges to Afrocentrism: A Letter to My Egyptological Colleagues." In Gross, Levitt, and Lewis 313–326.

Rubin, Sylvia. "Odyssey of a New Playwright: Homer inspires panoramic work on black themes." *San Francisco Chronicle*. 12 February 1996. E1.

Rutherford, Jonathan, ed. *Identity: Community, Culture, Difference*. London: Lawrence & Wishart, 1990.

Said, Edward. *Orientalism*. New York: Vintage, 1979.

———. "Reflections on Exile." In Ferguson, Geser, Minh-ha, and West 357–366.

Sartre, Jean-Paul. "Black Orpheus." Trans. John MacCombie. In *Race*. Ed. Robert Bernasconi. Malden: Blackwell, 2001. 115–142. Reprint of "Orphée Noir." *Anthologie de la nouvelle poésie nègre et malgache de langue française*. Ed. Léopold Sédar Senghor. Paris: Presses Universitaires de France, 1948.

Schondorff, Joachim, ed. *Medea*. Munich: Albert Langen, 1963.

Sellar, Tom. "Making History: Suzan Lori-Parks." *Theatre Forum* 9 (Summer/Fall 1996): 37–39.

———. "Suzan Lori Park's *Venus*: the Shape of the Past." *Theatre Forum* 9 (Summer/Fall 1996): 35–36.

Seneca. "Medea." *Three Tragedies*. Trans. Frederick Ahl. Ithaca: Cornell University Press, 1986.

Sharp, S. Pearl. "Beloved Beah and Medea." *Black Masks*. 14.4 (Feb/Mar 2001): 9, 15–6.

Sharpley-Whiting, T. Denean. *Black Venus: Sexualized Savages, Primal Fears, and Primitive Narratives in French*. Durham: Duke University Press, 1999.

Shewey, Don. "Not Either/Or but And: Fragmentation and Consolidation in the Post-Modern Theatre of Peter Sellars." In *Contemporary American Theatre*. Ed. Bruce King. New York: St. Martin's, 1991. 263–282.

Simawe, Saadi A., ed. *Black Orpheus: Music in African-American Fiction from the Harlem Renaissance to Toni Morrison*. New York: Garland, 2000.

Simon, John. "The Gospel Untruth." *New York Magazine* April 18, 1988: 96–7.

Smethurst, Mae. *The Artistry of Aeschylus and Zeami: A Comparative Study of Greek Tragedy and Nō*. Princeton: Princeton University Press, 1989.

Smith, Iris. "The 'Intercultural' Work of Lee Breuer." *Theatre Topics* 1.7 (1997): 36–58.

Snowden, Frank M. Jr. *Before Color Prejudice: The Ancient View of Blacks*. Cambridge:

Harvard University Press, 1983.

Sobel, Mechal. *Trabelin' On: The Slave Journey to an Afro-Baptist Faith.* Westport: Greenwood, 1979.

Southern, Elieen. *The Music of Black Americans: A History.* 3rd ed. New York: W.W. Norton, 1997.

Soyinka, Wole. *The Burden of Memory, the Muse of Forgiveness.* New York: Oxford University Press, 1999.

Spencer, Jon Michael. *Protest and Praise: Sacred Music of Black Religion.* Minneapolis: Fortress, 1990.

Stein, Howard. "An Interview with Michael Kahn." In Bryant-Jackson and Overbeck, *Intersecting* 189–198.

Stone, Judy S.J. *Studies in West Indian Literature: Theatre.* London: Macmillan, 1994.

Sun, William H. "Power and Problems of Performance across Ethnic Lines: An Alternative Approach to Nontraditional Casting." *The Drama Review* 44.4 (2000): 86–95.

Sutherland, Efua Theaodora. "The Second Phase of the National Theatre Movement in Ghana." In *FonTomFrom: Contemporary Ghanan Literature, Theatre, and Film.* Eds Kofi Anyidoho and James Gibbs. Amsterdam: Rodopi, 2000. 45–57.

Tallant, Robert. *Voodoo in the New Orleans.* New York: Macmillan, 1946.

Taplin, Oliver. "Derek Walcott's *Omeros* and Derek Walcott's Homer." In *Homer.* Ed. Katherine Callen King. New York: Garland, 1994. 311–323.

_____. *Greek Fire* New York: Atheneum, 1990.

Tatlow, Anthony. *Shakespeare, Brecht, and the Intercultural Sign.* Durham: Duke University Press, 2001.

Tetrel, Sophie. "Abused African's Remains Go Home." *Columbus Dispatch.* 5 May 2002. B6.

Thompson, Robert Farris. "Kongo Influences on African-American Artistic Culture." In Holloway 148–184.

Tuttle, Kate. "Just, Ernest Everett." In Appiah and Gates 1072.

Van Doren, Charles. *The Joy of Reading.* New York: Harmony, 1985.

Vernant, Jean-Pierre. "The Tragic Subject: Historicity and Transhistoricity." In *Myth and Tragedy in Ancient Greece.* Jean Pierre Vernant and Pierre Vidal-Naquet. Trans. Janet Lloyd. New York: Zone, 1988. 237–247.

Walcott, Derek. *Collected Poems: 1948–1984.* New York: Noonday, 1986.

_____. "The Muse of History: An Essay." In *Is Massa Day Dead? Black Moods in the Caribbean.* Ed. Orde Coombs. New York: Anchor Books, 1974. 1–27.

_____. *The Odyssey.* New York: Noonday, 1993.

_____. *Omeros.* New York: Farrar, Straus, Giroux, 1990.

Walton, J. Michael. *The Greek Sense of Theatre.* London: Methuen, 1984.

_____. *Greek Theatre Practice.* Westport: Greenwood, 1980.

_____. *Living Greek Theatre.* Westport: Greenwood, 1987.

Washington, Joseph R. Jr. *Black Sects and Cults.* Garden City: Anchor, 1973.

Watney, Simon. "Missionary Positions: AIDS, 'Africa,' and Race." In Ferguson, Gever, Minh-ha, and West 89–103.

Weatherford, J. McIver. *Indian Giver.* New York: Crown, 1988.

Weaver, Michael S. "Makers and Redeemers: The Theatricality of the Black Church." *Black American Literature Forum* 25 (1991) 53–61.

Weber, Bruce. "*Oedipus the King*: Timeless Tragedy, Transported in Time." *New*

York Times. 30 January 2001.

Weber, Carl. "AC/TC: Currents of Theatrical Exchange." In *Interculturalism and Performance.* Eds. Bonnie Marranca and Gautam Dasgupta. New York: PAJ, 1991.

Wecht, Cyril, Mark Curriden, and Benjamin Wecht. *Grave Secrets.* New York: Onyx, 1998.

Weisenburger, Steven. *Modern Medea.* New York: Hill and Wang, 1998.

Weiss, Rick. "War on Disease." *National Geographic* 201.2 (February 2002): 5–15, 26–31.

West, Cornell. *Race Matters.* New York: Vintage, 1994.

Wetmore, Kevin J. Jr. *The Athenian Sun in an African Sky: Modern African Adaptations of Classical Greek Tragedy.* Jefferson: McFarland, 2001.

White, Jack E. "My Dungeon Shook." *Time* 30 March 1998: 46.

Williams, John. "Hip Hop Homer." *American Theatre* May–June 1996: 6–7.

Williams, Patrick, and Laura Chrisman, eds. *Colonial Discourse and Post-Colonial Theory.* New York: Columbia University Press, 1994.

Wilson, August. *The Ground on Which I Stand.* New York: Theatre Communications Group, 2000.

Wilson, Edward, and Alvin Goldfarb. *Living Theatre: A History.* 3rd ed. New York: McGraw-Hill, 2000.

Wilson, Michael. "From the Artistic Director." In Pensak 7.

Winn, Steven. "Caribbean *Pecong* Is Brilliant in Bursts." *San Francisco Chronicle* 22 October 1993: C1.

Wren, Celia. "In Medea Res." *American Theatre.* 19.4 (April 2002): 22–25, 60–61.

Wolfe, George C. *The Colored Museum.* New York: Broadway, 1987.

Woods, Alan. "*The Ohio State Murders*: From the Dramaturg." Internet. Ohio State University Department of Theatre. 17 December 2001. <http://www.the.ohio_state.edu/Production/0001/Murders/Murttoutt.htm>.

Woods, Randall Bennett, *A Black Odyssey: John Lewis Waller and the Promise of American Life, 1878–1900.* Lawrence: Regents Press of Kansas, 1981.

X, Malcolm. *The Autobiography of Malcolm X.* New York: Ballantine, 1965.

Zeitlin, Froma I. *Playing the Other: Gender and Society in Classical Greek Literature.* Chicago: University of Chicago Press, 1996.

Index

259